SIEGE

DAVID L. WILLIAMS

IAN ALLAN *Publishing*

First published 1993

ISBN 0 7110 2177 5

Design by Ian Allan Studio

Published by Ian Allan Publishing,
an imprint of Ian Allan Ltd, Terminal House,
Station Approach, Shepperton, Middx
TW17 8AS, and printed by Ian Allan
Printing, Coombelands House, Coombelands
Lane, Addlestone, Surrey KT15 1HY

Contents

Introduction

According to psychologists, each and every one of us has his own private worst fear. George Orwell certainly demonstrated the point in his book *1984* with the spectre of the hidden horrors contained in the dreaded room 101 which could compel the most loyal into betraying their dearest compatriot. According to surveys carried out on the subject, some sources of personal dread are more common than others. Apparently, among the most 'popular' bogeymen are the fear of drowning, fear of rats, the fear of being involved in an aircrash and the fear of being trapped in a burning building or a submerged and sinking vessel. Now, perhaps not so surprisingly, the 'top ten' list has had added to it a new subject as one of the most widely held causes of personal anxiety — the fear of being taken and held hostage by terrorists, in a hijacking or some other form of siege.

It is a series of real-life siege experiences of various types, not all of them related to acts of terrorism, that comprise the contents of this book. These are ordeals of human suffering that go beyond the comprehension and imagination of the average person. They are stories of extreme suffering and degradation and, at times, of almost animal survival and endurance against all the odds; they are stories of subjection to squalor and deprivation, and of coping with unimaginable terror, constantly confronting the prospect of imminent death.

Equally, though, they are stories of extreme bravery, fortitude and resolution; stories of irrepressible human spirit, strength of character and indomitable will power which have enabled the victims of these experiences to survive the most challenging of personal trials.

Strictly speaking, 'siege' is a military term, referring to the encirclement and containment of a garrison or a force of soldiers for the purpose of compelling its surrender, either through denying replenishment of supplies, in effect 'starving them out', or through causing their resources of defensive ammunition to be exhausted.

The Oxford English Dictionary provides the following, specific definition for the word 'siege':

> 'The surrounding or hemming-in of a fortified place by a military force, to compel its surrender or to take it by direct attack; period during which this lasts.'

In essence, however, this book is not concerned with military sieges and it only contains one account that falls into this category, although, even in this case, those incarcerated by the siege were primarily civilians. This was the prolonged blockade of the Mediterranean island of Malta during World War 2, an episode which has a special significance in the context of this subject. The enduring courage and resilience of the island and its people earned them special recognition, culminating in decoration with the George Cross medal, a unique distinction as far as any siege incident is concerned.

Through common usage, the term 'siege' has come also to refer to similar non-military situations in which, for a variety of reasons, civilians have been trapped and surrounded in such a way that a siege has ensued. For example, when terrorists or criminals have been caught red-handed in the course of their deeds or been trapped, while being pursued by law enforcement officers; when the sanctuary sought by victims of religious or political persecution, rightly or wrongly, has been threatened with violation or when it has been politically expedient to apply coercive pressure on a population by subjecting them to starvation and hardship through blockading their lines of supply or by cutting off vital services.

It is primarily with this kind of civilian siege that this book is concerned. Along with hijackings, with which they are often associated, sieges are highly frightening experiences which have become something of a phenomenon of life in the late 20th century. This is an age in which outrage and atrocity, often the product of stifled political expression, have become regrettably commonplace, in which the playing with human lives as if they are no more than pawns in a chess game has become somehow acceptable if the ends are considered to justify the means, and in which religious and political intolerance has come to condone outrageous deeds that challenge the most basic principles of civilised behaviour. Worse still, these types of incident appear to be on the increase.

Fundamental to sieges of this kind, in the majority of cases, has been the taking of hostages — innocent bystanders caught up unwittingly in the events concerned or captives taken expressly for the purpose of being used as bargaining chips to be traded for safe passage or as human shields to deter a direct assault by the surrounding forces.

For the most part these have been ordinary people who found themselves hostage victims through sheer misfortune, whilst going about their lives in a routine, everyday manner. Quite literally they were people who found themselves in the wrong place at the wrong time. One minute, everything was as normal, the next minute, violence and fear had burst upon them, changing their lives irreversibly.

Imagine yourself, the reader, sat perhaps as you are now in the quiet and security of your own home. Perhaps it is the evening. You have had your dinner and are now taking it easy, relaxed in an armchair reading this book, content in the knowledge that sometime later you will go to bed in the full expectation of getting up tomorrow as usual to go to work. Suddenly, there is a loud, agitated knocking at the front door. Just as you are opening it, the door is burst open by a number of rough-looking men brandishing guns who threaten you and your family with physical harm unless you co-operate with them. It turns out they are escaped convicts who have been cornered by the police, men with a history of violent behaviour who have been serving long sentences for crimes of this nature. Within an hour your house is surrounded and a long ordeal commences in which attempts are made to trade your safety in exchange for the release of the wanted men. Protracted negotiations ensue, during which you and your family are compelled to endure conditions of indescribable mental anguish along with the embarrassing need to perform publicly those acts of a private nature which hastily improvised sanitary arrangements have now imposed.

The full horror of such an intrusion into your personal and private sanctuary is hard to imagine and it is an experience that would not end with the conclusion of the siege. Afterwards, quite apart from the obvious problems of emotional adjustment to come to terms with such a traumatic experience, you may be unable ever to feel the same again about your home, the scene of the affair. Painful memories, constantly evoked by every image around you, would be difficult, if not impossible, to eradicate.

Alternatively, another, equally plausible imaginary siege situation, worth contemplating as a preamble to the true-life stories that follow, could see you involved as a hostage victim during a routine rail journey. Sat in the crowded commuter train that you take every day, heading home after a long and tiring day in the office, you have no reason to believe that the apparently insignificant gentleman sat opposite you, with whom you exchanged a few pleasantries on entering the compartment, poses any sort of threat to you or your fellow passengers. But then, quite without warning, a short while after leaving the station on a quiet and remote stretch of the track, the train lurches to a halt and the 'passenger' opposite leaps to his feet, confronting you all with an automatic weapon. Along with a number of accomplices, who by now have also revealed themselves, instructions are barked out advising you that the train has been hijacked by the People's Organisation for the Liberation of somewhere or other. One of the gang members indicates that he is holding a primed hand grenade which will be exploded if any attempt is made to overpower him or his associates. They are clearly fanatical terrorists, quite prepared to martyr themselves for their cause. Everyone's life is in danger and it is quite probable, with such unstable characters that you may never again see your family and loved ones. In short order, the stationary train is surrounded by crack units of Scotland Yard's Anti-Terrorist Squad and a siege has begun.

Two weeks later, dirty, hungry and exhausted, your remaining, tenuous grip on sanity is subjected to its final test when, in the face of intransigence from the terrorists, the train is stormed by commandos to end the affair. Fortunately, they are able to prevent a bloodbath but, until the situation is brought under control, you are at a peak of fear.

Such vivid imaginary descriptions may seem, on the face of it, to be unduly emotive and melodramatic. The fact is, though, that they are not untypical of the real incidents which a significant number of ordinary individuals have been forced to endure and which have shattered the otherwise tranquillity of their lives.

In a sense, it is that dimension of these nightmare episodes, the experience of extreme terror in familiar surroundings, which makes them so compelling. There is a certain morbid curiosity in the majority of us which makes the very things that most disturb us or that most frighten us somehow intriguing. It is this same compulsion that is responsible for the enduring fascination with the *Titanic* disaster and numerous other famous human tragedies, as well as murder mysteries and even the occult. So it is too with the modern menace of the terrorist hijacking.

Of course, not all the stories related here were quite as dramatic as this, in the sense of the extreme suddenness in which they intruded into the lives of their victims or, indeed, the method by which they were resolved. In other cases, much the same end result of mental anguish and utter exhaustion was achieved insidiously, over a longer period. By a process of inexorable corrosion, the lives of those affected was systematically reduced to an extent where they were compelled to endure acute deprivation and a subsistence-level of existence, dreading constantly the prospect of sudden, violent death if some minor irritation or act of belligerence from outside should precipitate a fickle captor into venting his frustrations. Although the Yugoslav Civil War is a military confrontation, nevertheless the misery being inflicted by the Serbs and Croats upon Muslims besieged in Bosnian enclaves provides a very recent and very graphic example of this kind of situation.

Having made the distinction between military sieges and other siege-like situations it becomes apparent that there are a wide variety of incidents of this type that fall into the latter category. Each is distinguished by the peculiar circumstances and motives that initiated it and each is characterised by distinctive features such as the behaviour displayed by the persons or groups involved as well as by the method used to resolve the situation in each case. A siege incident, by its very nature, is highly confrontational and once in place presents considerable difficulties in achieving its resolution. This is owing to the general distrust and suspicion that arises as well as the risks posed to all parties in making concessions in order to bargain a return to normality.

To set the scene for the reader, prior to commencing the main chapters ahead, it is fitting here to briefly review some of these variations on the siege theme and highlight some of the different kinds of situation in which ordinary people have found themselves besieged or compelled to endure siege-like conditions. In doing this, I have chosen to include within the range of the occurrences under discussion certain affairs which do not in the strictest sense fall within the scope of the book's subject range but which serve nevertheless to convey particularly well the circumstances which typify the state of siege.

There are many different aspects of siege incidents by which they can be compared, one of the most critical being the primary cause or catalyst in each case.

Sieges are complex affairs which arise for many reasons. They can be the result of either the actions taken by those who are responsible for imposing the siege or those who are ultimately trapped by it. It is possible, in analysing sieges, to demonstrate when a given situation has arisen primarily from within the besieged group or outside of it. On the one hand a siege might be the outcome of a necessary response to a terrorist outrage. On the other hand, a siege may be imposed as a calculated act by an apparently legitimate but authoritarian organisation to insulate deliberately a group of people in order to coerce them, for instance, into conceding to unpopular and unwelcome political demands. In these circumstances the siege has not been directly triggered by the actions of those who, as a consequence, became the besieged. The Berlin Airlift, dealt with in Chapter 2, is an example of this.

Another situation in which the authorities may be compelled, for good reason, to impose siege-like circumstances upon a community is when it is necessary to quarantine it from the outside world for reasons of health or safety, in effect to create a 'cordon sanitaire'. A recent case of this type was the police action to cut off the town of Hungerford in Berkshire when the gunman Michael Ryan was at large, indiscriminately shooting residents in an unprecedented act of insane violence. Although of limited duration, for all practical purposes the police cordon temporarily imposed siege conditions on the community in order for the situation to be more effectively contained. It enabled the police to restrict the ingress of further persons who could have become additional victims and, with Ryan trapped within the cordon, it permitted them to bring the incident to a swifter conclusion.

Quite evidently, sieges are affairs that do not follow any convenient or customary pattern. Just as the catalyst for a siege incident can originate on either side of the siege line, so too it is with the disposition of integrity in so far as it relates to the motives of the various individuals and groups of persons involved, be they those who are trapped on the inside or those who have implemented and are enforcing the containment. One thing is certain, as the reader will soon discover, that virtue is not always on the same side of the siege equation. In fact, sometimes it is not really clear whether virtue is on either side, while at other times it appears, when considering all the evidence objectively, that virtue may actually be present on both sides simultaneously.

Having said that, certain patterns of consistency in siege situations can be identified. For instance, those sieges that are primarily initiated externally are, in the main, incidents in which the aims of the besieging force are hostile, oppressive or malicious. By way of example, the siege of Malta in World War 2, related in Chapter 1, as well as the Soviet blockade of Berlin in the period from 1948 to 1949, which has already been mentioned, were both instigated externally for strategic reasons of a hostile or coercive nature. In both these cases, the behaviour of the people who were subsequently besieged had little bearing on the decision to blockade. In fairness, of course, where the siege of Malta is concerned, judgement as to the merits of the besieging forces' motives depends, quite naturally, on whether one's loyalty was to the Allied or to the Axis cause.

Further examples of sieges triggered externally for what might be regarded as unsavoury reasons are the siege of the United States Embassy in Tehran, the capital of Iran, between November 1979 and January 1981, described in detail in Chapter 7; also, the Yangtse Incident, as it was called, when for four months in 1949, the Royal Navy frigate HMS *Amethyst* was trapped in the River Yangtse by Chinese Communist forces. This latter affair is one of those borderline cases which may not legitimately qualify as a true siege but which nevertheless contains all the classic elements of a siege, including those aspects of deprivation and degradation to which victims are typically subjected. For reasons of its borderline qualification, I have not devoted a full chapter to this subject but the substance of the affair is well worth relating in condensed form here.

It began in April 1949 when HMS *Amethyst* was steaming up the River Yangtse bound for Nanking where she was to relieve the destroyer HMS *Consort*, the guard ship for the British Embassy there. The conduct of the operation was surrounded in an air of tension and expectation, as the Civil War between the Nationalist and Communist Chinese forces was approaching its climax. For this reason the *Amethyst*'s orders contained contingency instructions for the evacuation of the embassy staff in the event that the city, then the seat of the Nationalist Government, fell to the Communists.

In the event, the *Amethyst* never reached her destination for some 60 miles from Nanking she came under fire from Communist forces. Seventeen of the ship's complement were killed and a further 10 were critically injured. Among the latter was the Captain, who later died of his wounds. The *Amethyst* ran aground, later being refloated and moved to a safe anchorage while her release was negotiated. Surrounded by hostile forces, the blockaded ship had no other means of securing her freedom. Attempts to bring aid to the besieged ship were unsuccessful. The *Consort*, as well as the cruiser *London* and the frigate *Black Swan*, were each repelled in turn, forced to retreat to Shanghai, having sustained further casualties. The helpless *Amethyst* was left to resolve her predicament alone.

Lt Geoffrey Lee Weston, who had assumed temporary command of the *Amethyst*, was subsequently relieved by Lt-Cdr John Kerans, the naval attaché at Nanking, and it was the latter who took charge of negotiations with the Chinese. It soon became evident, however, that the commander of the Communist forces, a Col Kang, was not interested in compromises, insisting that the ship's release would only be granted if a written apology was made for the wrongful and criminal invasion of Chinese territorial waters, a request which was, of course, refused.

Replenishments of fresh food and fuel were immediately denied and, with dwindling provisions, conditions on board the beleaguered vessel rapidly deteriorated. Apart from shortages, there were also rats, cockroaches, flies and

Above: **The British Frigate HMS *Amethyst* steaming into Hong Kong after breaking through the Communist Chinese blockade of the River Yangtse on 1 August 1949. Artillery hits can be seen on her side.**
Associated Press

Left: **The German motorship *St Louis*.**
World Ship Photo Library

intolerable heat to contend with, all of which placed an unbearable strain on the crew, whose enforced idleness exacerbated the intensity of their desperate situation and their apparent inability to resolve it.

Realising that Kang would never willingly permit the release of the ship, Lt-Cdr Kerans resolved to make an escape bid under cover of darkness before there was any danger of his men becoming totally demoralised. Despite great fortitude and the maintenance of a disciplined régime on board, the strain would perhaps inevitably have told. Already it had been necessary to reduce the crew to half rations and fuel supplies were so low there was barely sufficient to maintain onboard services let alone to complete a dash for freedom. Hence, the timing of the escape attempt was vitally critical.

It is said that desperate situations call for desperate measures. Even so, it required a quite daring plan to attempt escape in the circumstances, for the navigable channel was restricted, and the ship was neither carrying a pilot nor charts and her gyro compass was inoperable. Yet another difficulty that had to be faced was the need to break through the booms that the Chinese had placed at intervals across the river, while, for much of the passage, the *Amethyst* would be within the range of Chinese shore batteries positioned along either bank. In dauntless fashion, the British crew manfully prepared to confront these difficulties. Other than finding these obstacles intimidating, the very fact that positive action was being taken, regardless of the prospects for success, had a profound effect upon the crew, immediately lifting their spirits.

The break-out bid was made during the night of 31 July 1949, almost four months after the blockade had commenced. As soon as darkness fell, all shiny and metallic surfaces on the ship were rapidly painted black. Then the mooring cables were quietly slipped, allowing the ship to drift away on the current. Once underway, the *Amethyst*'s engines were started and, in short order, they were working flat out, pushing her along at a speed of 20kt.

Initially, all went well but a Chinese vessel spotted the *Amethyst* as she passed on her way down river and opened fire on the frigate as it took up pursuit. Luckily, the shore batteries, which also joined in the action, fired on and sank their own ship, mistaking it for the *Amethyst* in all the confusion. This stroke of fortune allowed the *Amethyst* to get away and she cleared her final obstacle, the searchlights of the Woosung forts, early the following morning. Appropriately enough, the *Amethyst* headed out to sea as dawn was breaking, her ordeal finally over. To announce their deliverance, her commander transmitted one of those now-famous, typically measured, tongue-in-cheek naval signals for which the British are so renowned: 'Have rejoined the fleet. No damage or casualties. God Save The King'.

Despite the down-beat turn of phrase used by Lt-Cdr Kerans, the Yangtse Incident had ended in high drama, a feature of the conclusion of a great many siege affairs, as will be seen.

Another case of a blockaded ship which is worthy of mention here, even though it again only marginally relates to the book's central theme, is the case of the Jewish refugees who were trapped aboard the German passenger liner *St Louis* off the entrance to Havana harbour, Cuba, in May 1939.

These pitiful victims of anti-semitic tyranny had been able to escape the menace of the Nazi terror in their homeland, with all that that implied for them, thanks to a mercy voyage funded and arranged by the Association of Jewish Refugees. The poignant mission, embarked upon with such commendably humane objectives was, however, to fall foul of bureaucracy and political horse-trading half way across the world, in the West Indies, when the

Cuban authorities refused the refugees the right to land. This was a bitter irony for, having been aided in their flight by German nationals, their potential enemy, they found themselves rejected in Cuba, where they were perhaps entitled to expect a friendly reception and a temporary safe haven. Obliged to moor outside the harbour entrance, the *St Louis* was without exception the saddest vessel afloat, for not even a plague ship had received a sorrier welcome.

As days of bargaining and negotiation passed, the *St Louis*'s decks became the stage for a drama of human misery without precedent. Relatives and friends ashore clamoured to get aboard but were held back. The weeping refugees, in earnest to reach refuge ashore, were halted at guarded gangways. For a week the desperate affair continued with no hint of a relaxation of strict, new Cuban immigration regulations. The fact that many of the refugees had been granted consular visas, permitting them to land, made no difference. Others, who, in good faith, had purchased special landing permits back in Germany found that these too had been declared void. Their every appeal for concessions was refused.

Trapped in this nightmarish situation, unable to reach the freedom and safety that beckoned ashore in Havana and on which their survival depended, and dreading a return to further persecution under the Nazi régime, some chose to take the ultimate means of escape from their ordeal. One attempted suicide victim was dragged from the water with his wrists slashed. Other suicide bids followed and, fearing a wave of self-destruction, the senior representatives of the party of refugees were compelled to organise deck patrols to prevent this from happening.

Yet, it was all to no avail and finally, after an equally abortive attempt to land her cargo of despair in Miami, Florida, the *St Louis* was compelled reluctantly, to return to Europe.

Virtually all these unfortunate men, women and children had been registered under the quota provisions of various 'free' nations. But rejection by these self-declared champions of human rights meant that once more they risked subjection to the horror of the Nazi death camps, a horror whose full extent was not revealed until 1945 with the defeat of Germany.

The only minor redemption to this sad affair was the offer of asylum for a small number of the *St Louis*'s refugees in Great Britain, the Netherlands, Belgium and France.

While the *St Louis*'s 'voyage of the damned' was not a siege in the strict sense of the word, the Jewish refugees were undoubtedly besieged aboard the vessel for its duration. In their unique circumstances, they more than most had to endure the anxieties and suffering that are associated with enforced confinement in the face of imminent personal danger.

Persecution and repression, and the maltreatment of oppressed or disenfranchised peoples in general, have regularly been contributory factors to sieges, especially where the passions and emotions of frustrated political expression have exploded into direct action. Sieges of this type fall almost exclusively into that category where the catalyst takes the form of confrontational or provocative action on the part of those who ultimately become the besieged. In other words they are incidents that are primarily initiated by the besieged rather than the besiegers.

The depth of public sympathy for the aspirations of minority nationalist, racial or religious groups has, quite naturally, tended to be influenced by the character of the actions that they have taken to promote their causes. A certain solidarity may perhaps be felt towards those who, while pursuing a non-violent campaign to increase public awareness of their plight, are suppressed by intimidatory official reaction. Quite the reverse is the case when it is the perpetration of a blatant and murderous atrocity that provokes police or military intervention in order to trap those responsible.

Unfortunately, the evidence clearly demonstrates that the majority of sieges involving extremist minorities have been of the latter variety. Even in cases where the original intention was only to make a gesture of defiance, in a restrained fashion, to challenge authority, matters often became complicated as the taking of hostages introduced an element of violence.

An example of this occurred in February 1973 when, in an intentionally peaceful occupation, a large group of disenfranchised North American Indians took over the town of Wounded Knee, South Dakota. Wounded Knee has a special, symbolic importance to the Indians in their struggle for fair and equal treatment as citizens of the United States and the recognition of their traditional rights. Just as the treaty provisions of the past were not honoured, so too Indian affairs have been neglected in the modern era.

With no protection under the constitution, the Wounded Knee Indians found themselves challenged when they exercised the basic right of demonstrating about their grievances. Confronted by heavily armed federal agents, hostages were taken in an act of desperation. Finally, though, with the prospect of a bloody shoot-out, a two-month long siege was ended when the Indians reluctantly but peacefully submitted.

It has to be said that most of the sieges which have involved revolutionary or direct-action groups resulted from actions which, right from the start, had no peaceful intent or motivation whatsoever. Such incidents feature prominently in this book, being the subject of no less than seven chapters. In the majority of these cases, the stimulus of the incident was a politically motivated action although cases of a religious and criminal origin are also described.

Among the sieges covered here which arose out of an extremist political action is the attack on the Israeli athletes at the Munich Olympics in 1972 which is believed to have launched the bloody career of Carlos, 'The Jackal', as well as others which are linked to terrorist outrages perpetrated in the name of Palestinian liberation. Other extremist political groups caught up in sieges featured in this book are the IRA and South Moluccan nationalists.

Chapter 3, which recounts the perpetration of many atrocities which resulted in sieges, is to some extent a profile of the career of Carlos, a man described by international police as the most wanted terrorist in the world. The terrorist track record of Carlos epitomises particularly well the kind of manic, extremist practices which often result in siege confrontations.

Of the incidents described in this book which are of a violent but non-political nature, there is the account of an otherwise ordinary criminal raid on a restaurant in London's West End which, when interrupted, resulted in a siege. Another interesting, recent siege which resulted from a criminally motivated incident was the taking hostage of a French schoolteacher, Laurence Dreyfus, and 15 children of a very tender age at their school in Neuilly, a Paris suburb. The siege was ended after two days, when a French anti-terrorist squad raided the building, shooting dead the gunman, Eric Schmidt, who had apparently threatened to detonate sticks of dynamite attached to his body if his demands were not met. At first, it seemed that this was a straightforward ransom case because one of Schmidt's demands had been for £12 million worth of used bank notes. Later, though, it was hinted that Schmidt may have been an AIDS victim

Images of siege: a hooded terrorist. This terrorist from the Arab commando group who seized the Israeli Olympic team quarters at the Munich Olympic village in 1972 was captured on film as he appeared briefly on the balcony of the building in which Israeli team members were being held hostage. *Associated Press*

seeking a vindictive vengeance for his own personal predicament. For her bravery in dealing with the crisis, Laurence Dreyfus received the Legion D'honneur, France's highest decoration.

Chapter 10 deals with two siege affairs of a religious origin. The first of these occurred in June 1984 when heavily-armed Sikh militants occupied the holy shrine of the Golden Temple in Amritsar as part of their campaign for an independent state of Khalistan. The other arose when members of the extremist religious cult, the Branch Davidians of the Seventh Day Adventist Church, barricaded themselves into their fortified compound at Waco, Texas after federal agents attempted to serve an arrest warrant on their leader.

Many siege incidents have arisen as a result of the hijacking of a vehicle of one sort or another, either an aircraft, a train or a ship, and examples of all three are related here. This in itself is a matter of some interest for several reasons. For one thing, the hijacking of vehicles gave the terrorists concerned the scope for an element of surprise which was not always possible with a fixed structure. Each mode of transport provided what was, in effect, a detached, self-contained environment that could be intercepted and controlled in a remote, inaccessible location. In some respects it gave them better scope for consolidating their position to resist a siege before the authorities could respond, allowing them in effect to manage the siege on their terms.

As a mobile platform, a hijacked vehicle also served another useful purpose for the terrorists in that it offered immense scope for exploiting the publicity angle, an objective that often seems to have been fundamental to many of these activities. It certainly seems that at times the precipitation of a siege was actually desired, if not intended, because, given the much reduced capability for escaping from an open and exposed vehicle, publicity was the only tangible and valuable trade-off. Thus, the whole exercise could almost be stage-managed, ensuring that the drama was played out as conspicuously as possible, to the appropriate audience, against a suitable back-drop free from other extraneous surroundings. Certainly some of the terrorists' antics, performing for the cameras of the worlds' media, suggest that this may have been a predetermined aim.

Hijackings have been beneficial to terrorists for another reason, providing them with the means of achieving what was invariably their main objective, securing the release of other, already imprisoned associates.

The seized passengers, held as hostages, became a convenient source of barter, to trade for the extremist prisoners whose freedom was sought. On more than one occasion, too, these desperadoes showed the ruthless extremes to which they were prepared to go in the treatment of their hostages to emphasise their determination to have their demands met.

Aircraft hijackings commenced in earnest in the early 1970s with some spectacularly outrageous acts of piracy, notably the blowing-up of three captured airliners at Dawson's Field, Jordan in September 1970. More than 20 years on, even with quite strict security measures imposed at airports, it has been impossible to eradicate them altogether. The travelling public has now come to accept as normal the rather intrusive measures that are necessary to prevent such acts of terror, the trade-off of added security being seen as more than adequate compensation for any inconvenience experienced.

No matter how difficult it may be to achieve fully effective security to protect passengers travelling by air, it is almost impossible to prevent the hijacking of trains. Railway passengers occupy train seats on a largely *ad hoc* basis and there is an absence of security barriers at stations to screen passengers before they are allowed access to platforms. Indeed, in order to meet the schedules which are

Jordan on 12 September 1970 by Palestinian guerillas. The BOAC VC-10 on the left, which had been hijacked on a flight from Karachi to London, had first landed at Beirut airport before being forced to fly on to the desert airstrip. *Associated Press*

Left: The full extent of the trauma suffered by victims caught-up in siege incidents may only be revealed at a later date. Young children show greater resilience to these kinds of experience than adults, as demonstrated here by smiling six-year old Jewish boy, Yaron Rabb. He sports the headgear and sub-machine gun of an Arab terrorist who, only a short time earlier, had been threatening his life and that of other hostages. The photograph was taken at an hotel in Amman after the hijacked passengers had been released. *Associated Press*

nowadays necessary for profitable railway operation, stations usually have to be open and freely accessible and, increasingly, trains are operated without guards or even ticket inspectors.

Though much rarer, ships too have become the target for hijackings and two such incidents which resulted in sieges on the open sea, as tracking warships surrounded the seized vessels, are described in this book. These are the cases of the *Santa Maria* in 1961 and the *Achille Lauro* in October 1985. Although passenger ships enjoy rather better security controls than trains, assisted further by the legal requirement to maintain a full passenger manifest, nevertheless, they present a number of concerns to security officers. First, through the sheer numbers of persons embarking at sailing time who in themselves present a monumental security challenge. Appropriate means of screening and filtering have to be employed, in effect forms of security sampling, if departure times are not to be unreasonably delayed. By virtue of what the circumstances permit, a significant security loophole can inevitably be left unplugged. Secondly, there are all the processes of stores replenishment direct from the quayside, which usually take place simultaneously with passenger embarkation, and thirdly the scheduled routes or cruise itineraries that ships operate on. Vessels often call at ports in what can only be described as 'politically-dubious' countries, exposing them to danger at a time when they are furthest removed from the friendly forces of law and order which could prevent or intervene to deal with a hostile incursion.

It is easy to see that ships are perhaps more vulnerable to this kind of insurgence than other modes of transport and it is perhaps surprising, therefore, that more incidents of this kind, involving passenger vessels, have not occurred. This may be due to the fact that maintaining control over the larger number of accosted persons aboard a ship and preventing their access to the more numerous means of raising alarm presents a challenge to terrorists which cannot easily be overcome.

The prevention of hijackings, whatever the form of transportation concerned, is difficult to achieve because operators are naturally reluctant to allow an over obvious security presence. No matter what reassurance the traveller may derive from the presence of armed guards patrolling passenger termini, it is a fact that security personnel also ultimately act as a reminder of the potential risks involved in taking a journey in an age of international terrorism. Thus, they can actually act as a deterrent to potential passengers, undermining the normality that they are seeking to protect. It is constantly necessary to strike a balance between, on the one hand, ensuring that the travelling public is not needlessly exposed to danger and, on the other, the need to adopt a low profile 'business-as-usual' mode of operation, refusing to submit to the terrorists' negative intrusion into everyday life.

Just as it is necessary to establish an acceptable equilibrium between adequate security and a reasonable level of normality, so too, in the methods of handling sieges involving extremist groups, it is essential to balance the needs of urgency to resolve an incident against the risk of introducing an increased level of danger to those who are held hostage. Some firm views have been expressed by politicians cautioning against conceding in any way to the demands of terrorists for fear of encouraging recurrences of the same crimes. But such intransigence in the face of equivalent obduracy on the part of the extremists can often worsen the situation unnecessarily.

Professionals who are experienced in siege breaking tend to counsel against this style of response, urging instead a more cautious and calculated approach, less overtly uncompromising and more inclined to patient negotiation.

There are others who strongly advocate a pre-emptive, interventionist approach to raising sieges. Operations of this kind, involving taking the siege site by storm, have resulted in both spectacular successes and equally spectacular failures.

Two chapters of this book are specifically devoted to describing incidents which were resolved by the alternative approaches of negotiation and physical assault, allowing the reader a measure of comparison. There are further examples in other chapters. It is not suggested that either approach is right or wrong, or better or worse than the other, but it is appropriate to consider by actual examples the alternative methods used as well as their merits and disadvantages. In these instances I have considered it best to let the facts speak for themselves; after all a failed operation may not have been so much a reflection on the approach adopted as on the method of its implementation.

Ending a siege by force, particularly one involving unstable, suicidally-committed opponents, clearly increases the physical dangers to any hostages who are being held. To be successful, such operations depend on precise preparations and, if it is possible, on achieving an element of surprise. Meticulous debriefing of any escaped hostages is essential in these circumstances as well as thorough research of the besieged building or vehicle and the particular group being confronted, its members, their track record and known pattern of behaviour. A detailed knowledge of the layout of the siege location and accurate intelligence on the numbers of adversaries being faced and the nature and strength of the weapons they hold are all vital ingredients to the planning of a successful siege-busting raid.

It may also be desirable to distract temporarily the besieged rebels, exploiting the fact that these groups often lack the discipline of trained military units. If it is not possible to employ some diversionary measure, then it may be necessary to employ other tactics to buy time for the raiding party by causing a state of disorientation and confusion among the terrorists. This may be achieved by the use of stun grenades, tear gas or other similar tools. Clearly the primary aim here is to secure the safe release of the hostages. Loss of life among the terrorists, while undesirable, is not necessarily a paramount consideration.

In contrast, the processes employed to negotiate the peaceful conclusion of a siege are aimed at securing both the safe release of any hostages and the surrender of the terrorists within the framework of a peaceful and injury-free settlement of the incident as a whole. This depends absolutely on having inexhaustible patience. The techniques employed to achieve negotiated settlements can be equally sophisticated and, similarly, are equally dependant on developing a comprehensive understanding of the character of the extremist group being faced and any established or predictable pattern of behaviour. Police and para-military units engaged in these operations now routinely have psychologists attached to them and, as information on the abductors is gathered, psychological profiling is performed to determine those areas of character weakness which can be exploited to advantage.

The process of negotiation itself is a business that has to be carefully managed, never in effect conceding anything but equally never quite refusing demands; always spinning things out, playing for time and seeking opportunities to trade minor favours, such as providing food and water, in exchange for the release of captives. Here too, opportunity is taken to disorient the besieged gang through both physiological and psychological means such as denying them sleep or rest, by causing disturbance around the clock or by making the siege location as unpleasant and unbearable as possible by isolating power, leaving the occupants in darkness after sunset and without access to sources of news information. In this respect too, a delicate balance has to be pursued between constantly keeping the terrorists on the defensive, cultivating an air of uncertainty without so provoking the group's latent paranoia that a calamitous and suicidal outbreak of savagery could result.

The emphasis in this introduction to *Siege!* has so far been on the intrusion of these affairs into ordinary lives. There have, in fact, also been sieges which have involved not-so-ordinary persons such as ambassadors, consular officials, government ministers and the like, targets consciously selected to demonstrate that even the heart of the establishment is far from invulnerable from terrorist attacks. Embassies and consuls, of course, do not only represent part of the fabric of civilised government and political administration but are also sanctuaries in which oppressed persons may seek refuge. As extensions of the sovereignty of foreign governments they are granted diplomatic immunity and, as such, should be inviolable from any form of demonstration or subversive attack. The fact is, though, that this has not always been the case, either in the distant past or today. A number of embassy sieges have occurred over the last dozen years or so for both justifiable and unjustifiable reasons. Three of these cases are related in this book.

There is the lengthy siege of the United States Embassy in Tehran along with the abortive attempt at resolving it by force which effectively terminated the presidency of Jimmy Carter. Also, there are the sieges of the Iranian and Libyan Embassies in London. The first followed the take-over of the building by representatives of an ethnic minority group seeking the release of political prisoners held in Iran, and the second resulted from the shooting of WPC Yvonne Fletcher while she was engaged in supervising a legitimate demonstration in the road adjacent to the building.

In writing about this subject, I have tried to avoid a shallow or superficial approach to describing the incidents concerned although I must confess that only a limited analysis has been made of the circumstances surrounding the cause of each siege. Equally, I have tried to avoid a sensationalist or over-dramatic presentation of the events. Instead, I have endeavoured to present the facts from all angles with any emphasis placed on the civilian experience in each case. I have also attempted to highlight the differences which have characterised each of these incidents as well as the method by which each was resolved. It should also be noted that, wherever possible, I have avoided the inclusion of spoken dialogue, the exceptions being certain quotations which I have con-sidered to be particularly pertinent to given situations.

For the most part these will be familiar stories, most likely remembered in general terms from contemporary press accounts and news bulletins. Too often though, at the time, particularly when they were inclined to linger on, these affairs tended to lose their front-page coverage, as they became obscured by subsequent news events. Occasionally, when there was a dramatic climax, they were temporarily restored to top billing but more typically the final outcome was not as prominently broadcast as the initial incident. Consequently, the detail of many of these siege incidents or the circumstances in which they were resolved has long been forgotten. Equally, the aftermath for the victims and the perpetrators may not even be known. I trust, therefore, that the reader will not only find these accounts stimulating reading but will appreciate the fact that each has been encapsulated here as a complete story.

The bulk of my research for this book was based on newspaper articles but for the student interested in exploring a given siege in greater detail, I have listed published sources, where they exist, at the back of the book.

Their Finest Hour

Winston Churchill's famous wartime speech 'Never in the field of human conflict has so much been owed by so many to so few', addressed to the Royal Air Force's Fighter Command in recognition of its stalwart defence of the British Isles during the Battle of Britain, could have applied, just as fittingly, to the people of Malta. Their resolute endurance and irrepressible fortitude in the face of the determined Axis bid to conquer their small, insignificant but strategically vital Mediterranean island is an epic story which had just as profound an impact on the course of the conflict.

Certainly no book on the subject of siege worth having, whether military or otherwise, could possibly exclude the great siege of Malta during World War 2 which earned the award of Great Britain's highest honour for civilian courage — the George Cross. Undoubtedly, the siege of Malta originated for military reasons, an inevitable consequence of the war between the United Kingdom and Germany and Italy and the fact that Malta's geographic position happened to straddle the Axis supply routes to North Africa. The British base there, operated like a vast, static aircraft carrier and floating depot, was able to harass enemy convoys largely unhindered with an impact disproportionate to the size of the forces that were deployed. Malta was like a small stone, waiting to trip the unwary or as the German Admiral Eberhard Weichold expressed it 'like a small but very sharp and painful thorn in the side of the Axis forces'.

In a determined bid to eradicate the 'painful thorn', Germany conceived Operation 'Hercules' as part of a bid to conquer the island, setting the tone for the Mediterranean campaign for the 24 months from January 1941. Naturally enough, therefore, the majority of the accounts written about Malta's wartime experience have been slanted to this military campaign. Yet the resistance of the Axis onslaught was ultimately only made possible by the courage and fortitude of the Maltese people, ordinary civilians though committed allies, who as a small nation resigned themselves to enduring the most extreme hardships in order to support the Allied cause. Had their spirit or resolve been broken, then the performance of the defending military forces would probably have been irrelevant. Consequently, this account of the siege of Malta, while fundamentally complete in all respects, is rather more inclined to the viewpoint of the Maltese civilians who survived it.

This was in fact the second major siege to which the Maltese islands had been subjected. In 1565, after years of attacks on Malta by the Turks, who were determined to take possession of the tiny island for its strategic value, Suleiman the Magnificent assembled a fleet of galleys and landed a 38,000-strong invasion force at Marsaxlokk Bay. Malta's defence was entrusted to Grand Master Jean de la Valette, the head of the Knights of the Order of St John, after whom the capital of Valetta is named. Able to muster only 600 knights and 9,000 troops and with requests for help from the powers of Christendom unheeded, it seemed that the island was doomed. The defiant resistance of the defenders, supported by the whole Maltese population, managed to repel the Turks' initial attacks and, though besieged within the citadel in the Grand Harbour, it seemed a glimmer of hope remained.

Throughout the summer of 1565, heat, disease and dwindling food supplies increasingly afflicted the Maltese forces as they fought off successive assaults by the invaders, always inflicting greater casualties than they sustained themselves. When all seemed lost, desperately needed reinforcements and supplies arrived with the Sicilian Viceroy, Garcia de Toledo. By the late summer, the Turks themselves were starting to run out of provisions. Unable to sustain their offensive, with fragmented leadership and broken spirit amongst the troops, and having suffered heavy casualties, the Turks finally withdrew, lifting the siege on 8 September 1565, 113 days after it had started. What remained of the large, original Ottoman invasion force sailed away. Historians have calculated that more than 26,000 Turkish soldiers were lost in the campaign.

There are a number of parallels between the great siege of Malta of 1565 and the siege that occurred almost four centuries later, during World War 2. On both occasions, resistance depended on a defensive force that was heavily outnumbered by its adversary, but, as before, the inferiority in numbers was more than offset by their indomitability of spirit. Likewise, during both sieges, the contribution of the entire population was essential for survival, if not through direct military action, through bearing collectively the brunt of hardship, in providing the care and treatment of the sick and injured and in toiling with the island's meagre resources to provide additional sustenance wherever it could be gleaned.

Ultimately, Malta's ability to continue to repel the attackers depended both times on the replenishment of supplies from the outside. An island, like a castle, can be an impregnable fortification but its ability to survive and fight is, in the final analysis, totally dependent on its reserves of food, water and munitions. So it was too for Malta. In 1565, the Sicilian Christians had come to the island's aid in the very nick of time. During World War 2, it was the Allied convoys that had to battle through the Mediterranean with desperately needed supplies. These comprised ammunition, fuel, military equipment and spare parts, certainly, but also food, clothes and oil for electricity generation, heating and cooking as well as to drive buses and tractors in order to maintain the island's capability for life-sustaining existence.

While there are marked similarities between the two great sieges, there are also some important differences. For one thing, the siege during World War 2 lasted considerably longer, for approximately 23 months in comparison to the 3½ months of the 1565 siege. Secondly, throughout the Ottoman siege it was primarily the military forces on either side who were engaged in the fighting. Although, as it turned out, the planned Axis invasion of Malta did not transpire, nevertheless, throughout the constant, heavy aerial bombardment, the civilian population was directly affected by the conflict as their homes were pounded by bombs and their lives endangered. Finally, the Ottoman invasion had posed an immediate threat to the sovereignty and self-determination of the Maltese. In contrast, World War 2 was not, in that respect, Malta's war. That is not to say that the Maltese were not, as a population, committed to the Allied cause, or that they were not vehemently opposed to the fascist régimes of Germany and Italy. The fact is, though, that Malta's involvement in this war, which led to the Axis siege, was the result of its being a British Colony, a relationship which in itself was more a function of Britain's interest in Malta's military facilities than of a benevolent support of a small and defenceless country threatened by a common enemy.

Having said that, the British interest in Malta went beyond the simple preservation of its military capability there and certainly extended to a genuine concern for the well being of the Maltese people. The British also had an enormous respect for the indomitable character and resolve of the Maltese people in the way they cheerfully endured with spirit this most challenging of physical and emotional trials on their behalf, in the necessary execution of the war against Germany and Italy. At that time, Britain stood alone in confronting the forces of the 'Pact of Steel'. In these circumstances it was critical to exploit every strategic advantage they had, wherever it was, in order to tip the balance of odds against the enemy in every way possible until, hopefully, other support was forthcoming.

In the Mediterranean theatre of war, the island of Malta had an immense strategic value that enabled Britain to keep on the defensive an adversary who, since the capitulation of France, was numerically superior. This aided the armies in North Africa in their battles with Rommel's Afrika Corps and allowed the Royal Navy to dictate the course of the naval war.

Using Malta as the base of operations, naval reconnaissance aircraft enabled the British to monitor closely the movements of the Italian surface fleet permitting the implementation of a plan to destroy the heavy battle units in their home base. This occurred on 11 November 1940 when naval torpedo bombers destroyed four of the Italian Navy's six battleships in the port of Taranto. Thereafter, although Italy retained a huge dominance in submarines and aircraft, her naval threat was largely neutralised, through timidity in the wake of the Taranto experience, and as a result of other costly surface engagements in which the British were able to score major successes through the exploitation of other tactical advantages, notably shipborne radar.

This reluctance to engage the British fleet further disadvantaged the Italians when the ambitious but unwise campaign in North Africa compelled them to establish supply routes to replenish their armies who had overextended themselves by advancing into Egypt. As the Italians suffered embarrassing setbacks in their engagements with Wavell's 8th Army at Sidi Barrani, Tobruk and Benghasi, the Germans felt compelled to go to the aid of their humiliated ally. Thus, Erwin Rommel was sent to Africa where he took command of the Axis campaign.

Maintaining the logistical support of his German fighting units was equally critical if Rommel was to sustain any sort of lasting counter-offensive but interruption to supplies forced him to hold his advances for four vital months in the spring of 1941. This was still partly due to the impotence of the truly powerful Italian Navy but more fundamentally it was the existence of the British-controlled island of Malta from which the convoy routes to Tripoli and Benghasi were being constantly harassed.

An incident which graphically illustrated the Axis dilemma occurred during a night attack on a convoy on 18 September 1941, when the British submarine HMS *Upholder*, under Cdr M. D. Wanklyn VC, torpedoed and sank the twin Italian troopships *Neptunia* and *Oceania* which were bound for Tripoli. Representing 39,000 tons of lost shipping, their sinking also denied the Axis forces in North Africa 7,000 replacement troops, either dead or incapacitated.

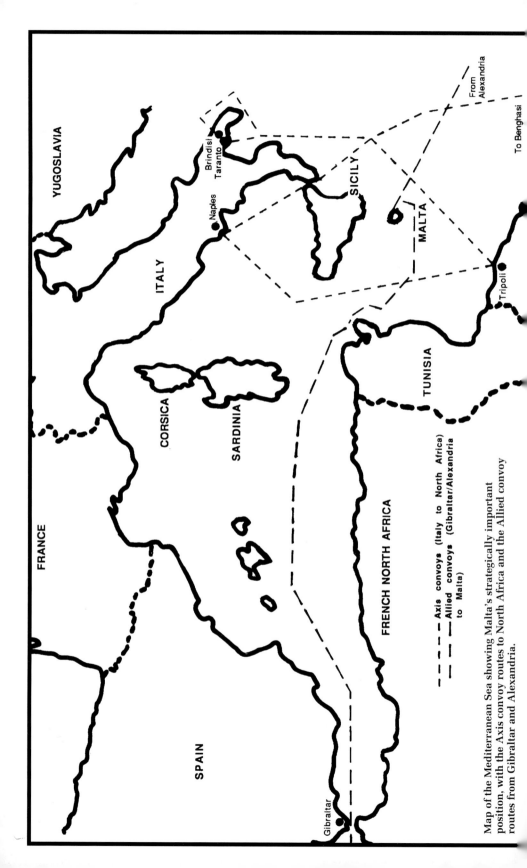

Map of the Mediterranean Sea showing Malta's strategically important position, with the Axis convoy routes to North Africa and the Allied convoy routes from Gibraltar and Alexandria.

Later, on 8 November 1941, seven cargo ships escorted by 10 destroyers and two cruisers, effectively two escorts for each merchantman, were intercepted 135 miles east of Syracuse, by a small British force of two light cruisers and two destroyers, and sunk with the loss of 60,000 tons of supplies.

So it had been for month after month, the figures maintained by the German Admiralty emphasising the graveness of the Axis predicament:

- July 1941 — 21 cargo ships and tankers lost totalling 78,000 tons.
- August 1941 — 25 cargo ships and tankers lost totalling 85,000 tons.
- September 1941 (first 2 weeks) — 10 cargo ships and tankers lost totalling 40,000 tons.

In order to stop this strangulation of the arteries of supply, the Germans were compelled to take action to neutralise Malta's threat. Grand Admiral Raeder had been advocating such an offensive for some time but, until late in 1941, his arguments in favour of such an offensive had not been received with any measure of enthusiasm. A decision in support of action was finally made in November 1941 when a forced suspension to the progress of the war on the Eastern Front, caused by appalling weather, allowed the attention of the German High Command to be diverted to the Mediterranean theatre and the difficulties being experienced there.

The transfer of large numbers of frontline aircraft from their advanced bases on the outskirts of the Russian capital to the islands of Sicily and Crete was agreed upon as being the essential first step to achieving German control over the vital central section of the Mediterranean. They joined other air groups already relocated in Greece, providing Field Marshal Kesselring, who had been appointed Commander in Chief of the operation, a force of over 2,000 combat aircraft. By securing a position of supremacy in the skies over this sea area, a number of key objectives could be achieved which in turn would have a positive influence over the subsequent conduct of the North African campaign and the pursuit of other German military goals in the Mediterranean area. The objectives which Kesselring was set had three broad thrusts:

- To eliminate Malta's strike and defensive capability as a prelude to the planned invasion of the island, codenamed Operation 'Hercules', in order to keep it under subjection.
- To close or restrict the Mediterranean to British shipping traffic and naval operations.
- To safeguard the convoy routes to Cyrenaica and Libya in order to resume full replenishment of the Axis land forces preparing for the final drive on Egypt.

Fundamental to the success of the whole programme was the achievement of the first of these objectives, for the position of Malta as a strategic keypoint was decisively important.

Kesselring took some time to prepare for the offensive, consolidating his air groups in their new bases and having detailed plans drawn up which first identified critical bombing targets on Malta and the small adjacent island, Gozo. At the top of the list were airfields, harbour and dock installations and any ships that were laid up or berthed within the Grand Harbour complex. It was not anticipated that Malta would capitulate immediately and that it would probably be necessary to starve the island into submission as well as destroy its defensive capacity. To reinforce the blockade that would be imposed as part of the overall offensive, the coastal waters around the island would also be intensively mined

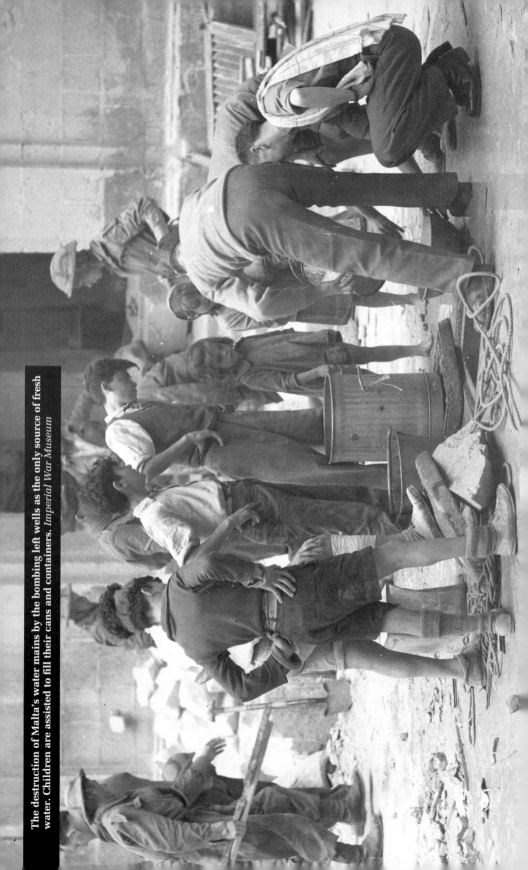

The destruction of Malta's water mains by the bombing left wells as the only source of fresh water. Children are assisted to fill their cans and containers. *Imperial War Museum*

to prevent resupply or relief from the sea. Kesselring calculated that the initial phase, the concentrated air assault on the island, would take approximately six weeks to complete. It commenced in earnest on 1 April 1942, heralding a period of terror which is indelibly etched in the memories of those who experienced it.

Some description of the extent of the onslaught is necessary to give the reader an impression of the scale of devastation inflicted upon Malta in the period to 10 May 1942. The islands had already endured two years of sporadic bombing from which there had been significant damage and, inevitably, the islanders were already suffering a measure of inconvenience. The 8 April 1942 witnessed the 2,000th air raid on Malta. Over the following month 6,700 tons of bombs were dropped, mainly around the dockyard area. The effects of this overwhelming weight of bombs was devastation and havoc at an extreme level.

More than 10,000 houses were destroyed while a further 30,000 were badly damaged and left structurally unsafe. The rubble caused by this destruction blocked up the streets, restricting passage and severely hampering movement and communication in the islands as well as hindering rescue operations. The islands' reservoirs and the water they held, an essential resource for survival in the island's hot climate, were totally obliterated and food stores distributed around Malta and Gozo were gutted. Over 800 persons were killed and another 1,000 or more were injured to a serious extent. Protection from the bombing was found in ancient caves and new air-raid shelters chiselled deep into the island's natural limestone rock strata. Caverns were also carved out for the rapid construction of secure underground hospitals affording refuge for the injured from the onslaught above.

The dockyard suffered too, with cranes and other ship repair facilities damaged beyond repair, warehouses burnt-out along with their valuable contents and helpless ships, berthed within the Valetta harbour complex, seriously incapacitated.

Life for the Maltese people was reduced to a bare existence of day to day survival, although in spite of all the terror being inflicted upon them they managed to remain cheerful and courageous. The effects of the bombing impacted on all aspects of daily life. Families were compelled to live and sleep in improvised shelters among the rubble, meals were prepared and eaten in the open air and, with school buildings destroyed, so too, children's lessons were taken *al fresco*.

Apart from the loss of the reservoirs, water mains in the towns were damaged without exception, causing great inconvenience to the population. Old wells had to be recommissioned and new ones sunk and it became a common everyday sight to see people carrying around buckets of water for sanitary purposes, cooking, washing and, most vitally, for watering the crops of tomatoes and other locally-grown produce.

Gozo, always more verdant and fertile than the larger island of Malta, now became the kitchen garden for the whole Maltese community and distributions of food produce cultivated by the Gozitans became a regular occurrence.

Despite all the improvisation and industry of the quarter million population, a grave situation still threatened, for the island was in reality grinding inexorably to a halt and widespread starvation and disease were dangerously close at hand. Already, all food and other commodities, including milk and water, were strictly rationed to an extent that made the rationing in Great Britain seem quite mild by comparison. Even before the enemy's bombing campaign had begun the supplies position had been critical, as the report issued on 1 April 1942 by Lt-Gen Sir William Dobbie, Malta's Governor, emphasises:

'Our supply position has been reassessed and may be summarised as follows:

a) *Wheat and flour*: No material cuts seem possible as these are staple foods. Present stocks will, with care, last until early June.

b) *Fodder*: Issues already inadequate were recently cut; stocks will now last until the end of June.

c) *Minor Foodstuffs*: Meat stocks are entirely exhausted. Most other stocks will last until June.

d) *White Oils*: Aviation fuel till mid-August; Benzene till mid-June; Kerosene till early June.

e) *Black Oils*: We have only 920 tons of diesel oil — five weeks supply — and 2,000 tons of furnace fuel, all of which will be needed for fuelling HM Ships now in dock. The black oil position is thus becoming precarious and very urgent action appears necessary to restore it.

f) *Coal*: Welsh coal will last only until the end of May, other grades until mid-June.

g) *Ammunition*: Consumption of ack-ack ammunition has greatly increased and we have only one and a half months' stock left.'

Besides the items listed in the report, the island also desperately needed replenishment of its meagre defensive force of fighter aircraft, which, at one point, had been reduced to the now legendary three Gloster Gladiator aircraft which were dubbed *Faith*, *Hope* and *Charity* in an oblique reference to the island's state of spirited resistance. While a series of combined operations by the Royal Navy and United States Navy enabled the island's garrison to be reinforced by Spitfire aircraft, the supplies position remained critically depleted and survival depended upon the arrival of provisions from outside, shipped to Malta by convoy. The alarm signals had been clearly sounded and the Government in London was warned that it would be impossible for Malta to endure any longer without food and ammunition as well as the replenishment of other vital needs.

Reacting to these most urgent calls for relief from Malta's senior figures, the Royal Navy planned a double relief convoy from either end of the Mediterranean — Operation 'Harpoon' from Gibraltar and Operation 'Vigorous' nominally from Alexandria but in actuality from Haifa and Port Suez. Even though the level of losses that had been sustained by the Navy meant that at this time it was hard-pressed to provide adequate escorts, the go-ahead was given for these operations to proceed regardless, even though the fleets would be more vulnerable to attack, in itself a reflection of the urgency of the situation.

The 'Harpoon' convoy comprised five fully loaded cargo ships, three British vessels, one American and one Dutch, plus a single, fast tanker which was supplied by the United States. 'Vigorous' was organised around a similar number of cargo freighters of various nationalities. All these vessels, with their naval escorts, could expect to be kept under sustained attack for the entire voyage, as well as to be exposed to continuous danger from German E-boats and enemy submarines.

As things turned out, the combined exercise was a depressing failure. It must be emphasised that this was through no fault of any of the merchant crews or naval servicemen. They were simply confronted by overwhelmingly superior enemy forces with an escort that was known to be inadequate for the task. Apart from those losses to ships that occurred during the passage of the convoys, the 'Vigorous' convoy was ultimately forced to turn back to Alexandria, totally depriving Malta of all its vital cargo. The 'Harpoon' convoy was slightly more

Above: The Maltese endeavoured in all respects to carry on as normal. Here, an open-air market is held among the wreckage of the buildings. Note the distinctively camouflaged car. *Imperial War Museum*

Left: Neither the bombing, nor the general effects of the siege were allowed to interfere with wash-day. The usual lines of clean clothes hang outside damaged houses. *Imperial War Museum*

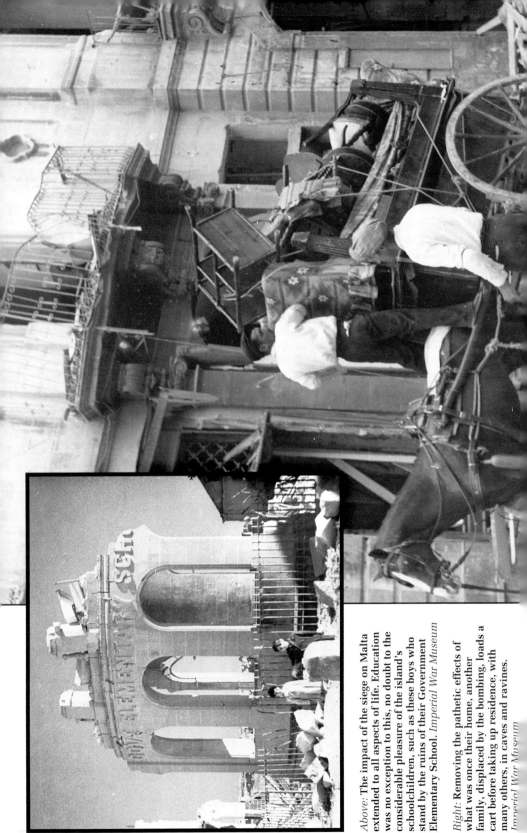

Above: The impact of the siege on Malta extended to all aspects of life. Education was no exception to this, no doubt to the considerable pleasure of the island's schoolchildren, such as these boys who stand by the ruins of their Government Elementary School. *Imperial War Museum*

Right: Removing the pathetic effects of what was once their home, another family, displaced by the bombing, loads a cart before taking up residence, with many others, in caves and ravines. *Imperial War Museum*

successful, fighting its way through to the beleaguered island with just two surviving cargo ships, but at an unacceptable price in naval losses. With 20,000 tons of new supplies unloaded, Malta's resistance could continue, albeit briefly, but it was hard to see how the British could continue to justify this level of sacrifice in order to prolong the island's defiant stand.

Quite apart from the continuing deprivation for the Maltese that the convoy's failure meant, the Axis dominance of the sealanes had permitted the resumption of unhindered resupply of its own North African forces. Within weeks Rommel had advanced decisively — Tobruk was taken and the British Army of the Nile had been driven back to Mersa Matruk. Cairo was threatened and serious consideration was given to the evacuation of the naval base at Alexandria. Malta must surely be next. With the Luftwaffe's softening-up process complete, the launch of Operation 'Hercules' was anticipated at any time.

Despite the fact that Malta was quite evidently on its knees, for no definite reason Operation 'Hercules' never happened. It is possible, perhaps, that the successes in impeding the resupply of Malta by sea may have led to the mistaken belief that the objectives of 'Hercules' could be achieved without the need to force an occupation. The neutralisation of the island was presumably considered to be adequate.

The respite afforded by the absence of this immediate assault was small comfort, for the civilian population was under continuing strain due to the inadequate replenishment of supplies. Following the minimal contribution of the 'Harpoon' convoy and the totally aborted 'Vigorous', the position of the island's supplies was again reviewed. This confirmed that the situation had worsened, for consumption, even at the reduced level, had outstripped the meagre replenishment. This led to the Deputy Governor, Sir Edward Jackson, introducing the concept of the 'Target Date', notionally the date by which it was essential that further supplies reached the island garrison but, in reality, the date at which, if new supplies did not arrive, surrender and capitulation were inevitable. Putting a brave face on the situation, the 'Target Date' was used as the basis for making further adjustments to rationing levels in a bid to conserve remaining supplies for as long as possible. Optimistically, it was stated that this provided ample opportunity for more convoy runs to be made with fresh supplies before stocks were totally exhausted.

The 'Target Date' was in fact, 7 September 1942, a piece of information that was closely guarded for had it reached the enemy, a final concerted effort to conquer Malta would most certainly have been inevitable.

With or without further enemy action directed at the island, everything depended on the next convoy. This was Operation 'Pedestal', planned for August 1942, which turned out to be one of the two greatest convoy operations of World War 2. The other was the disastrous Arctic supply convoy, PQ17.

'Pedestal' was organised along the lines of 'Harpoon' but as a single big convoy from the west with a second, simultaneous operation from Alexandria as a purely diversionary decoy exercise. Operation 'Pedestal', officially identified as convoy WS.5.21.S, consisted of 13 cargo ships and one tanker. Assembled east of the Straits of Gibraltar, during the night of 10-11 August 1942, the convoy moved east accompanied by a veritable armada of escort vessels. Over the next five days it was subjected to the most intensive enemy action as the Germans and Italians made every effort to prevent the convoy getting through to Malta, throwing all the offensive resources at their disposal against it.

Right from the outset the convoy had to run the gauntlet of enemy submarines as they lurked menacingly in their patrol zones between the Balearics and the coast of Algeria and, further on, in the area north of Tunisia. These attacks were concentrated throughout the nights of the convoy's passage during the hours when aircraft were grounded and their crews enjoying the benefit of a period of relaxation, an opportunity which was denied to the convoy personnel.

During daylight hours the convoy was subjected to remorseless aerial attack from aircraft based in Sardinia and Sicily. As the 'Pedestal' ships passed southwards through the Sicilian Narrows, they had to negotiate their way through an enemy minefield and here too, after darkness, they were harassed by E-boats when the convoy's ability to manoeuvre was severely restricted.

Finally, as the convoy approached the coastal waters of Malta, they were exposed to the hazards of more mines that had been laid around the island. Even as the surviving five ships — from the 14 that had set out — were entering Grand Harbour, Valletta, the enemy onslaught continued as Junkers Ju87 Stukas rained bombs down on the helpless targets below. Yet the convoy had managed to reach Malta, even though it had been reduced to barely a third of its original capacity, and the fact that the Germans and Italians did not press home their advantage while the ships were unloading and at their most vulnerable, meant that a significant level of replenishment was achieved. It might not have been sufficient to meet all the islander's needs but it was adequate to sustain the beleaguered island during this critical period. Most importantly it permitted the strategic advantage in the chess game of the Mediterranean War to transfer back to the British.

Not only did the convoy's supplies bring renewed sustenance to the Maltese people but they also permitted the revival of the British offensive against the Axis convoy supply lines. In particular the precious consignment of fuel brought in on the crippled tanker *Ohio* allowed the level of patrols by Allied warships and warplanes to be increased. And this time it was decisive.

When the British counter-offensive in North Africa got underway, marked by the spectacular success at El Alamein, it was unstoppable, and following the Operation 'Torch' landings, the Axis forces were irrevocably swept from the African continent.

In turn, the reverses in Africa resulted in a declining enemy interest in achieving the subjugation of Malta. There was no longer any benefit to be derived from taking the British stronghold that warranted the consumption of men, equipment and ammunition that would be necessary to secure such an objective.

The cancellation of Operation 'Hercules' became most evident in the enemy's reduced commitment to preventing further replenishment of Malta. So it was that when the next convoy, Operation 'Stoneage', sailed for the island stronghold, it reached its destination largely unscathed.

In the final analysis, none of this would have been possible, of course, had it not been for the courageous endurance of the Maltese people in the face of an assault of unprecedented magnitude. In recognition of this, the British Government decorated the island with the George Cross medal, Britain's highest honour for civilian bravery. The award had been announced by King George VI on 16 April 1942, at a point when the island had already experienced almost four months of daily air attacks and its future survival was still far from certain. In his message to the island's Governor, the King spoke of the magnificent resistance to the German efforts to bomb Malta into submission and reaffirmed the acclaim of the British for 'the heroism and devotion of a brave people that will long be famous in history'.

The medal was presented by His Excellency Viscount Gort VC, the island's new Governor and Commander-in-Chief, to Sir George Borg, the Chief Justice

other example of how the Maltese struggled to continue their lives normally despite the terror visited
on them and the deprivation of the continuing siege — a family meal is cooked amidst the debris.
erial War Museum

ODENAME	NUMBER	DATE	ASSEMBLY PORT OF DEPARTURE	TOTAL MERCHANT SHIPS	MERCHANT SHIPS TO MALTA	SUCCESS RATE	NOTES
EXCESS	-	Jan. 1941	Gibraltar	4	1	25% (100%)	Three ships diverted to Piraeus
JBSTANCE	GM1	July 1941	Gibraltar	6	6	100%	
IALBERD	GM2	Sep. 1941	Gibraltar	9	8	89%	
Jnnamed		Mar. 1942	Alexandria	4	2	50%	5,000 tons supplies delivered out of 26,000 tons shipped
ARPOON		June 1942	Gibraltar	6	2	33%	20,000 tons supplies delivered; no fuel
GOROUS	MW11	June 1942	Alexandria	11	0	0%	
EDESTAL	WS.5.21.S	Aug. 1942	Gibraltar	14	5	36%	32,000 tons supplies delivered, including enough fuel for 2 months
ONEAGE	MW13	Nov. 1942	Alexandria	4	4	100%	
RTCULLIS	RES MW14	Dec. 1942	Alexandria	4	4	100%	

Total Malta supply convoys up to 31 December 1942: ex Gibraltar = 40+
ex Alexandria = 27
plus fast minelayer runs and submarine operations

le of selected, key supply convoys that sailed to Malta between January 1941 and December 1942.

and President of the Court of Appeal, who received it on behalf of the people of Malta, in a ceremony at Valletta on 6 October 1942.

Within the context of the accounts in this book, the experience of the beleaguered island of Malta in World War 2 represents a distinctive and very different dimension to civilian siege, far removed from the terrorist inspired incidents of more recent times that are described elsewhere.

There is a uniquely important lesson to be learnt from the siege of Malta that remains applicable today, particularly for the United Kingdom. Britain, like Malta, is an island and, despite the tenacious resistance that would inevitably confront any enemy that attempted to conquer her, her survival in such circumstances would ultimately depend, as it did for Malta, on the ability to keep open the sea routes for supply and replenishment. This should be a matter of great concern at a time when the 'Options for Change' policy is substantially reducing our capability to protect convoys if the need was ever again to arise.

In recognition of its stalwart resistance, Malta was decorated with the George Cross, the highest award for civilian valour. Here the ceremony reaches its climax as the case containing the medal is handed by His Excellency Viscount Gort VC, on the left, to Sir George Borg, the Chief Justice and President of the Court of Appeal, who received it on behalf the people of Malta. *Imperial War Museum*

Bridge Across the Sky 2

When the postwar map of Europe was effectively, if unintentionally, redrawn by the Allied powers at Yalta, in February 1945, quite apart from the understandable objections of those peoples whose futures had been decided without their even being consulted, it inevitably introduced complications that caused strains to international relations in the period immediately following the end of World War 2. The former German capital city Berlin was a particular case in point.

Besides the wider issues of political alignment that were discussed at Yalta, it had already been agreed in London in 1944 that, after the war was over, Berlin, and Germany as a whole, would be placed under the occupational control of the four Allied powers — the United States, Great Britain, the Soviet Union and France — divided into administrative zones and sectors under an Allied Control Council.

While the politicians may have broadly agreed their spheres of influence in this grand plan for the new Europe, including the fundamental aspects of the occupation of Germany, this did not incorporate explicit written provisions and guarantees for the unimpeded access to those sectors of Berlin which would come under the jurisdiction of the Western Allies, in the event that the city as a whole was isolated within a Soviet zone of Germany.

Such an outcome was always in prospect given the more rapid advance of the Russian forces which were spearheaded on the German capital in the drive to complete the defeat of the Third Reich. By contrast the American and British advance which was continuing on a broad front and meeting stiffer resistance was making considerably slower progress.

Gen Eisenhower, the Allied Supreme Commander, stated later that the Western Allies could have taken Berlin first if they had wanted to but that he had no instructions to do this. In reality this probably saved the lives of many American, British and French servicemen who would needlessly, but certainly, have been killed if such an objective had been pursued. The fact was that the seizure of Berlin was of no importance to the Western Allies since those functions of the German government that were of interest, both administrative and technical, had already been moved to the west.

Regrettably, this otherwise sound policy took no account of the symbolic importance the city would attract in the ensuing Cold War which would give it a strategic value that far outweighed all other considerations. This was hinted at when, after the official instrument of Germany's unconditional surrender was signed at Rheims on 7 May 1945, the Russians insisted on having a second, token ceremony of surrender held in Berlin.

Hence, after the end of hostilities in Europe, the line along which the victorious armies finally met left the German capital stranded some 160km (100 miles) within the eastern or Soviet zone of occupation, effectively an island of democracy, in three of its sectors, in an ocean of communism.

In these circumstances, West Berlin became a thorn in the side of the Soviet Union. Its continued, separate existence, blatantly representing free democratic and economic values, was seen as a threat to the stability of the communist block as a whole. Equally, as a magnet, attracting disaffected East Germans, it threatened to undermine the very life blood of the infant communist state.

The Soviet Union and, later, its puppet East German government therefore sought increasingly to isolate the western sectors of Berlin from the rest of the city's population by employing tactics of intimidation and harassment towards West Berlin citizens and the personnel of the occupying forces, in pursuit of the objective of totally absorbing West Berlin as an extension of its own territory. For their part, as the Soviets' intentions became clearer, the Western powers determined to resist this contrived expulsion most vigorously, resolving to maintain their presence and influence in West Berlin whatever the cost.

Thus, as a potential weakness in the fabric of the Iron Curtain, Berlin became the focal point of east/west tensions and a symbol of the idealogical conflict of the Cold War that developed between the Soviet Block and the West after World War 2.

Before the war had even ended both the USA and the USSR had realised that Germany would be pivotal in establishing control over Europe. Later, both feared being taken advantage of by the other if they adopted any position of concession or compromise in their dealings with the other over Germany. Although both sides expressed support for the reunification of Germany, even a commitment to the achievement of this goal, clearly, the circumstances of intense suspicion and insecurity that now dominated their relationships led to extreme reluctance to see this happen unless it could be realised totally according to their own conditions. In the developing climate of entrenched polarity, which realistically condemned Germany to remaining divided for the foreseeable future, neither side could afford to show weakness in its dealings with the other and the occupation of Berlin was no exception to this.

It was against this emerging political background that the confrontation between the former wartime allies over the status of Berlin developed into a major incident in the summer of 1948.

The carving up of the German capital had given eight of Berlin's districts in the east to the Soviet Union. The city's New West End, the area that had developed as older Berlin outgrew its space, was placed under the authority of the Western powers. The United States' sector comprised the southern districts of Zehlendorf, Steglitz, Templehof, Neukölln, Kreuzberg and Schöneberg. The British sector embraced the central western districts of the Tiergarten, Wilmersdorf, Charlottenburg and Spandau, while the French were allocated the northern districts of the city at Wedding and Reinickendorf. Internal borders were set up between the sectors, essentially between the Soviet zone and the rest. Berlin acquired the aura of a city of espionage and counter-espionage, of spies and black marketeers as exemplified so perfectly in Graham Greene's classic Cold War novel *The Third Man*.

In essence it was the contrasting approaches of the respective allied power blocks in their treatment of the defeated German nation that provided the catalyst for the confrontation over Berlin. The Soviet Union for its part was determined to suppress Germany's economic and industrial capability, presumably to neutralise its future military threat, in much the same way that France had intended after World War 1. The Communist authorities set about systematically stripping the eastern zone bare of anything of monetary or industrial value, leaving the citizens of eastern Germany impoverished, resentful and with a severely reduced capability to provide for their own basic needs of life. It seems too that, given the massive destruction suffered by the Soviet Union during World War 2, it intended that any future war would be fought on territory beyond its own frontiers. Hence, East Germany, along with a string of other eastern European countries, were to be used to provide a protective buffer around Mother Russia's boundaries.

America, France and Britain had, by contrast, learnt a valuable lesson from World War 1 and had no intention of allowing the mistakes of Versailles to be repeated. The economic reconstruction of Germany was, therefore, seen as paramount, to restore the dignity of the German people and to allow them as soon as possible to recover their position of respect among the family of nations. Financial support, in the form of currency reforms, democratic rebirth and assistance with industrial regeneration formed the cornerstone of the Western powers policy towards the western zone of Germany, the direct opposite of what was happening in the east over which they were powerless to exert any influence.

The implementation of these starkly contrasting policies led to increasing tensions between the former allies which intensified acutely in 1947 when the Western powers took the first tentative steps under the Marshall Plan to establishing the economic independence of their own zones of Germany from that occupied by the Soviet Union. The fact was that the countries of eastern Europe were not deliberately excluded from the Marshall Plan initiative. Rather, they collectively elected to decline the aid on offer on the basis that it was essentially an anti-Communist stratagem.

George Marshall, the Truman administration's Secretary of State, presented his plan himself in what can only be described as benevolent terms, though with perhaps a thinly disguised wider intent, in a speech on 5 June 1947:

'Our policy is directed not against any country or doctrine but against hunger, poverty, desperation and chaos. Its purpose should be the revival of a working economy in the world so as to permit the emergence of political and social conditions in which free institutions can exist.'

Whatever the reaction of the Soviet block, the Western Allies saw no justification for delaying the implementation of the plan or any impediment which prevented its adoption. In March 1948, therefore, it was decided that their zones of Germany should be united into a single economic unit, including, of course, the western sectors of Berlin. In protest, the Soviets withdrew their representatives from the Allied Control Council.

Three months later, the West introduced a reform to the German currency in the western sectors of the country creating the Deutschmark and inflaming the already difficult political situation. The Russians did not accept the currency change and refused to allow the new money into East Germany, seeing it as a threat to the East German currency. More critically they blocked its introduction into any part of Berlin.

On 24 June 1948, in an act of deliberate brinkmanship, the Soviet Union unilaterally announced that the four power administration of Berlin had ceased to exist and that the Western Allies no longer had any rights in the city. Simultaneously they closed all land routes into Berlin from the West. The aim was to deprive both the population and the occupying forces of the basic necessities of life to compel the Western powers to make concessions, though these were unspecified and probably amounted only to the relinquishing of their entire interest in Berlin.

Until that time Berlin had been linked to the rest of Western Germany by a recognised network of road and rail routes, as well as canals and rivers, allowing continuous access for supply and renewal.

America, Britain and France collectively saw the Russian action as highly provocative, threatening direct conflict and evidently a move aimed at forcing them to abandon their jurisdiction over Berlin.

Given that the West now viewed the continued existence of West Berlin as a beacon of freedom glowing in the repressive darkness of the Communist zone, there was not even the remotest possibility that the West would capitulate. Instead, their response was to commence the transportation of all supplies into Berlin by air.

To elect to breach the Russian blockade by an airlift was no light decision for it represented a logistical challenge of immense proportions. For its part, the Soviet Union considered it an impossible objective to achieve and presumably, on the basis of this assumption, made no attempt to interfere with the aircraft operations that now started. For the same reason they made no hostile military counter move. Berlin's western sectors had approximately two and a half million inhabitants for whom the provision of the most basic rations required the conveyance of a minimum of 4,000 tons of cargo each day. Based upon the numbers of aircraft that were immediately available it was calculated that this was initially an attainable target. West Berlin could survive, it seemed, but only under siege conditions.

Much has been written on the operational side of the airlift to Berlin that commenced in June 1948. In fact the airlift consisted of three distinct operations: the British and American military operations, Operation 'Plainfare' and Operation 'Vittles' (the latter, a name selected in preference to the original choice of Operation 'Lifeline'), managed respectively by the Royal Air Force and the US Air Force. Later, when it was realised that there were inadequate military aircraft available to maintain the required level of supplies, a civil airlift operation was formally commenced on 4 August 1948. A number of well-known aircraft operators of that period assisted with this civilian supply effort, among them Flight Refuelling Ltd with its fleet of Lancastrian tankers (converted Lancaster bombers), Aquila Airways with its Hythe class (ex-Sunderland) flying boats and Silver City Airways whose Bristol Freighters offered a large cargo capacity which was ideal for the airlift operation. In all 25 private airlines, including BOAC, the forerunner of British Airways, contributed to the civilian Berlin Airlift which continued in earnest until late July/early August 1949. The civil airlift was placed under the overall direction of BEAs' General Manager in Germany.

To achieve the delivery of the maximum volume of supplies, the airlift operation required careful planning and precise control. It was based on the use of three air corridors into the beleaguered city.

The corridor from Hamburg in the northwest was followed by aircraft operating out of the RAF bases at Schleswigland, Fuhlsbüttel (Hamburg's civil airport) and Lübeck. The reception point was the combined RAF/USAF base at Tegel in the French sector of Berlin. The returning, empty aircraft were routed initially to Schleswigland. Also operated along the northwestern corridor were flying boats from Finkenwerde, on the River Elbe, which terminated on the Havel See, one of the large lakes in West Berlin.

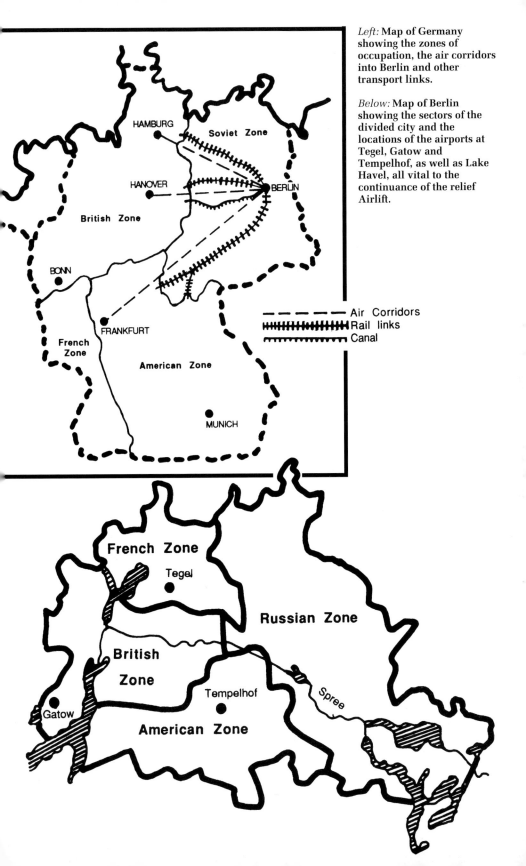

Left: **Map of Germany showing the zones of occupation, the air corridors into Berlin and other transport links.**

Below: **Map of Berlin showing the sectors of the divided city and the locations of the airports at Tegel, Gatow and Tempelhof, as well as Lake Havel, all vital to the continuance of the relief Airlift.**

HAMBURG

Soviet Zone

HANOVER

BERLIN

British Zone

BONN

FRANKFURT

French Zone

American Zone

MUNICH

- - - - - Air Corridors
++++++++++ Rail links
~~~~~~~~~~ Canal

French Zone

Tegel

Russian Zone

British Zone

Tempelhof

Spree

Gatow

American Zone

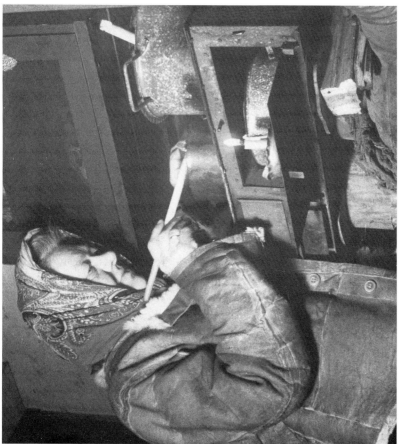

Left: The shortages experienced during the blockade of Berlin caused inconvenience and discomfort rather than anything more immediately life-threatening. Resourcefulness became the key to bearable existence in the beleaguered city. Typical examples are shown here: Old and young alike scour the refuse for scraps of food that could supplement the population's insubstantial diet. *Source unknown*

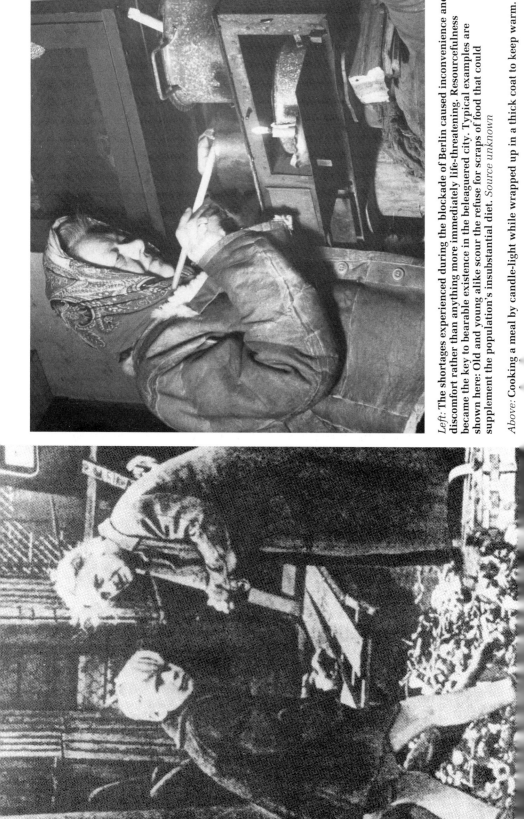

Above: Cooking a meal by candle-light while wrapped up in a thick coat to keep warm.

From the direction of Hannover in the west, the central air corridor was used by aircraft leaving the RAF base at Wünstorf and the combined RAF/USAF bases at Celle and Fassberg. These aircraft, too, terminated at Tegel before returning to their bases of departure either direct or via RAF Gatow in Berlin's British sector.

Finally from the southwest, the corridor from Frankfurt handled planes from the USAF bases at Wiesbaden and Rhein-Main which flew into the USAF base at Templehof in Berlin's American sector. The returning aircraft were routed through Gatow back to Wiesbaden.

There were also flights into and out of Gatow direct.

Control of the vast armada of aircraft amassed for the airlift was managed by Allied air traffic controllers from the Operations Room of the Berlin Air Safety Centre which was housed in the Allied Control Commission building in Berlin.

In total, many hundreds of aircraft were involved in these operations, among them some of the latest and largest aircraft of the time. These included the Douglas C-74 Globemaster which, at the time, was the largest aircraft to land in Berlin, carrying a record single aircraft load of some 25 tons of goods. The new British aircraft, the Avro Tudor Mk IV and the Handley Page Hastings, also cut their teeth on the Berlin Airlift. Nevertheless, the mainstay throughout the entire operation was the amaranthine and ubiquitous Douglas C-47 Dakota which saw service in both RAF Transport Command and USAF Military Air Transport Service colours, as well as in the form of civil variants.

Of course, central to all this was the relief and sustenance of the beleaguered population of West Berlin, a population which, through the decimation of the war years, now comprised mainly the elderly and the very young, the most vulnerable sections of the community. It must be remembered too that, despite some rebuilding effort, Berlin was still largely a city devastated by the war, with bomb damage and rubble everywhere. Many of the buildings that were inhabited had cracked masonry and either broken panes in the windows or no glass at all, and hence, were difficult to keep warm.

The Allied reaction to the blockade imposed by the Soviet forces had assured Berliners, the 'Islanders' as they were obliquely referred to, that sufficient food to satisfy their basic needs would be supplied by the airlift, which was of some comfort during the summer months of 1948 when the operation started. But there were grave concerns about how they would survive during the harsh winter months, for a diet that was barely adequate in the warm weather would not sustain them through the cold of a Berlin winter, and the winter of 1948 was particularly cold throughout Europe! Great emphasis was placed, therefore, on the building up of stock piles of fuel during the autumn for, initially, all the coal flown into Berlin was destined for consumption by hospitals and industry, as well as to provide power for any food production processes. During the winter of 1948 each family received a weekly ration of just one shopping bag half full of coal for domestic heating.

In itself, this act of contingency planning was interesting for, apart from the practical common sense behind organising it, it also demonstrated that the people of Berlin had already resigned themselves to the reality that the blockade would not be a short-lived affair.

As a consequence, West Berlin became a city of foragers, as the population regularly searched the district, like maggots stripping clean the carcass of a dead animal, searching for anything which could supplement their meagre diet or be added to the fuel stocks for winter. Refuse tips were scoured for anything that could be safely recovered and consumed such as carrot and turnip tops, cabbage leaves and even rotten potatoes that had been jettisoned in better times and which could now be pared down less selectively to leave a residue that could be used to thicken up stews.

Similarly, the suburbs of the city were systematically stripped of all dead wood. Permission was granted for citizens to dig out of the ground the stumps of trees that had already been cut down or that had died, all of which when chopped up could be used for firewood. However, there remained throughout the blockade a strict ban on the felling of more trees. A dangerous but, by force of necessity, essential practice involved the removal of combustible material from the city's many ruins. Roof timbers, joists, floorboards, doors and window-frames all provided an excellent supplementary source of fuel and indirectly, of course, this process of stripping the ruins aided the process of clearance of the city's bomb sites.

Two kinds of processed food commodity now became a part of the West Berliner's regular eating habits as well as introducing new words to the international vocabulary. Though hardly welcome from a culinary point of view, they were seen as necessary dietary supplements to maintain a healthy level of nourishment in the population and they were thus shipped to the city in large quantities. These were SPAM and POM, the former being tinned SPiced hAM manufactured in the United States, the latter being a form of dehydrated potato compound which, when mixed with water, produced a creamy substance which did not exactly taste of potatoes but which did bulk-out many an otherwise insubstantial meal.

At this time, West Berliners still had free access to the Soviet zone of the city and could, if they so desired and at the price of submission to the Soviet's objectives, receive East Berlin ration cards which entitled them to a share of the food which on the eastern side was, by comparison, in plentiful supply. Few took up this offer and, of those who did, many subsequently rejected the cards, valuing much higher their personal freedom and liberty.

Apart from shortages of food and fuel, West Berliners suffered power restrictions and frequent interruptions to the electrical supply when it was supposed to be operating normally. This situation requires little comprehension when it is explained that the bulk of the city's power stations were located in the eastern sector, permitting the Soviet authorities to control virtually the generation and supply of electricity. The output of those stations which were located in West Berlin depended critically on the supply of fuel which, because it could never be guaranteed, resulted in intermittent power generation. Candles and vacuum flasks became as scarce as gold dust and the West Berlin womenfolk were forced to adopt a nocturnal lifestyle, rising in the middle of the night, when supplies were usually on, in order to wash and iron clothes or to heat water and cook food for their families.

The rest of free Germany rallied to the support of their beleaguered compatriots and numerous initiatives were launched to raise funds to purchase supplies or to make donations of provisions of food and coal. Postage rates in West Germany were temporarily increased by virtue of the need to purchase a special two pfennig stamp in addition to the normal postage stamp. All proceeds from the sale of these special stamps went towards assisting West Berlin. Later, as part of a special 'Help Berlin' campaign, 10 and 20 pfennig stamps were made available for voluntary purchase. In some western provinces, a one-day fast was organised and each day's food ration thus saved was contributed to the needy cause. In cities across Germany collections were made of commodities which the people could hardly spare themselves but which they willingly went without in

ove: **Ironing the washing while the rest of the family sleeps — no doubt a posed photograph intended** convey the impression of the actual interference to normal daily routine experienced by many. *ndesbildstelle*

ove right: **Cutting up twigs and treestumps for firewood. Note the bomb-damaged ruins in the** *ckground. Landesbildstelle*

low: **Issuing meagre coal rations in the street — only a bag full per family per week!** *Landesbildstelle*

The end of the blockade was celebrated by all with great enthusiasm. Here one of the first road convoys has reached Berlin from the west. The sign says: 'Hurrah, we are still living'. *Landesbildstelle*

order to provide aid to their countryfolk in Berlin who needed it even more. From Westphalia and Saxony came donations of 100,000 tons of coal and 10,000 candles; from the city of Bremen, a consignment of 20 million cigarettes, presumably to help temper the nerves; from Hamburg in the north and Munich in the south, tons of desperately needed medical supplies. And so it continued from just about every corner of western Germany.

The airlift continued through the winter months, the flight crews and traffic management people on the ground constantly improving their performance so that the records for the numbers of flights and the volumes of supplies transported were repeatedly being broken. Each important milestone was given due publicity as it was clocked up: the exceeding of 500 average daily flights for the first time in November 1948; 'Plainfare's' 50,000th landing in December 1948; a million tons of supplies overall in February 1949, and so on. It was essential, too, for each of these achievements to be attended with appropriate ceremony and public acclamation for not only did it lift the morale of West Berliners as the long months of tedium and anxiety were punctuated by these high points, but it was an effective counter to the negative publicity pumped out daily by the Soviet-controlled Berlin Radio.

During the winter months when Lake Havel froze over, the flying boat operation from Finkenwerder had to be suspended. At this time it became something of a daily battle to keep Berlin's three airports open as the winter weather constantly threatened to interfere with flight operations. Gangs of workmen toiled endlessly to keep the runways free of ice and snow and all this was achieved on the most meagre food rations. As it turned out the greatest impact on the airlift operation for which the weather was responsible came in November 1948 and this was principally long spells of foggy conditions.

As the Allied operations to break the blockade of Berlin emerged from winter and continued into spring, it was evident that the Russian's attempted stronghold on the city was not succeeding. Equally, though, and in spite of the commitment to maintain the airlift *ad infinitum* if necessary and the almost clockwork smoothness of the conduct of the operation, it was obvious that the Allies had in fact only created a stalemate situation, for there was no sign of the blockade being lifted. For such a situation to continue in perpetuity would have been intolerable for the citizens of West Berlin. To bring the blockade to an end required, in addition to the Allies continued unwavering solidarity to Berlin, a political initiative that would apply pressure on the Soviet Union.

Discussions on lifting the blockade had commenced under the auspices of the United Nations in early spring 1949 and these were given a major impetus by two events that occurred that April. On 4 April 1949 the North Atlantic Treaty Organisation (NATO) was formally created when 12 nations signed the treaty of mutual support in Washington. These were: Belgium, Canada, Denmark, France, Great Britain, Iceland, Italy, Luxembourg, The Netherlands, Norway, Portugal and the United States of America. The treaty declared in part that an act of aggression against any one of the signatories would be treated as an attack against them all and would be met by a collective military response. The treaty also stated that any such aggression would be treated in the same way whether it occurred within sovereign boundaries or against the forces of any of the signatories anywhere in the North Atlantic or the continent of Europe under their jurisdiction in which occupational forces were stationed.

Almost simultaneously, it was announced by the Airlift Command that during the 24-hour period from noon on 15 April to noon on 16 April 1949, the Combined Airlift Task Force had achieved the magnificent new daily record of conveying 12,940 tons of food, coal, oil and machinery into Berlin over the course of 1,398 flights. Gen Lucius D. Clay, the US Military Governor in Germany, announced that, if this rate was sustained, the Allies would be easily able to transport to Berlin by air more food and fuel than had been conveyed by road and rail vehicles prior to the blockade. In addition, a significant amount of material was now also reaching the city on barges brought along the network of canals linking Berlin to West Germany.

The Russians knew that their blockade had been defeated. They knew too that they dared not resort to military means to impede the airlift for fear of precipitating direct conflict with all the countries of the NATO alliance. On top of this, they were suffering the effects of a trade embargo on their own products which had been imposed in retaliation for the Berlin blockade.

Progressively, Soviet preconditions for the settlement of the dispute over Berlin were relaxed. They no longer insisted on the prior resolution of the long-standing currency question or the postponement of new constitutional plans for West Germany. On 4 May 1949 it was announced that the four occupational powers had reached agreement to bring the end to the blockade and this time they contained guarantees for the inviolable rights of access to Berlin from the west. Four days later, in Bonn, the Parliamentary Council representing the merged American, British and French sectors of West Germany, adopted a constitution for a new Federal Republic of Germany. Four days later, yet again, at one minute past midnight on 12 May 1949, the blockade of Berlin was lifted. Convoys of waiting vehicles proceeded through the borders into the Soviet zone and along the autobahns to the long-beleaguered city, while, simultaneously, the railway line to Berlin was also reopened. The arrival of these first blockade-busting supply vehicles was met with a rapturous welcome. The relief and jubilation was savoured by all concerned and the party spirit that followed was long in subsiding.

The airlift itself did not immediately end at this date. Determined not to be caught unawares in the event that the Soviet Union once more attempted to isolate the city and as a further demonstration of the unequivocable resolve of the West to maintain the democratic freedom of West Berlin, the airlift was continued for another five or so months to build up a huge stockpile of essential supplies. For all practical purposes, the Airlift finally ended on 30 September.

Of the resounding and unqualified success of the Berlin Airlift, there could be no doubt, whether it was viewed logistically, organisationally or politically. In terms of its physical achievements, the statistics that were announced after the completion of all operations were impressive to say the very least.

The total deliveries of food, fuel, machinery and other supplies amounted to 2,323,738 tons, of which 1,831,200 tons had been transported by air. This total figure comprised 1,586,530 tons of coal, 538,016 tons of food produce and 92,282 tons of fuel oil, the balance accounting for machinery, spare parts, clothes and household goods etc. Of this total, 76.7% had been handled by the USAF, 17.0% by the RAF and 6.3% by the civil airlift. A further 34,240 tons of freight had been conveyed back from Berlin by RAF aircraft, principally manufactured goods, as part of a drive intended to help sustain West Berlin's own capability for economic self-sufficiency.

There had been a total of 21,921 civil aircraft sorties and well over a quarter million military aircraft flights into Berlin over the course of the 463 days of the airlift operation, a daily average of some 590 flights. On the down side, there had been a number of aircraft accidents which in most cases resulted in heavy casualties among the crews.

The permanent memorial to the Berlin Airlift at the Place of the Airlift by Tempelhof Airport.
andesbildstelle

It was estimated that maintaining the airlift to Berlin had cost the Allies $224 million at contemporary values.

Viewed in retrospect, the blockade of Berlin and the operations organised to supply it by an air bridge had a profound impact on the world political scene, both positive and negative, as well as on subsequent military operations.

On the plus side, it cemented good relationships between West Germany and the victorious Western Allies at a time when defeat could have created deep and bitter resentment, as had been the case after World War 1. This was to be of great assistance to the NATO alliance in its continuing posture of stand-off with the Soviet block and it eventually smoothed the way for the admission into the alliance of the Federal Republic of Germany.

From a military standpoint, the airlift taught the USAF and the RAF innumerable, valuable lessons in the handling of major logistical air support exercises, all of which were applied later during the conflicts in Korea, Vietnam, Suez and even the Falklands.

Against this, the blockade and its legacy soured east/west relationships for more than a generation. It drove a deep wedge between the two halves of Germany, a division confirmed as a political fact with the formation of the German Democratic Republic (East Germany) and it led to the creation of the Warsaw Pact alliance, the Soviet block's answer to NATO. Nor, too, did the antagonism over Berlin come to an end. Conflicts frequently arose as the communists maintained their campaign of interference and intimidation, albeit for the most part on a lower key. This culminated in the erection of the Berlin Wall in 1960 as a physical manifestation of the division between the two sides of the city. Intended as a permanent barrier, it was demolished when Germany was finally reunified in 1990 accompanied with a relish and enthusiasm which was equal to that which had witnessed the end of the blockade in 1949.

Despite these unfortunate spin-offs of the Berlin affair, the Allies could not, in all honesty, have handled the situation any differently. Indeed, perhaps the greatest legacy of the blockade of Berlin was the Allies oneness of purpose in their response, a united front which they continued to present in the face of the Communist threat. This sentiment was neatly encapsulated in an inscription attached to the nose of one of the last RAF Dakota's to leave Lübeck for Berlin under Operation 'Plainfare'. The inscription was a reference to a biblical text in the Book of Psalms, Chapter 21, Verse 11. This read: 'For they intended evil against thee, they imagined a mischievous device, which they are not able to perform'.

ITEM	R.A.F. Operation Plainfare	Civil Airlift	U.S.A.F. Operation Vittles
TOTAL FLIGHTS (to and from Berlin)	49,733	13,879	131,378
TOTAL MILES FLOWN	18,205,284	4,866,093	69,257,475
TOTAL SUPPLIES TONNAGE (flown into Berlin)	281,727	87,619	1,214,339
TOTAL FREIGHT TONNAGE (flown back from Berlin)	29,532	1,541	28,836
TOTAL GERMAN CIVILIAN PASSENGERS (flown out of Berlin)	67,373	Nil	Nil

Table of key statistics for the Berlin Airlift, by Operation.

Mark of the Jackal 3

The early 1970s witnessed the onset of a sharply increased level of worldwide terrorist activity as many ultra-left wing, subversive organisations and extremist nationalist groups resorted to the perpetration of atrocities against civilian targets in the furtherence of their political aims. Almost overnight, through newspaper and television reports, the names of numerous radical organisations had entered everyday language: the Angry Brigade, Black September, Baader-Meinhof, the Symbionese Liberation Army, the Red Brigade and the Red Army Faction to name but a few. Similarly, certain of the key individuals engaged in subversive activities with these groups began to attract increasing personal publicity, unintentionally presenting them as latter-day Robin Hood's, so-called heroes of the common man, sinisterly appealing as icons to a generation of disaffected western youth. The likes of Che Guevara, Malcolm X, and Wadia Hadad among the better known, were attributed with a legendary prowess and cult image status, as champions of a proletarian revolution. Less well-known, but equally surrounded in the same sort of fictional mysticism that was more appropriate to the villain of a James Bond thriller were Miguel Enriques and Mohammed Abbas. Perhaps the most evil of these characters, a man who was soon notorious for the cynical insensitivity with which he administered cold-blooded death, a heartless mercenary who had no ideological interest in the causes he represented, was one Carlos Martinez, born Ilich Ramirez Sanchez Navas and known as the 'Jackal'.

His unfortunate alias was acquired as a result of what was, in retrospect, a careless revelation following a raid by British police on one of Carlos's safe houses in London. It seems that in sifting through the contents of the flat, a copy of Frederick Forsyth's novel about an assassin, *The Day of the Jackal*, was discovered. Unfortunately, this quite trivial find was blown out of proportion by the press who, of course, used it to maximum effect in casting the headlines for the morning editions presenting the story in the style of a cheap spy thriller.

Carlos was born in Caracas, Venezuela on 12 October 1949, the son of a wealthy Communist lawyer. His family background was one of indoctrination in revolutionary ideals from an early age, hence both he and his brother were given the Christian names of Lenin and Stalin. As a young man he came to London in 1966 with his mother and brothers where they took up residence in Kensington. The next few years in the British capital were used to good purpose with his subsequent career as an active terrorist in mind, providing him with the opportunity to get to know the city in detail, selecting suitable locations for future safe houses.

From this point Carlos's movements became unclear and it is a factor of the reputation that he has attracted that much has been attributed to him which he may have had no involvement in, while there is much besides in which he was almost certainly involved for which there is no definite proof. The characteristic signs of a Carlos-inspired attack, the mark of the Jackal, are, however, often unmistakeable.

He exhibited the personality of a psychopathic killer, a cold-blooded assassin who showed no remorse in his violent treatment of his victims. Those who fell into his clutches, in terrorist attacks or sieges, knew that their chances of survival were greatly diminished, depending as they did on the magnanimity of a man who, by experience, had shown no mercy. He was the ultimate mercenary, having no immediate doctrinaire interest in any of the causes he espoused but ever willing to offer his services to any subversive or anarchist group whose activities would contribute to the de-stabilisation of international affairs and help to hasten a Communist world order.

Recent research into the career of Carlos has revealed that, as a willing recruit into the world of international terrorism, he joined the pro-Palestinian group of Wadia Hadad in the early 1970s receiving small arms training in Aden and Jordan. Hadad, as it was collectively known, was a branch of the Popular Front for the Liberation of Palestine and enjoyed links or at least close associations with the Baader-Meinhof gang, Black September, the Italian Red Brigade and the Red Army Faction of Japanese terrorists.

By comparison with the 'troubles' in Northern Ireland, the Palestinian problem has been a matter for concern for twice as long, having originated some 20 years earlier, although realistically the root issues in both cases go back many years in history. The formal creation of the state of Israel in May 1948, in the former protectorate of Palestine, led overnight to the Arab section of the population becoming second-class citizens, if not virtual aliens, in their own homeland. Any faint hope that peaceful co-existence between the Jewish and Arab sections of the population could be achieved were dashed when armed conflict erupted almost immediately. An exodus of Palestinian refugees into the neighbouring Arab states of Lebanon, Jordan and Syria followed and the 'Intifada' or Holy War against Israel was launched. It had a single objective — the eradication of the Jewish nation and its replacement by a wholly Arab sovereign state of Palestine.

To attract worldwide public attention to the Palestinian cause and their long-held and, as it was felt, long-neglected grievances, Hadad and the other Palestinian extremists embarked upon a campaign of terror in the 1970s. Carlos was a willing accomplice. He was soon masterminding operations.

As spectacular evidence of the terrorist's intentions, the mass hijacking of five aircraft was attempted between 6 and 9 September 1970. The first three aircraft to be seized were a TWA Boeing 707, a Pan Am Boeing 747 Jumbo, and a Swissair DC-8, all taken during flights over northern Europe. The hijack of a fourth aircraft, an El-Al Boeing 707, was foiled when the terrorists were overpowered by members of the crew. One of the terrorists was killed, the other, Leila Khaled, was released into the custody of British police after the aircraft safely landed at Heathrow airport. Of the three captured aircraft, the Jumbo jet was flown to Cairo airport while the remaining two were taken to Dawson's Field in Jordan. Dubbed 'Liberation Airport' by the terrorists it was in fact a disused former RAF wartime airstrip. Three days later, a third aircraft joined them when a hijacked BOAC VC-10 was flown to the abandoned desert airstrip. The hijackers were met in this remote desert location by a gang of accomplices, clear evidence of the careful pre-planning of this major terrorist crime. There they proceeded to release 255 of the 311 hostages, both passengers and crew, who had been seized with the three aircraft. The aircraft were then blown up where they stood as the world's press and impotent Jordanian officials looked on, leaving them as shattered and blackened skeletons. Meanwhile, the remaining 56 hostages were taken to a secret location while their safe return was negotiated in exchange for the release of a number of captive terrorists, including Leila Khaled.

After 18 days of resisting the terrorist's demands, the German, Swiss and British governments finally conceded, fearing otherwise that the hostages would be executed without exception. The exchange was made after an RAF Comet jet delivered Khaled and six other terrorist prisoners, who had been held in Germany and Switzerland, to Beirut in the Lebanon. The relief which accompanied the safe release of the hostages was muted by great unease about the capitulation to the terrorists' demands by these Western governments.

The reaction of the official Palestinian resistance under Yasser Arafat was, apparently, one of disapproval of the Dawson's Field action, although ultimately Fatah, the active branch of the Palestine Liberation Organisation (PLO), was itself to become directly engaged in, if not involved in sponsoring and encouraging, similar atrocities. As to whether Carlos masterminded the multiple hijacking, as has been suggested, this will never be known for certain but it is more likely that this was an exercise on which he cut his teeth as he pursued his apprenticeship of terror.

What is more certain is that, two years later, the black legend of Carlos may have commenced in earnest with his alleged involvement in the raid on the apartment of the Israeli athletes in the Olympic Village at the Munich Olympics, although this has been vigorously denied. Whether or not he was actually present during this raid, it displayed all the hallmarks of a Carlos inspired and directed attack.

Regrettably, too, it became one of the first of many examples of a backfired attempt to end a siege by force when, as a result of impatience and misunderstandings, a premature and inadequately thought through intervention was ordered.

It all began on 5 September 1972 at around 5am local time, Munich. Five unopposed terrorist commandos entered the Olympic Village dressed in sportswear with their weapons concealed in sportsbags. The group were seen entering the village by a telephone engineer who was testing some equipment nearby. He watched a number of men climbing over the seven feet high perimeter fence that surrounded the village. He took no action because they were carrying sportsbags and he assumed therefore that they were athletes who were returning from a night on the town and who were sneaking back into the village secretly to avoid being reported to their team manager.

Shortly after, at 6am, the men stormed an apartment in the three-storey block occupied by the Israeli athletics team, killing two of the team members and taking another nine hostage. The two who were killed were Moishe Weinberg, the Israeli wrestling coach, and Joseph Romano, a weight lifter. By 7.30am the building had been surrounded by German police and security guards from the Olympic village while marksmen had taken up positions on the rooftops. Athletes of other nationalities, trapped elsewhere in the apartment block, were led to safety across rooftop parapets and balconies. A classic siege ensued.

Negotiations began between the German authorities and the terrorists who were identified as members of the Black September guerilla organisation, the secret cell of Al Fatah. Heading the team of German negotiators were Walther Troeger, 'mayor' of the Olympic Village, and Manfred Schreiber, the Munich police chief. The West German Minister of the Interior, Hans-Dieter Genscher, assumed overall control of the operation until, later on the first day, the West

Left: Map of the Olympic Village showing the site of the siege in the Israeli quarters in relation to the other principal features of the sports complex.

Above: Unidentified residents of the Olympic Village building, in which Arab terrorists held Israeli team members captive, making their escape as they pick their way carefully across the rooftops to

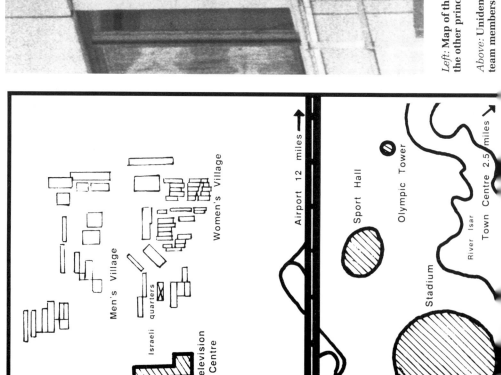

Men's Village

Israeli quarters

Women's Village

Television Centre

Airport 12 miles

Sport Hall

Stadium

Olympic Tower

River Isar

Town Centre 2.5 miles

German Chancellor, Willy Brandt, took personal charge of the negotiations and the total handling of the operation, following his arrival from Kiel. In these talks, the terrorists were allowed to believe that a peaceful settlement was sought. Simultaneously though, Manfred Schreiber instructed his men to shoot the gunmen down if the opportunity presented itself.

The terrorists were demanding the release of 230 Palestinian Arab prisoners held in Israel. These demands were backed up by an ultimatum to the German authorities: if the prisoners were not released, one hostage would be killed every two hours after which the Arabs themselves would commit suicide. The deadline for acceptance of these terms was set by the guerillas at 12 Noon after which the process of summary executions would begin. This was later extended to 1pm, local time.

The callousness displayed by this group of violent Arab renegades, a matter which was the cause of great concern as far as the safety of the remaining hostages was concerned, had been evident from the very outset of the siege. The Arabs had burst into a room in Block 31 firing shots from Kalashnikov automatic rifles as they entered, immediately hitting two of the Israelis as they lay in their beds. A warning to other athletes in adjacent rooms had permitted some of them to escape. Moishe Weinberg, who was already bleeding from a bullet wound in the side of his face, along with the other captured Israelis, was ordered to take the terrorists to where the remainder of the team were accommodated. Fearing for the well-being of their comrades, in spite of the critical injuries they had already sustained, Moishe Weinberg and the others attempted to steer the terrorists away from the fencers, swimmers and athletes to the quarters of the weightlifters and wrestlers who they hoped would overpower them.

Regrettably, the Arabs understood the verbal exchanges between the Israelis and forced them to go instead in single file to the entrance of the building where they could be transferred to a car. It seems that it was here that Moishe Weinberg died trying to escape, for the Arabs were seen later cold-bloodedly dumping his body outside the building. A similar fate befell Joseph Romano, but Tuvia Sokolovsky, one of the weightlifting coaches did manage to escape, using to good effect his army training, zig-zagging as he ran away under a hail of automatic fire.

The terrorists' first deadline was reached and passed without their sinister threats being carried out. Negotiations continued, interrupted only by the delivery of food at lunch time. The transfer of the food was a bizarre affair involving one of the terrorists who presented an incongruous figure dressed in the disguise adopted to gain entry to the Olympic Village — white flannels and blazer with white Panama-type hat. This contrasted starkly with the image of some of the other terrorists who appeared on the balcony of the apartment block wearing hoods with sinister looking eye slits that covered all of their head. As the drama unfolded, Avery Bundage, on behalf of the International Olympic Committee, announced that the decision had been made to postpone the Olympic Games pending the resolution of the siege. Meanwhile, the Egyptians, Kuwaitis and Syrians decided to withdraw their teams from any further competition.

At 3pm, local time, on 5 September, the terrorists' third deadline passed as, simultaneously, a virtually total news black-out was imposed to deny them outside information. Later, a fourth deadline, set at 5pm that day, was reached again with no sign that the Arab's death threats would be implemented.

The outside impression of stalemate belied the reality behind the scenes. Mrs Golda Meir, the Israeli Prime Minister, had already signified that the terrorists ultimatums would be ignored and no prisoners would be released. However committed the Arab terrorists were, in the face of this uncompromising stance, their objectives were thus modified to one of escape. The safety of the hostages was now to be traded in exchange for the safe getaway of the terrorists. The German authorities agreed in principle to this and were prepared to make an airliner available for this purpose but the concern now was which country would be prepared to offer safe haven to the terrorists which could also be relied upon to honour the commitment to release the hostages unharmed. The West German organisers of the Olympic Games had offered themselves as substitutes for the Israeli prisoners but this was refused.

A dialogue between the German and Egyptian governments had been proceeding in parallel with the negotiations with the guerillas and the Egyptian Prime Minister, Aziz Sidky, now apparently advised that Egypt was prepared to act as honest broker to resolve the impasse. Egypt would allow the terrorists to fly to Cairo and would take responsibility for guaranteeing the safe return of the Israeli athletes. Later, it appeared that this offer may have been reversed. Certainly there was confusion and misunderstanding between the two governments as to the precise nature of the Egyptian proposals. In the event, this was of critical importance to the decisions that followed and had a direct bearing on the German handling of the terrorist incident at its climax.

By the evening of the 5 September, some 12hr after the siege had commenced, the Olympic Village had been almost completely sealed off as armoured cars arrived to strengthen the police cordon which had already been reinforced by over 100 soldiers. Suddenly, at 8.30pm, things began to happen. Three Frontier Defence Force military helicopters landed in the grounds of the Olympic compound to collect the terrorists and their hostages and take them to the Furstenfeldbruck military airport, 24 miles from Munich, where a Lufthansa Boeing 707 airliner was waiting on the tarmac to take them to the agreed destination.

At 10.45pm, immediately after the helicopter had landed at the military airfield, a gun battle broke out between the terrorists and armed German security forces, in the course of which all nine Israeli hostages were killed as well as four of the guerillas and a policeman. The pilot of one of the helicopters was also gravely injured. Two other Arab terrorists, who had survived the gunfire, were captured as they attempted to escape from the airfield. A further three Arabs suffering with knife wounds were said to have been found in the Israeli quarters following the evacuation but the police declined to confirm or deny this report.

So how had this incident ended so disastrously, particularly when, prior to its bloody climax at Furstenfeldruck, Chancellor Brandt had announced to the world's press that his Government was concentrating on avoiding bloodshed?

There were conflicting views as to the precise sequence of events at the airfield on the fateful night of 5 September 1972. There were contradictions as to who had first opened fire, even erroneous announcements by the Munich police authorities that first advised that the Israeli athletes had all survived the onslaught. Just how the drama unfolded that night 20 years ago may never be known exactly but most probably it was as follows.

The German authorities felt, with good reason so they believed, that there was significant reason to doubt whether the hostages safe release could be assured if the terrorists and their captives were permitted to leave on the Lufthansa jet. Plans were hastily hatched, therefore, to make a rescue attempt. Any possibility that this could have been made at the Olympic Village, while the terrorists and hostages were being transferred by bus to the helicopter, was ruled out when it was realised that the hostages were tied and blindfolded. The only opportunity

52

Israeli sportsmen were kept hostage for 18hr by Arab extremists. *Associated Press*

that remained was to pick off the Arab guerillas at the airport when they arrived there and Army marksmen took up positions in readiness.

As the Arab gunmen emerged from the helicopters and proceeded to walk towards the airliner, apparently to check it out before boarding, Manfred Schreiber signalled to his officers to open fire. At this point the hostages remained bound up within the stationary helicopters. Unfortunately, in the darkness, the German sharpshooters were unable to hit all their targets, the single objective of the surprise attack that was more critical than any other to get right if a successful conclusion to the operation was to be ensured. Those terrorists who had not been hit turned their weapons on the helicopters, both guns and grenades, spraying them with bullets and blowing one up complete with its occupants.

Thereafter, a gun battle broke out between the surviving Arabs and the German security forces who were evidently anxious to secure the situation as swiftly as possible. Eye witnesses saw one of the West German helicopter pilots, who was caught in the crossfire, fall to the ground. When it was all over and the realisation had dawned that the operation had been a costly failure, the West German authorities were understandably reluctant to announce the outcome.

The names of the other dead Israeli team members were announced during 6 September. They were:

- Mark Slavin (18) — wrestler;
- Eliezer Halfin (24) — wrestler;
- David Berger (28) — weightlifter;
- Zeev Friedmann (28) — weightlifter;
- Jacob Springer (52) — weightlifting and wrestling referee;
- Joseph Gotfreund (40) — wrestling referee;
- Kehat Shoor (53) — shooting coach;
- André Spitzer (30) — fencing coach;
- Amitzur Shapira (40) — track and field coach.

The death of Zeev Friedmann was particularly tragic for he was the only son of parents whose entire families had been murdered in Poland by the Nazis.

The three guerillas captured by the West German police were also named as Ibrahim Badran (21), Abd Kadir el-Dnaoui (21) and Samer Mohammad Abdullah (22), all three identified as unmarried students.

The atrocity at the Munich Olympics was destined to be recorded for posterity in the history books, if not for the scale of the bloodshed certainly for the stage upon which it was perpetrated. Despite the condemnation piled upon them, the Palestinians had secured the publicity they sought. Relationships between West Germany and Egypt were strained in the wake of the affair and appeals for joint action by the United States and the European Community in the fight against terrorism attracted a great deal of popular support but, in the fullness of time, produced very little in the form of practical measures that were adopted and implemented.

What was not evident at the time was that Carlos's campaign of subversion had barely begun. Over the next few years anti-terrorist forces around the world would be kept fully occupied as outrage after outrage was committed almost with arrogant impunity. There were so many incidents that it serves no valuable purpose here to do other than make mention of a representative selection to demonstrate the range, scope and scale of his deeds which kept national authorities worldwide constantly on the alert. It was with good reason that Carlos became identified as the world's most wanted terrorist.

From a base somewhere in Paris he recruited a team of Palestinian fanatics and proceeded to perpetrate a sequence of crimes throughout 1973 and 1974. This catalogue of terror encompassed the raiding of the Saudi Embassy in Paris, the hijacking of a train and its passengers in Vienna, the blowing up of a Paris drugstore and an attack on the French Embassy in Amsterdam.

In late December 1973, Carlos struck in London when he gunned down Joseph Edward Sieff, the president of Marks & Spencer, at point blank range at his home in St John's Wood. Incredibly, Mr Sieff survived the attack, after undergoing emergency surgery to remove a bullet lodged in his jawbone, but it was revealed soon after that he had actually been only the first name on an assassination hit-list of other prominent Jewish persons which included Yehudi Menuhin, the impressario Bernard Delfont and Lord Sainsbury. Carlos fled the scene of the shooting, evading the police, so it seemed, with consummate ease.

Despite co-operation through Interpol, Carlos remained at large, slipping through every net laid by the police to trap him. The year 1975 began with an audacious bid to blow up an El-Al passenger airliner at Paris's Orly airport, an attack commissioned by Saddam Hussein, now the President of Iraq. On 13 January, Carlos and his accomplices slipped through the security barriers and attempted to shoot down the aircraft with a shoulder-launched missile. The rocket missed the Israeli jet, hitting instead a Yugoslav cargo plane. Barely two weeks later, Carlos, again with his gang and hoping to make good the earlier failure, attempted to repeat the exercise. This time the French airport security forces intercepted the terrorists and cornered them within a toilet block where they took hostages. Briefly besieged there, Carlos managed somehow to negotiate himself out of the predicament and, having managed to conclude a deal that was hard to justify given the urgency of the need to terminate his campaign of mindless violence, he once more fled the scene to conceal himself within the protective security of the Arab countries sympathetic to him or sponsoring his activities.

Never more was the release of Carlos more regretted than in late December 1975 when, in his next major offensive, he committed an attack aimed at undermining the economic stability of the whole world. Again, it was a case in which there was clear evidence of collusion by Saddam Hussein. Indeed, following police investigations at the time, it was claimed that Carlos had been recruited by the Iraqi leader for the primary purpose of assassinating Sheikh Ahmed Zaki Yamani, the Saudi Arabian Oil Minister along with his Iranian opposite number.

Four days before Christmas, Carlos coolly walked into the Vienna offices of the Organisation of Petroleum Exporting Countries (OPEC) with a handful of Arab gunmen, four men and a woman. They seized as hostages virtually all the Arab oil ministers and their senior staffs. Three men were killed during the take-over of the offices which were situated on the first and second floors of the Texaco Building on Vienna's Ringstrasse, opposite the University. The terrorists then threatened to commence killing the hostages if their demands were not met.

Prior to the violent intrusion, since 10am that morning, the OPEC ministers had been debating, somewhat heatedly, an agreement over price differentials between the major and minor producers. Not without coincidence, given the apparent objectives of Carlos's mission, the OPEC group was seeking to avert a price cutting battle between Iraq and the other Gulf area producers, principally Kuwait, which would have been potentially damaging to all concerned.

The terrorist group entered the building from the street at around 11.40am, wearing nondescript clothing and unchallenged by security personnel. This was presumably because it was assumed that, with their swarthy complexions, they were members of one of the national delegations. A joke passed among a scattering of journalists who were waiting for a press statement on the OPEC talks, to the effect that, with such a dishevelled appearance, they must surely be the Angolan delegation. Angola, a small producer and a poor third-world country, had been expected to apply for OPEC membership.

There was a near total absence of any formal security controls in the lobby to prevent entrance to the building as a whole or to the offices of the occupying concerns to any undesirable or dangerous persons. Had there been, it may have revealed the weaponry concealed within the sports bags carried by the gang members and may have thwarted the attack before it began. Instead, the terrorists were able to reach the lift on the first floor before they were challenged by an elderly Austrian doorman whereupon they produced their weapons and shot him dead. Later, the police revealed that the gunmen rode up one floor in the lift and then sent it back down to the first floor with the body of the dead man in it. Subsequently, the lives of two other victims, both security guards, were claimed in the immediate shoot out. When they had reached the second floor, the terrorists burst in on the OPEC minister's meeting, discharging bursts of fire from automatic weapons followed by a single loud explosion as a grenade was detonated, blowing up the OPEC office's telephone exchange.

Having seized their hostages, they were sinisterly divided up into two groups representing countries sympathetic and unsympathetic to the Palestinian cause. Carlos's group then proceeded to occupy positions at the exterior windows of the building where they opened fire on the police reinforcements which were already arriving at the scene with their sirens blaring and warning lights flashing.

The ministers and senior officials held in the raid represented countries who, collectively, controlled 90% of the world's oil production. Apart from Sheikh Yamani, they were:

- Dr Jamshed Amouzegar (Iran)
- Mr Belaid Abdessalem (Algeria)
- Mr Ezzedin Mabruk (Libya)
- Mr Abdul Mutalib al-Kazimi (Kuwait)
- Mr Tayeh Abdul-Karim (Iraq)
- Mr Ali Jaidah (Qatar)
- Dr Valentine Hernandez-Acosta (Venezuela)
- Dr Mofia Topio Akoba (Nigeria)
- Mr Edward-Alexis Mbouy-Boutzit (Gabon)

plus the representatives of Indonesia and Ecuador. With them, some 60 members of their combined staffs and advisers were also held.

The whole area around the OPEC building was swiftly cordoned off by hundreds of steel helmeted policemen while marksmen took up position on the roofs of surrounding buildings. Members of the staff of the Canadian Embassy, which was located on the top two floors of the building, were effectively trapped there for the duration of the siege, not so much because they were unable to make their way down to the ground floor but rather because they were definitely disinclined to attempt an evacuation in the circumstances.

Ambulances that now arrived on the scene took away the bodies of the casualties plus a wounded terrorist who required urgent hospital treatment after he had been hit by police gun fire during a foray into the building by the Austrian militia. At 12.30pm and again, a short time after, two of the female secretaries were released, one an Austrian girl employed at OPEC, the other Miss

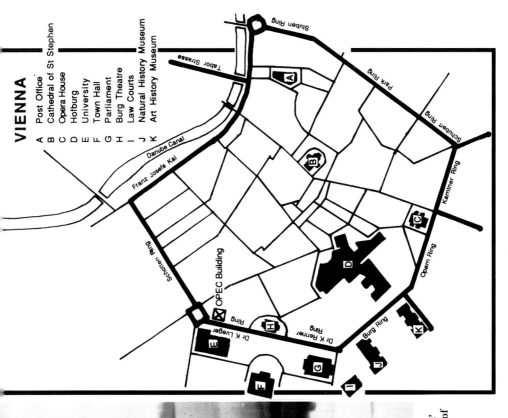

VIENNA

A Post Office
B Cathedral of St Stephen
C Opera House
D Hofburg
E University
F Town Hall
G Parliament
H Burg Theatre
I Law Courts
J Natural History Museum
K Art History Museum

Stuben Ring
Tabor Strasse
Park Ring
Schubert Ring
Danube Canal
Franz Josefs Kai
Kärntner Ring
Schotten Ring
OPEC Building
Opern Ring
Burg Ring
Dr K Lueger Ring
Dr Renner Ring

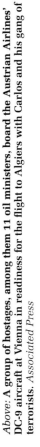

OE-LDB

Above: A group of hostages, among them 11 oil ministers, board the Austrian Airlines' DC-9 aircraft at Vienna in readiness for the flight to Algiers with Carlos and his gang of terrorists. *Associated Press*

Right: Map of Vienna showing the OPEC building on the Dr Karl Lüger Ring at left, facing the University.

Griselda Carey, the personal secretary to the OPEC Secretary General, Chief O. M. Feyide of Nigeria. Both were in a state of shock. Both, it was later revealed, conveyed elements of the terrorists' demands to the Austrian authorities. Progressively, other hostages carried out more comprehensive statements of the terrorists' demands. These encompassed the identity of preferred mediators, specific arrangements to permit the gang to get away from Vienna with their hostages and, effectively, appeals to Arab states to express oaths of allegiance to the Palestinian cause and to renounce any peace agreements which were unsympathetic to the achievement of the fundamental objective of the reconstitution of an Arab state in Palestine. They were referring, of course, to the Sinai Peace Pact being negotiated between Israel and Egypt, which would be signed later by Menachem Begin and President Sadat.

The terrorists first insisted that the Libyan Ambassador in Austria should be called upon to act as negotiator. Up until then, Austria's security chief, Oswald Peterlungen had taken personal charge of negotiations with the gunmen. Meanwhile, Dr Bruno Kreisky, the Austrian Chancellor, decided to return from a winter holiday to take direct control of the affair.

The terrorists also demanded that a jet airliner should be made available for them at Schwechat airport as well as a bus to convey them and a selected group of hostages there. Scissors, ropes and knives were also demanded, all of which had to be ready by 7am on 22 December otherwise they would blow-up the building with its occupants.

Several hours after the siege began the Venezuelan Mines Minister, Valentine Hernandez Acosta, was briefly released and came down from the besieged offices on the second floor seeking a radio and carrying a note which advised that one oil minister would be sent down every two hours in succession with a new demand.

The first of these was delivered at 4.30pm by one of the members of the Iraqi delegation. It insisted that a seven-page statement, written in French and described as the communiqué from the Arm of the Arab Revolution, must be read over the Austrian radio network by 5.30pm that day or one of the hostages would be shot. The statement defined a minimal, eight-point programme for national salvation, fundamentally calling for the reaffirmation of those basic commitments agreed at the 1967 Khartoum Arab summit, ie: no treaty with, no negotiation with and no recognition of the state of Zionist aggression (Israel).

In the event, the broadcast of the statement did not commence until 6.20pm but this significant deviation from the terrorists' instructions did not elicit any violent response. The fact that the gunmens' threat had not been carried out, clearly indicated that they were not, perhaps, as inflexibly committed as had at first been concluded. There seemed to be a possibility, no matter how tenuous or remote, that they could be reasoned with to agree terms for a peaceful end to the siege. Nevertheless, Dr Kreisky, who had stated that he was concerned first and foremost with avoiding bloodshed, did not pursue this option with any zeal. As he put it 'It is my conviction that human lives must be saved at all costs. Other things have been tried in the past and have failed.' Instead, the Austrian authorities effectively completely capitulated, conceding to all the demands made by Carlos's gang including the return of their wounded accomplice, even though the stomach wound he had received was serious and potentially life-threatening.

Arrangements were hastily made to prepare an aircraft for the gang's getaway, along with a selected number of the hostages. Although the terrorists did not advise the Austrians where they wanted to fly to, the destination turned out to be

Algiers, for the Algerian Government had agreed to allow them to fly there in the interests of seeing the affair concluded peacefully.

At 7.30am on 22 December, as duly requested, a cream bus, with drawn blinds, arrived at the OPEC building's back entrance where it was boarded by the terrorists along with the selected party from the hostages, the 11 ministers plus two of their advisers in each case, a total of 38 persons. The injured terrorist was accompanied by an Austrian nurse who had declared her willingness to travel on the dangerous mission in order to provide care and assistance to the wounded man. This terrorist was subsequently identified as a German — Peter Klein. The loading of the bus occupied more than an hour. When it left for the airport, Carlos could be recognised as the gang leader, sitting in the front seat by the driver wearing a black beret and dark glasses, waving and smiling to journalists. Awaiting the bus party at a remote part of the airport was an Austrian Airlines Douglas DC-9 aircraft which, as soon as it had been promptly occupied, took off. The whole operation was covered live on local television, a matter which may have been known by the terrorists for they appeared to perform suitably for the cameras and gave every impression that they were thoroughly enjoying the experience.

It seems that Carlos was in fact planning a round trip of visits to Arab capitals to milk the maximum publicity from the operation and that Algiers was only the first of seven planned calls. This was thwarted, however, due to the the limited range of the DC-9 jet, as well as through the later refusal to have it replaced by a larger Boeing aircraft. After arriving at Algiers' Dar al Beida airport in mid-morning and following further consultation, the captive OPEC delegates from Nigeria, Gabon, Ecuador, Indonesia and Venezuela, along with the Nigerian Foreign Minister, Mr Bouteflika, were then released. The wounded guerilla and nurse who had travelled with him from the Austrian capital also left the aircraft. The released hostages confirmed the police suspicions that the gang leader was indeed Carlos Martinez but advised that they had not been personally threatened or mistreated by the gang.

The DC-9 then took off for its next port of call, Tripoli airport, Libya, where a further eight hostages were released. These were Mr Belaid Abdessalem, the Algerian Oil Minister, Mr Ezzedin Mabruk, his Libyan counterpart, and six other hostages of lesser status — another Libyan, two Saudi Arabians and one each from Iran, the United Arab Emirates and Qatar. It was here that attempts to switch aircraft in order to permit the terrorists to fly on to Baghdad, the next planned stop, were frustrated by a lack of compromise on the part of Libyan officials. It seems that they may have been prepared to do a deal in exchange for the release of more hostages but this was refused.

It emerged, too, that there was strong hostility to the terrorists' action across the Arab world. In connection with this, the Iraqi authorities advised the group that they were denied permission to land in Baghdad but whether this was intended as a genuine rebuke, as part of the chorus of condemnation, or whether it was intended to distance Iraq from any reprisals for the raid, either economic or military, will never be known.

The obstacles blocking the release of the remaining hostages were finally resolved when Algeria allowed the DC-9 airliner to return to Dar el Beida airport where it arrived during 23 December, following a refusal to allow it to land in Tunis. The Algerian Energy Minister, Mr Abdessalem, who had been released in Libya and who had reboarded the aircraft for the next leg of the planned tour of the Middle East as 'a sign of human solidarity' now regained his freedom, released along with all the remaining hostages.

In a deal concluded with the Algerian Foreign Minister, Mr Abdul Aziz Bouteflika, which effectively granted political asylum for Carlos and the other terrorists, they were whisked away to an undisclosed destination not to be seen again, at least not immediately anyway. They were evidently not under arrest and Austrian efforts to have them extradited were brushed aside by the Algerian authorities who seemed anxious to end quickly the affair and restore, as far as possible, a situation of business as usual.

Carlos was, no doubt, soon back in his home base planning the next operation in a campaign that continued up to the mid-1980s with an assault on an Israeli ferry. Since that time, according to reports by leading experts on Middle East and Arab terrorist affairs, Carlos has been living in Damascus with his wife, Magdalena Koch, trading guns and other armaments to any and all interested subversive organisations. He remains beyond the reach of anti-terrorist squads wishing to apprehend him.

Alarmingly, at the time of the OPEC siege, the PFLP claimed that Carlos was just one of a large array of European, Latin American, Asian and African guerillas who formed a 'terror bank' from which specific people could be drawn for operations planned by various revolutionary groups of diverse political or religious persuasion.

It seems that for as long as these groups of extremists, in pursuit of their own ends and regardless of consequences, are prepared to gun down innocent people or violently take them hostage they will somehow find the opportunity. Terrorists with machine guns can just as easily turn their weapons on people in the street as in any public place. The fact that those who live by the gun may ultimately die by the gun is of little consolation in the wake of the slaughter of innocent people they inflict. The tragedy of those deaths can never be expunged. Ultimately, it will only be by the negotiation and adoption of an international convention against terrorism that these extremist organisations and their practices can be defeated.

Whether or not Ilich Ramirez Sanchez Navas, alias Carlos Martinez, is directly or indirectly involved in future outrages, they will always be viewed in the broader context of the campaign of revolutionary terrorism in which he has been such a prominent figure. Thus, collectively, they will always bear the mark of the Jackal.

Siege Breaking – the Kid Glove Approach

The accounts described in this and the next chapter illustrate contrasting approaches to raising sieges; either by a process of patient negotiation or by forceful direct intervention. In all four of the cases related, central to the concerns of the authorities acting to resolve these affairs was the safety of the ordinary citizens who had been taken hostage by persons who were responsible for the crime or act of terrorism that had precipitated the siege. All four cases occurred in the period from 1975 to 1977, when public alarm about terrorist crimes that victimised innocent civilians was most acute.

On Sunday, 28 September 1975, at about 1.45am, a number of senior managers and deputy managers of restaurants in the Spaghetti House chain were at the Knightsbridge branch checking the accounts of the Saturday night's takings. It was long after the restaurant had closed and it echoed with emptiness in stark contrast to a few hours earlier when it had been thronging with revellers out for a night on the town, taking a late meal before heading off to the West End for a theatre performance or a visit to a night club.

Suddenly, three gunmen burst into the restaurant armed with a double-barrelled shotgun and two pistols. Holding the Italian restaurateurs at gun-point they proceeded to bag more than £11,000 of the evening's takings. Preoccupied with grabbing the money, the gang's attention to the group of accosted managers was allowed to waver and one of them, Signor Giovanni Mai, managed to escape, taking care, as he went, to stash away much more of the money that had prompted the crime as possible. He alerted the police and, within a minute, no less than four cars, which were on duty in the area, arrived on the scene. The gunmen managed to hold off the police and withdrew into the restaurant's basement storeroom taking the other managers with them as hostages. The eight men that were held were: Signor Mario Rosselli, Signor Gino Berni, his brother Signor Bruno Berni, Signor Pasquale Cernicola, Signor Giovanni Scrano, Signor Enrico Mainini, Signor Renato Nasta and Signor Alfredo Olivelli.

Shortly afterwards, armed units of Scotland Yard's Special Patrol Group reached the restaurant, reinforcing the uniformed police already there and taking over control of the siege. Wearing a distinctive attire of black jackets and berets, these were men specially trained to handle terrorist crimes, ready-organised in the wake of a series of extremist attacks on civilian targets in European capitals and major towns. British police had feared that sooner or later political activists would employ the same methods in London and they intended to be prepared when the event arose. Thus, it was no mere coincidence that these special task forces happened to be in the area, conveniently placed to be able to respond at lightning speed. The fact was that the gang of robbers, a Nigerian and two West

Indians, had inadvertently chosen as the location for their crime, that branch of the Spaghetti House chain which was situated in the most sensitive area of London where, within a radius of half a mile, could be found the embassies and consulates of the majority of the world's governments.

Of course the police actions were not intended to imply that they were dealing with a terrorist incident; rather, that the procedures and techniques developed for handling such a situation were equally applicable to this case where a criminal raid had been badly bungled and, in desperation, the perpetrators had holed up with captives. Indeed, from the police point of view, while they did not seek to diminish the seriousness of this particular case, its occurrence presented them with an ideal training exercise which could be used to help prepare them for any future incident involving diplomatic prisoners. With all the benefit of hindsight, it was evident that the police were in fact handling the 'real thing' at the Spaghetti House for the experiences of successive sieges has shown that they invariably involve ordinary citizens rather than VIPs.

The later pronouncement by the gangsters that they were representatives of the Black Liberation Front, working under orders, did not dissuade the police from believing that they were only dealing with a straightforward robbery that had backfired; in other words, a routine police matter. Right from the start, the police team had an advantage over the besieged gunmen because they were able to listen in to their conversations through the grill of a basement ventilator located at the rear of the building.

While showing a willingness to engage the gunmen in a dialogue, in a bid to bring the siege to a swift and violence-free conclusion, the authorities made it quite clear from the outset that there would be no bargains of any kind and that, provided the gang threw out their weapons and came out of the basement peacefully, they would come to no harm. The gunmen countered this with demands for a radio, which was granted, and an escape car, which was not, as well as the involvement of Lord Pitt, the West Indian chairman of the Greater London Council, to act as a mediator. The Italian Consul General in London, Signor Mario Manca, also placed himself at the disposal of the police team in order to assist in monitoring the state of health and well-being of the hostages. After he had made contact with the gunmen and the hostages for the first time, Signor Manca made a disturbing assessment of the siege predicament. In his judgement the gunmen were suicidally resolved in their defiance of the law and prepared to play their trump cards, the lives of the hostages, right up to the last.

One of the eight Italians, Alfredo Olivelli, was suffering from an acute gastric complaint, no doubt aggravated by the anxiety and tension of the siege predicament. His release was negotiated after 15hr as a 'gesture of good faith' by the gunmen. Olivelli was able to advise the police that the other hostages, as far as he could tell, were generally fit and were being treated fairly well.

After the siege had been underway for 41hr, a second hostage was released after an appeal was delivered in person by Signor Manca to the Italian Ambassador, Signor Roberto Ducci. This called for him to take up the gunmen's case directly with Mr Roy Jenkins, the then Home Secretary, in order for them to be assured that they would be treated fairly. After arranging for confirmation of this to be broadcast over a news programme, the hostage, 34-year old Pasquale Cenicola, was allowed to go. He was suffering from extreme fatigue, shock and dehydration through lack of food and drink. Carried out on a chair stretcher, he was taken into hospital for treatment and observation.

Later, Signor Cenicola was able to assist the police as they tried to piece together the identities of the three gang members, although, with a shortage of clues and the absence of definitive identification by either of the released men, this could not be confirmed. The police also believed that there were other members of the gang, perhaps even that the raid had been an 'insider' job. While the siege proceeded, they followed up other leads as part of a broadening investigation. These led to the outside arrests on 2 October 1975, by Detective Chief Superintendent Ray Ranson and Detective Superintendent William Hucklesby, of Lillo Calogero Termina, a 33-year old Italian, and Norman Friedrich Waldberger, also known as Rondel, a 48-year old German. The police stated that other men were also being sought in connection with the incident.

Meanwhile, within the basement, conditions had deteriorated alarmingly. A police spokesman said they were about as bad as they could possibly get. The storeroom itself provided a more than ample source of food, some fresh but mostly uncooked or unheated produce. This consisted principally of crates of melons and tins of tomatoes, fish and peanuts as well as other foodstuffs, which was supplemented by water and coffee provided from outside, along with a substantial supply of cigarettes. A bucket had been handed in because there was no sanitation and it was this aspect of the situation that was giving rise to great concern for the health of the basement's occupants. The 12ft by 10ft basement provided far from ideal living quarters for this unforeseen and, as was hoped, temporary emergency. It was crowded and had become alarmingly hot. The improvised sleeping arrangements for the nine men were plastic bags that had been stuffed with torn-up newspaper.

From what had seemed a relaxed and conciliatory attitude on the part of the gang, when the second hostage was released, their mood began to harden and they expressed their firm refusal to surrender after demands for a car and an aircraft, to flee the country, were flatly rejected. At times the gunmen appeared willing to talk; at others they insisted on an end to all discussion and demanded immediate action. At these times, the remaining hostages feared intensely that they were all going to be shot dead.

By way of reassurance, not that it could necessarily be transmitted to the captives in terms they would have understood or appreciated, the police had set a clear tone for their handling of the operation. Their prime concern was to get both the kidnapped men and the robbers out alive. They calmly but firmly asserted that they would not concede any of the gunmen's demands but were prepared to keep talking for as long as it would take. The Italian Ambassador, representing the interests of the captive restaurant managers, expressed satisfaction with the handling of the situation and sought only assurances from the Home Secretary that everything was being done and would be done to safeguard the lives of his countrymen.

Later, a third hostage was taken ill with a stomach upset. Apparently he had vomited several times. This could hardly have improved the already offensive and foul-smelling atmosphere of the cramped storeroom which, by this time, all concerned were finding increasingly intolerable. Signor Manca offered himself as a replacement for the prisoner in question but Sir Robert Mark, the Metropolitan Police Commissioner, refused to allow such an exchange. While he recognised the bravery of such a gesture, he was concerned about endangering another life.

At this time, the Police were able to confirm that 28-year old Franklin Davis was one of the gunmen. The other two — the West Indian pair — were at that time known only as Bonzo and Wesley. Later, it transpired that Bonzo and Wesley were in fact, respectively, Anthony Gordon Munroe, aged 22, and Wesley Dick, aged 24.

During the morning of 30 September, the police allowed a young black woman representative of the Black Liberation Front, calling herself Sister Temmi, to enter the sealed off siege area, to make an appeal to the gunmen to surrender. She informed reporters that the BLF, whose aims were said to be peaceful, disassociated itself totally from the gunmen's crime of which there had been no prior knowledge. She also advised that there was no formal membership of the BLF though she believed that the men concerned may at some time have assisted with community projects organised by the BLF.

Despite her best intentions, her appeals were ignored and she left only with letters from the gunmen which they had signed in the name of the Black Liberation Army. The letters, which were immediately confiscated by the police, stated in part:

- that the three men were fighting to make white society realise that they could not push black people around any more;
- that they would either come out in an aircraft or a coffin (they had demanded yet again to have an aircraft provided to fly them to Jamaica, a demand which police had once again flatly refused);
- that the police had refused to provide food for the hostages, therefore they would also withdraw the water supply from the hostages at 3am (1 October).

In spite of police efforts to diffuse tension, the gunmen's attitude was gradually hardening further and, when they dug in for the fourth night of the siege, it was, seemingly, with a bitter determination. Sensing this, the anxiety of the hostages also heightened. This, coupled with the extreme deprivation and insanitary nature of their conditions of occupation, was rapidly breaking them both physically and mentally.

Like most sieges, this one was following a fairly predictable pattern and, in keeping with this pattern, it had now reached a critical point. Increasingly, there was a danger of a token execution from among the hostages. Equally, the manifest deterioration of their health, remained a matter of mounting concern. In the short term, for as long as a negotiated settlement remained a remote prospect, these were issues that could only be relieved by forceful intervention. The police had to weigh up the two equally unattractive options open to them: either to wait and take no action at all in the hope that the situation would stabilise rather than worsen further but in so doing risk the emotional break-down of the hostages; or attempt to storm the basement, which was most inaccessible, to pre-empt any violence by the gunmen, in the full realisation that the killing of the hostages could probably be accomplished in less time than it would take them to overcome the gang. The next few hours, during which the pros and cons of these alternatives were weighed up, were particularly tense and difficult.

In contrast, there had been other developments in the Spaghetti House siege which the police felt gave them reason for optimism in spite of the difficulties that were now manifested in the present potentially explosive situation. Judging by what were already regarded, in this period, as being the classic traditions of criminal and terrorist kidnappings, it was calculated that the gunmen and their victims had been together long enough, now some 96hr, for them to have established a degree of rapport and that, as that rapport increased, there would be a very marked reluctance on the part of the kidnappers to harm the hostages. As evidence that such a bond was developing, the hostages were being trusted completely to talk individually to the Consul General, for over half an hour at a time in Italian, a language which the gunmen did not understand. Similarly, the various transactions involved in making deliveries of coffee, water and other

Above: **Dirty, untidy and cramped, the basement storeroom at the Spaghetti House restaurant where three gunmen held six Italians for over 120hr. The limited space was restricted even further by refrigerators and racks of shelving.** *Press Association*

Left: **Signor Maignini, his face revealing the signs of stress and tiredness, is welcomed by his wife after the end of the long ordeal.** *Press Association*

supplies showed signs of relaxation. Although no food was being sent in, the police were permitted to arrange for the provision of improved sanitary equipment.

In spite of the continuing deadlock, the authorities reaffirmed their fundamental standpoint, hopeful that it would encourage the three gunmen to accept the futility of their circumstances and concede to the police. As Sir Robert Mark put it 'We have made it absolutely, unmistakably clear that they have everything to gain and nothing to lose by coming out'.

As things turned out, the police's 'softly, softly' approach paid off. At 3.40am on 3 October 1975, 122hr after the siege began, Franklyn Davis, the gangleader, was quite unexpectedly heard to call out from within the cellar storeroom, saying 'The hostages are coming out'. Cdr Christopher Payne, head of the Metropolitan Police Airport Division, who had been one of the principal negotiators throughout the siege replied: 'All right — send them out, one by one'.

Blinking nervously, as their eyes adjusted to the light, unshaven and barely holding back their tears of relief, the six Italians left their basement prison in turn, each peering around the heavy door behind which they had been held captive, hardly able to believe that they were free. Half carried to waiting ambulances, they were transported to a nearby hospital for a full health check.

After the hostages had all been taken away, Cdr Payne shouted further instructions to the gunmen: 'Now you come out — one by one. Throw down your guns and place your hands on your head'. Munroe and Dick duly complied, emerging under the concentrated attention of a dozen police marksmen who had been positioned in the cramped area around the storeroom entrance. They were taken to a nearby police van. While the third man, Franklyn Davis, was being awaited, a loud gun shot was heard. As their colleagues flung open the storeroom door, two officers, with their revolvers cocked, dashed inside. There they found Davis lying groaning on the floor, injured by a .22in bullet discharged from the pistol that lay beside him. Transferred to hospital, his condition was later described as 'serious, but not critical'. Surgeons successfully operated, without removing the bullet.

In later committal proceedings at the Horseferry Road Magistrates Court, six men were charged in connection with the Spaghetti House siege in Knightsbridge. All the arrested men were charged with conspiring to rob branch managers of the restaurant chain on or before 28 September 1975. Three were also charged with assaulting eight managers and 'injuriously imprisoning them' against their will. A fourth was accused of attempted robbery of £12,284. All the men were further charged with having firearms — a shotgun and two pistols — while two of them were charged with having illegally a gas-gun at their home. Found guilty, in the subsequent trial, all received heavy prison sentences.

Reviewing the handling of the siege, after its conclusion, it was stated that it had been the very kind of situation which had been feared and for which contingency plans had been specifically drawn up. Having studied similar police operations abroad and listened to lectures by foreign police officers who had experience of kidnappings, the Metropolitan Police's plan of action had been formulated accordingly. With the successful outcome to the Spaghetti House affair, it was declared that the basic principles of the contingency plans were entirely satisfactory. Less than three months later, they were put to an exacting test for a second time.

Later that same year, the Metropolitan Police were investigating the murder by IRA gunmen on 27 November 1975, on the doorstep of his home at Enfield, North London, of Mr Ross McWhirter. With his twin brother Norris McWhirter, they were the co-founders, with Arthur Guinness, of Guinness Superlatives Ltd, famous for the *Guinness Book of Records*. They were both also outspoken campaigners against the atrocities inflicted by Irish Republican terrorists. One of the two men wanted by the police in connection with the cold-blooded killing of Mr McWhirter was Michael Wilson, a known Irish gunman.

The autumn and winter of 1975 had witnessed a growing intensity in the Irish terrorist incidents in and around London with a number of gun attacks on West End restaurants and fire bombings on different department stores. The police recognised the pattern of these crimes as the work typical of a terrorist cell and they were convinced that this campaign of violence would continue with other, similar attacks. A carefully planned trap was therefore set to catch the gang.

Each of the previous attacks had followed what came to be recognised as a predetermined sequence of events. Armed with this knowledge, Scotland Yard prepared accordingly and hundreds of armed, plain-clothes officers were drafted into the central London area to cruise the streets, watching out for any signs of suspicious behaviour. They were all linked to a hot line for up-to-the-minute information on stolen cars.

At around 7.30pm on Saturday, 6 December 1975, the IRA gunmen made the move that had been expected, stealing a blue Ford Cortina car from outside a house in Porten Street, Notting Hill. This was duly reported to police headquarters and swiftly relayed to the patrolling officers. Shortly afterwards the stolen vehicle was seen being driven along Mount Street, Mayfair by one of many police 'Q' cars (incognito vehicles operating in a similar fashion to 'Q' ships during wartime), its very slow speed particularly drawing attention and arousing suspicion. The 'Q' car alerted all the other nearby police vehicles while keeping the stolen car under observation.

Suddenly, as the stolen Cortina was passing Scott's restaurant, which had already previously been a target for an IRA attack, shots were fired at the outside of the building and it then sped away at high speed. The 'Q' car gave chase, joined by a yellow Flying Squad Cortina and a police van occupied by members of the Metropolitan Police's Special Patrol Group. As the police vehicles pursued the gunmen's car, racing through the streets of the West End, they were shot at two or three times.

The stolen car was eventually abandoned in Park Road, Marylebone, and the chase continued on foot. On more than one occasion, as they followed in pursuit, the police discharged rounds from their hand-guns in return for volleys fired at them from the gunmen's weapons. During their flight a red canvas holdall had been dropped which was found to contain machine-gun parts and two magazines of bullets.

The four members of the terrorist gang were being driven towards the area adjacent to Marylebone station where they were soon completely surrounded. With their retreat cut off, the trapped gunmen ran into the first open doorway they could find, the entrance to a block of council flats in Balcombe Street. On the first floor of the building, they burst in on the occupants of apartment 22B, forcing them back with their weapons and taking them hostage. A short while after, just before 10pm, the terrorists phoned Scotland Yard from the flat they had occupied, which by then had also been besieged by police officers, to advise that they were a unit of the Provisional IRA — the infamous 'Provos'.

The middle-aged couple, who had been captured by the gunmen, had, until then, been enjoying a quiet evening at home, little realising how alarmingly the peace and security of their lives was to be shattered. The pair was John Henry Matthews, a 54-year old Chief Inspector at a Post Office district sorting office, and his 53-year old wife Sheila. This ordinary couple, like so many others who have suffered similar experiences, could never, in their wildest imagination, have contemplated the prospect of being trapped in their own home with a group of dangerously violent criminals, their very lives threatened; what person in their right mind could imagine or believe such a thing could happen to them. Yet here they were in such a nightmare, all the minor, everyday concerns of a trivial nature swept away as they were compelled to confront the only challenge that mattered — ensuring their survival. As it had turned out, Michael Wilson was not among the gunmen besieged in the flat with them, although this was not known by the police for certain until a lot later. In fact, the gunmen were Harry Duggan, a 23-year old, and Joseph O'Connell, one year older, both from County Clare, and Edward Butler, 26, from County Limerick. The fourth man was a 25-year old Glaswegian named Hugh Doherty.

The hostages and the four gunmen were barricaded inside the front living room of the apartment. The police, who had followed the men into the flat, had occupied all the spaces around the living room. They were in fact separated from the siege scene by only the thickness of the wooden sitting room door.

A direct land telephone line into the room was installed and a dialogue commenced with a man with a southern Irish accent. In no uncertain terms, he threatened to kill the hostages unless the gang's demands were met totally. These comprised a safe car to Heathrow, flights aboard Irish-registered aircraft to Ireland and, in the meantime, a supply of food and water.

All but one of these demands were rejected out of hand, with no hint of room for negotiation, in a most uncompromising response from the Commissioner of the Metropolitan Police, Sir Robert Mark. This appeared to conflict with the basic strategy of the terrorist contingency plan. Only some water and a portable chemical lavatory were supplied.

Sir Robert Mark described the gunmen, with evident distaste, as 'ordinary, vulgar criminals'. He stressed that when they were arrested, as most definitely they would be, the best they could expect was to be fairly treated and to receive a fair trial. Then, softening this hard line somewhat he added: 'Our prime consideration in the whole affair is to avoid bloodshed and to obtain the safe recovery of the two hostages. We are prepared to surround that flat until these people see reason'. Pressed to illuminate on the tactics the police would employ in the siege, he would only say that the police would play it by ear: 'Wherever human life is at stake it is always serious, whether threatened by armed criminals for profit or by terrorists for misguided political beliefs'.

The police were, of course, anxious to establish whether Michael Wilson, the man who was being hunted for the McWhirter killing, was among the four gang members in flat 22B. Listening devices were attached to the walls of the room and, after the remaining 309 tenants of the flats had been evacuated, between the floor and ceiling spaces, above and below, as well. The conversations between the gunmen were recorded and then played back to Ross McWhirter's widow, Rosemary, to see if she recognised any of the voices. Simultaneously, Detective Chief Superintendent Nigel Read, Head of Enfield CID and Cdr Roy Habershorn, Head of Scotland Yard's Bomb Squad, who were responsible for conducting the siege operation, interviewed all the police officers who had witnessed the original chase, in the hope of making a positive identification. Also, fingerprints taken from the stolen car and from the holdall dropped by the gang during the chase on foot were compared with records held at Scotland Yard in the quest for a match. Meanwhile, ballistics tests on the guns recovered by the police had linked them with IRA shootings at the Churchill Hotel, the Portman Hotel and

Two detectives run into the besieged flat at Balcombe Street while uniformed colleagues, wearing bullet-proof jackets, cover them with hand-held revolvers. *Popperfoto*

Above: **Sir Robert Mark, the Commissioner of the Metropolitan Police, confers with officers at the scene of the Balcombe Street siege.** *The Times*

Below left: **Street plan of the Balcombe Street area of London showing the block of flats in relation to Dorset Square and Marylebone station.**

Below right: **Plan of the siege apartment at 22b Balcombe Street, Marylebone.**

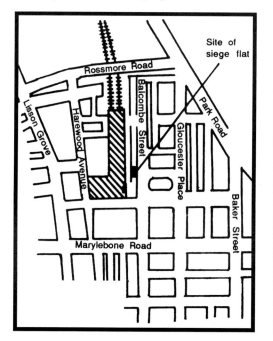

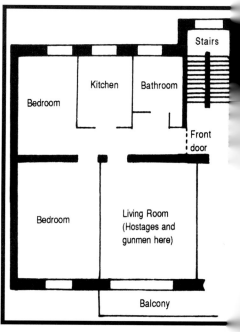

London's Cavalry Club. Without doubt, the police had cornered a particularly significant and highly active cell of Irish terrorists.

Other evidence from the ballistics tests was as alarming as it was informative. Analysis of the expended bullet cases revealed that the gunmen still had with them a number of .357in magnum automatics. These were of a similar type to the weapons used in the murder of Ross McWhirter. These men, if they were one and the same, had already demonstrated that they had the capability to kill and, if pushed, would no doubt do the same again.

From the outset, as a routine element of the police strategy for handling situations of this type, Dr Peter Scott, a Home Office consultant psychiatrist, had been attached to the police team. In view of the apparent mental character of the gunmen, he cautioned against an excessively uncompromising stance. Instead, he reminded all senior police officers of the need to defuse the situation in every way possible until such time as something of a sympathetic relationship had developed between the terrorists and their victims. He suggested that a hint of a deal should be left dangling as a carrot to encourage concessions by the gunmen which could, perhaps, be extended to include the release of the woman hostage. Equally, he counselled against refusing food outright, recommending that it be used instead to trade for Mrs Matthews' freedom.

The question of trading food for the release of the hostages was discussed at length with Deputy Assistant Commissioner of Police, Wilfred Gibson, who was in charge of the uniformed side of the police operation. In the event, it was not followed up as it was felt that this would compel the gunmen to make the next move. As things transpired, when a request for food was finally made, on the third day of the siege, and the police offered soup in return for Mrs Matthews, the gunmen declined, equally emphatically. Nevertheless, negotiations for Mrs Matthews release continued, even though, there were grounds to believe that, given the choice, she might elect in the circumstances to stay with her husband until the conclusion of the ordeal anyway.

It certainly was an ordeal, too! The police had been permitted to talk to the hostages via the telephone link, partly, as the gunmen hoped, so that they could apply pressure on the police to accede to their demands. From these snatched exchanges, the police were able to gauge an impression of how Mr and Mrs Matthews were coping with the frightening experience, both mentally and physically. Mrs Matthews had received dental treatment just prior to the commencement of the siege and complained of suffering from headaches, no doubt exacerbated by her extreme anguish. When asked how she was being treated, she said that they were well and 'doing all right' but that the lavatory facilities in the room in which she and her husband were confined with the gunmen were 'pretty awful'. Although it was evident that Mr and Mrs Matthews were coping magnificently, clearly determined not to let the terrorists believe they could be subdued, signs of weariness and weakness caused by unrelenting stress could be detected in her voice.

Dr Tiede Herrema, a Dutch business executive who had been subjected to a similar ordeal when he was held captive for two and a half weeks at Monasterevin, Eire, offered his advice to the Matthews couple on how to best cope with the situation. His words could have formed the basis of a general guidance on how to survive a siege for they were equally applicable to any person held in similar circumstances:

'If you cannot beat them, join them. Tell them about your background, tell them who you are and what you have done in your life. Ask them what they are thinking about, what is happening in the world. You have to find out why they are doing this. Try to move the aggression away from yourself to other people, maybe to the Government or maybe to other groups of people. (If you can) do the normal work in the house at the normal times. Do everything as normally and routinely as possible.'

As with the Spaghetti House siege, the affair at Balcombe Street gradually drifted into a protracted, lower-key stand-off between the respective parties, with little happening, apart from the occasional eruption as the temperature of the confrontation momentarily rose. The Balcombe Street siege seemed set to last at least as long.

Two incidents broke this period of relative inactivity — it would be quite wrong to imply that there was anything like boredom at these times, as a result of the absence of anything interesting happening, for that was hardly the way the kidnapped couple would have felt about it. For the police, too, these long quiet spells remained testing for other reasons, requiring the officers to maintain their concentration as sharp as ever. Nevertheless, the breaks that occurred in the monotonous proceedings, if not entertaining, were, in a strange sort of way, welcome to all concerned, helping to keep them alert and on their toes.

As a reminder of an earlier London siege, in Sidney Street in the East End in 1911, an old engine-less armoured car was wheeled out from nearby Huntsworth Mews and placed on a corner of Balcombe Street, opposite the siege flat. The vehicle was a collector's piece, placed at the disposal of the police by its proud owner for one final rota of active service. It proved to be very useful, its armoured plating providing ideal protection for the detectives who crouched behind it keeping watch.

Some time later, there was a moment of tension when the police cordon was broken. The police had feared that the IRA would make some countermove in order to strengthen the bargaining power of the trapped terrorists and were fully prepared for all eventualities. As with the Spaghetti House siege they had thrown a strict cordon around the area, preventing people from reaching their offices or business premises. Tenants from the area had been temporarily rehoused. At the time of the incident in Knightsbridge, shop owners there had complained about the inconvenience and the business they had lost so the police now issued passes to those persons who had a real need for access to the immediate Balcombe Street area. These required checking before entry was granted.

At 5.30pm on 7 December, Robert Alec Soaper of Cornwall Terrace, Regents Park was arrested after breaking the cordon tape in Rossmore Road in order to gain access, he claimed, to a telephone kiosk. Subsequently brought up before the Marylebone magistrates, he protested his innocence, claiming that he had no knowledge of the police operation and was completely unaware of the siege. For his trouble he was given 14 days in prison for 'obstructing the police in the execution of their duty'.

As the Balcombe Street siege was nearing the end of its first week, things suddenly began to happen. The mood of the gunmen had wavered throughout and even at times when they were apparently calm they displayed a command of invective. By the Wednesday, the abuse and belligerence had largely dissipated so the police also relented to some extent concerning the supply of food, providing it as an act of good faith in advance of the release of Mrs Matthews in the hope that the gunmen would respond reciprocally.

On Thursday, 11 December, the mood suddenly and drastically deteriorated. After much shouting, the gunmen hurled the food they had been given out of the

72

Bewildered but relieved, Mrs Sheila Matthews emerges from the besieged flat at the moment of her release. Behind her, on the balcony, is a hooded gunman; ahead is a policeman, beckoning her on. *Press Association*

flat into the street. The field telephone supplied by the police was also jettisoned, cutting off all means of communication. (Later, a clipboard and pencil was lowered from the flat above but this was far from ideal.) In response, the police cut off the electricity supply, throwing the flat into darkness and denying access to television news from outside. The police had considered imposing a complete news black-out earlier but the gunmen had the Matthews' portable transistor radio available to them.

Detective Superintendent Peter Imbert, who had been in charge of the telephone negotiations, worked swiftly to defuse the situation, offering hot soup and coffee and a supply of cigarettes. The terrorists refused. It seemed that on this occasion too, the siege had reached its critical point. There would be either a violent collapse to the episode or, within a very short while, it would be peacefully concluded. It was almost as if this outburst represented the final, frustrated but futile act of defiance prior to surrender.

As if to confirm this, the dawning of Friday brought with it an easing of the situation as the terrorists accepted both food and drink. At 2.15pm on 12 December 1975, Mrs Matthews was brought out on the balcony by a hooded but unarmed gunman. Deputy Assistant Commissioner Wilfred Gibson later said that the police had no idea that they were going to surrender right then. 'They must have realised the hopelessness of their position,' he added. Aided by a policeman, Mrs Matthews was directed along the balcony into the adjoining flat. A few minutes later she ran across the street to a waiting ambulance in Dorset Square.

Later, the field telephone link was restored and negotiations resumed in earnest. The siege was nearly over.

The police waited while the four gunmen and Mr Matthews had a meal, after which the talks recommenced. At 4.24pm the gang leader replaced the receiver on the field telephone after a lengthy talk with Detective Superintendent Imbert and the four men then calmly walked out into police custody.

The barricaded door of the sitting room was broken down by police officers. In the ramshackled room they found several hand-guns but no explosives. Apart from this there was only the settee and two armchairs which the Matthews had been compelled to share with the gunmen, the makeshift toilet and a lot of mess and an horrendous stench.

Considering what they had been through, the husband and wife couple were in remarkable shape. Mr Matthews was clearly physically stronger than his wife and in a state of elation that the siege was over. Both required medical attention for the lack of food and sleep and to cope with the inevitable psychological backlash that followed the ending of their harrowing experience but it was hoped that there was no permanent damage.

The police had reason to be proud. The conduct of two sieges in quick succession, according to a preconceived and carefully constructed plan, had resulted in success in both cases. In all, 10 hostages had been freed without harm and seven criminals apprehended, in the latter case clearing up a lot of open police business and bringing a halt to a wide campaign of terror against civilian targets. The case for the negotiated approach to settling siege incidents certainly had a lot going for it.

Siege Breaking
– the Mailed Fist
Approach

5

It was 9am on 27 June 1976. Air France flight AF139 was departing from Ben Gurion Airport, Tel Aviv, destined for Paris via Athens on what was to be a fateful flight. Earlier that same morning a Singapore Airlines flight 763 had landed at Athens *en route* from Bahrain via Kuwait. Four of the five passengers that disembarked from this aircraft crossed to the transit terminal to check in for the Air France flight, afterwards waiting in the transit lounge for the French Airbus A300, registration F-BVGG, to arrive.

As Air France AF139 was making its final approach into Athens, the four passengers from the Singapore Airlines' flight were in the process of being cleared through customs and passport formalities along with 54 others who were flying on to Paris. Next, they were required to clear the security controls but, regrettably, the metal detector which the passengers had to pass through was unmanned. There *was* someone on duty at the fluoroscope device, used for checking the contents of passengers' hand baggage, but insufficient attention was being paid to the screen. As a consequence of this inattentiveness, some very 'interesting' objects in the passengers' bags passed through undetected. All 58 passengers proceeded through security clearance without the slightest interruption. Outside the building, they joined the bus to take them to the aircraft that, by now, was waiting on the tarmac.

By 12.20pm local time, Air France AF139 was airborne again, steadily climbing to its cruising height of 31,000ft. There were now 246 passengers in total aboard the Airbus, including the 58 who had embarked at Athens. All but four of them were now settling down for lunch, which was already being prepared by the cabin crew. The meal was not served though, at least not right then.

Only eight minutes after take-off the four passengers who had started out from Bahrain left their seats. One, a young woman, took up a position at the front of the first-class cabin. Simultaneously, two others, dark-skinned males of Arab appearance, adopted a similar position overlooking the crowded tourist compartment, revolvers held in their hands ready for action. Meanwhile, the last of the quartet had forced his way into the aircraft's cockpit, through the unlocked dividing door. In one hand he had a revolver, in the other a grenade. The group's intentions were conveyed to the flight crew in a series of brief instructions delivered in staccato fashion.

Almost immediately radio contact with Air France AF139 was lost. Later in the afternoon, about 2pm, the suspicions on the ground as to the cause of this were confirmed when the lost aircraft contacted by radio the control tower at Benghazi Airport, Libya. Following the precise instructions that he had been given, the captain requested that sufficient fuel should be made available there for a four-hour onward flight and that the local representative of the Popular Front for the Liberation of Palestine (PFLP) should be summoned to the airport. Air France flight AF139 had been hijacked!

The identities of the four terrorists aboard the aircraft were now revealed or at least in so far as ticket details and the passports they were travelling under permitted. The group leader, the one who had taken over the cockpit, was a blond-haired man who, according to his passport, was a Peruvian named A. Garcia although he was in fact a German whose real name was Wilfried Boese. The young woman's passport gave her name as Ortega, and her nationality as Equadorian. The two men of Arabic extraction were carrying travel documents which gave their countries of origin as Bahrain and Kuwait respectively, the places from where the Singapore Airlines flight had set out. Clearly, all four gang members were travelling incognito.

After some deliberation, flight AF139 was given clearance to land at Benghazi where it was directed to a remote runway. Incredibly, one very bold female passenger succeeded in bluffing her way off the aircraft to freedom, persuading the terrorists that in her state of advanced pregnancy she was in danger of having an imminent miscarriage as she had a history of complications. Fully convinced, they allowed her to go. Mrs Patricia Hyman, who was *en route* to her mother's funeral in Manchester, was indeed pregnant but the crisis about her condition was a fabrication. After being detained for questioning by Libyan officials, she was allowed to continue on to England.

Air France AF139 was detained on the runway at Benghazi for nearly seven hours with no indication as to whether the extremists' demands would be met and the complement of terror-stricken passengers were becoming increasingly and acutely anxious about the fate that awaited them.

Then, almost unexpectedly, refuelling of the aircraft was permitted to proceed and, after taking on 42 tons of fuel, the aircraft took off once again, its destination unknown.

In France, the aircraft's country of registration, and in Israel, from where the aircraft had set out, there was already intensive diplomatic and political activity. For some reason, the Israeli Government concluded that the hijacked aircraft was going to be brought straight back to Ben Gurion International Airport where some grisly terrorist outrage was to be committed in a spectacular, public fashion for the benefit of a worldwide audience. Accordingly, a military contingency plan was activated and units from bases dispersed around Israel were hurriedly transferred to the airport in preparation to deal with whatever eventuality was in prospect. It gradually became clear though, as radar scanners across the eastern Mediterranean tracked the aircraft's movements, that it was actually heading south, away from Israel, so the anti-terrorist response units were stood down. The aircraft's range, with the fuel that had been loaded, was approximately 2,500 miles and it was a question of now seeing where it was going to end up.

The answer was not long in coming. At almost the very limit of its endurance, at 3.15am local time on 28 June, the Air France aircraft landed at Entebbe Airport in Uganda. Those watching the drama unfold now waited to see if this would turn out to be the final destination or whether it was yet another refuelling stop on a journey that was to take the hijacked hostages further afield.

By this time, it had been possible to establish the composition of the passengers aboard flight AF139. Of the 246 passengers, 145 were Jewish of whom 77 were Israeli nationals. It was soon evident that these were the prime targets of the terrorists.

Above: An Air France Airbus A300, similar to F-BVGG, the aircraft hijacked to Entebbe, Uganda by a unit of the PFLP.

Left: A Lockheed C-130 transport plane of the Israeli Defence Forces, typical of the aircraft used in the Entebbe raid.

As dawn broke at Entebbe, the hostages could see, looking down from the windows of the aircraft, yet more terrorists on the ground who were apparently mixing freely with Ugandan soldiers. Although it was not known at that time to anyone beyond those within the immediate confines of Entebbe airport it was clear to those incarcerated on the aircraft that they had indeed reached their destination and that there had been direct collaboration between the PFLP and the Ugandan Government in plotting the hijack. This was confirmed at midday when all the passengers and crew were removed from the aircraft and transferred to the airport's old terminal building, marched there between a cordon of armed Ugandan soldiers whose demeanour demonstrated that they, the passengers, and not the terrorists were being in effect arrested and forcibly detained.

Concerned about the terrorists' intentions with regard to the Jewish passengers, efforts were being made back in France and Israel to suppress information on the identities and nationalities of the hostages, in a bid to afford them whatever protection was possible in the circumstances. France had accepted responsibility for the safety of all those who were victims of this act of aerial piracy and French officials were endeavouring to establish contact with the Ugandan Government in order to register their demands for the passengers' release. That some unsavoury link existed between the terrorists and the Ugandan authorities was already suspected. If confirmed, it intimated that a dangerous new precedent had been established in the practice of international terrorist crime, for never previously had hijackers enjoyed the direct and overt assistance of a sovereign state in the perpetration of their deed. Uganda was not exactly on good terms with Israel, all diplomatic ties having been severed in March 1972, and the Ugandan dictator, President Idi Amin, who had come to power in a military coup in 1971, had on more than one occasion spoken in support of the PFLP.

At around this time the terrorists' demands were made known. That the act of terrorism had been carried out by members of Wadia Hadad's PFLP was also confirmed.

The hijackers were demanding the release of 53 fellow terrorists and sympathisers who were imprisoned in Israel, France, Germany, Switzerland and Kenya. On the assumption that these demands would be met, technical details for the exchange of prisoners were also supplied. The hijackers gave a deadline for the transaction: 2pm Israel time on Thursday, 1 July 1976, and an ultimatum: that if these demands were not met or if there was any interference they would blow up the aircraft and all of the captives. It was not known then that the passengers in fact had already been disembarked.

A very sinister turn of events for the hostages came during 29 June, the day after the arrival at Entebbe. Under the leadership of the flight crew, who had assumed local responsibility for the welfare of the passengers, efforts were being made to improve the cramped space of their confinement in the old terminal building to make it as comfortable as possible. Particular attention was paid to the needs of the very young and very old. Comfort and reassurance, as far as it could be provided, was also given to those who were suffering especially from fear for their survival.

During the afternoon, Ugandan soldiers commenced to demolish part of the wall between the hall in which the hostages were held and the adjoining room, ostensibly to alleviate the cramped conditions. However, before the work was completed, wooden planks were partially nailed across the opening, leaving only a very restricted access. The blond-haired terrorist, Wilfried Boese, now arrived on the scene, announcing that he had a complete list of all the passengers on the aircraft and that those whose names were called out were required to crawl through the opening into the next room. Not surprisingly, the only names called out were those of Jews and Israelis, this process of selection, conducted by a German, being frighteningly reminiscent to many of those present of the segregation at Auschwitz and other concentration camps which had determined who was to live and who was to die during the Nazi holocaust.

Later, 47 of the hostages from among the non-Jewish group were granted their freedom. They were loaded aboard another Air France plane which was to take them to Paris. The commander of flight AF139, Capt Michel Bacos, along with his full crew, was also offered the opportunity to leave but they all steadfastly declined, determined to stay with their passengers to the bitter end. A French nun who also offered her place among the released party to someone else, was totally ignored. Protesting vehemently, the Ugandans bundled her aboard the departing aircraft.

Kampala radio announced that the release had been achieved as a direct result of President Amin's efforts in negotiating with the terrorists to secure this 'humanitarian gesture'. The names of the released passengers were then announced, revealing that they comprised 33 French nationals, two Americans, two Greeks, two Dutch, three Moroccans, one Venezuelan, one Paraguayan, one Cypriot, one Canadian and one stateless person.

Back in Israel, where there were grave doubts as to whether the Jewish and Israeli hostages would ever be released alive, even if the terrorists' demands were conceded to, preliminary planning for a rescue raid on Entebbe airport had commenced. This involved both the assessment of the feasibility of such a raid, as well as the initiation of the process of detailed intelligence gathering. If, in the final reckoning, the release of the hostages depended on such a military intervention, the success of the operation would depend critically on the depth and detail of the pre-planning.

Information was needed on whether changes had been made to runways, taxi-ways and airport installations since the suspension of regular Israeli Air Force replenishment flights to the Israeli mission in Uganda in March 1972. Of course, this in itself indicated that Entebbe was well within the range of the Hercules transport aircraft operated by the Israeli Defence Forces. Besides up-to-date details about the airport's layout and any new construction work, the planners also needed to know whether any anti-aircraft measures had been installed at Entebbe. The Amin régime was, after all, most unpopular with both large sections of the domestic population as well as neighbouring countries. There was also a need to acquire information on the runway lighting system, the radar installations, and the air traffic control procedures. Military aircraft would have to be employed for a rescue mission but it would be necessary, for as long as possible, to convince Ugandan officials that any strange and unexpected aircraft were only civilian aircraft making unscheduled landings.

As soon as they could be reached, El-Al crew members were cross-examined for details of Entebbe and all senior Israeli Air Force personnel, active and retired, who had seen duty in Uganda, were contacted by the military planning team. As the option of a military-style rescue raid became increasingly attractive, every effort was made to obtain the latest information. This information was then used in turn to build a model of Entebbe airport with which aircrews and ground units could familiarise themselves and compare alternative operational sequences as well as rehearse the plan that was finally settled on.

In this context, there was a particularly beneficial revelation. While the intelligence gathering effort was proceeding, it came to light that a firm of Israeli civil engineering contractors had been engaged to design and erect many of the installations at Entebbe Airport including, fortuitously, the old terminal building in which the hostages were being held.

Simultaneously, steps were taken to obtain information on the present circumstances and location of the hostages, moves that depended on the formulation of an accurate perception of the complex personality of Idi Amin himself. Prior to the breakdown of relationships with Uganda, a number of senior ranking Israeli officers had enjoyed a close liaison with the Ugandan president, in particular a retired IDF Colonel — Burka Bar-Lev. Specialists working with the military planning team had put together a psychological profile of the Ugandan dictator. They believed that if Bar-Lev could open up a dialogue with him by telephone, playing on their personal friendship and exploiting the President's evident egotistical vanity besides suggesting that his 'peacemaking' efforts were recognised as sincere, it would be possible to persuade him to divulge useful information. And so, in the event, it proved to be. Over the course of a number of apparently innocuous and sympathetic calls to Kampala, Bar-Lev was able to extract critical details about the whereabouts of the hijack victims, the numbers of terrorists and the composition of Ugandan troops at the airport. He was also able to gain some valuable time — something which was fast running out. Amin was encouraged to request the terrorists to extend their deadline.

Meanwhile, the French had established a communications link with the terrorists via the offices of the Somali Ambassador to Uganda and through this channel they made it clear that neither they, nor the West Germans, were prepared to accede to the release of convicted terrorists. These rebuttals, consistent with established Israeli policy in the dealings with terrorists met with the approval of the Israeli Government. Uncharacteristically, though, the Israeli Government itself signified its willingness to enter into negotiations with the PFLP about the release of prisoners held in Israel in exchange for hostages. But there was more to this than met the eye.

Shimon Peres, the Israeli Defence Minister, had expressed a very profound view on the situation: that giving way to terrorist extortion was not the path that any sovereign state should choose. Having said that, though, it required time to outwit these criminals. To secure this, where the Entebbe incident was concerned, required an elaborate charade to be performed, as follows: first, a suitably rancorous debate in the Knesset, next a vote on a Government resolution in favour of negotiating a deal, all culminating with a sufficiently convincing majority in favour. It was purely a tactic to gain valuable time. It also happened to be a high risk manoeuvre to attempt, for at the time there were barely 90min to go before the terrorists' deadline expired. More importantly, though, it worked for seeing the possibility of achieving even a part of their objective accompanied with a humiliating climbdown by their arch enemy, the terrorists extended their ultimatum to 2pm on Sunday, 4 July 1976, in order to allow adequate opportunity for discussions. The tension that had been mounting among the hostages relaxed perceptibly at the announcement of their reprieve, even though it was only temporary.

The Israelis now knew exactly what had to be done and they knew precisely how long they had to accomplish it. The preparations for the commando raid rapidly gathered momentum. Three possible plans were taking shape:

- A parachute drop into Lake Victoria and a quiet landing at Entebbe from rubber boats.
- A large-scale amphibious landing, crossing Lake Victoria from the Kenyan

shore, utilising whatever waterborne craft could be conveyed, loaned, rented or, if all else failed, stolen.

● A direct airborne landing at Entebbe airport with a rapid deployment force to assault the terrorists' positions and remove the hostages by the same means as the commandos used to come in.

The latter was settled on, even though the main concern was the possibility of unidentified aircraft being fired on. It had been concluded that radar detection was of little consequence for the last thing that the Ugandans would suspect, in these circumstances, was Israeli aircraft so far from their normal sphere of operation. Critical to the success of the airborne assault was the requirement to secure, swiftly, four key objectives: the old terminal, the new terminal, the control tower and the airport's refuelling area.

Brig-Gen Dan Shomron, the IDF's Chief Paratroop and Infantry Officer, was appointed as commander of the operation which was code-named Operation 'Thunderball', and leader of the expedition on the ground. Later, after the death of Lt-Col Jonathan Netanyahu, his deputy who was killed during the raid, it was renamed Operation 'Jonathan'.

The pilots and aircrews who would fly the aircraft out to Entebbe and back were selected on the basis of one important credential — experience in long range flights over Africa. In some cases, for this reason, reservists were chosen in preference to active servicemen. The ground troops were drawn from three crack brigades of paratroopers and infantry, each recognised as an élite unit.

The 'mock' negotiations with the terrorists were advancing only very slowly, albeit without immediate risk of breakdown. This was, effectively, exactly what the Israeli defence planners wanted. The Israeli team for their part were insisting that the prisoner exchange, which had been agreed upon in principal could not take place at Entebbe airport as demanded by the terrorists. On 1 July, a second group of 101 non-Jewish hostages was released in a further so-called act of conciliation. Apart from the 12-person Airbus crew, all the remaining hostages were now of Jewish extraction, hinting at a genocidal end to the Entebbe siege in the event of a deal not being concluded. Foreign observers had already concluded that the PFLP was not really interested in negotiation, only in total satisfaction of their demands; otherwise the terrorists would mercilessly execute the captives. The incident was moving inexorably to a climax. To ensure the right outcome, the Israeli Defence Force team had to make its move!

Right up to the last minute, each stage of the operation was repeatedly drilled. There had even been trial landings on blacked-out runways at Ophir, at the southern tip of the Sinai Desert, so that, if it became necessary, the pilots would have a reasonable chance of safely bringing their aircraft down blind.

At last, all the rehearsals ended and the operation for real was launched on 3 July 1976 with the receipt of a signal to go from Israel's Prime Minister, Yitzhak Rabin.

At 1.20pm Israel time, five heavily laden Hercules C-130 transport aircraft took to the air from an unidentified air base. Four were required for the operation, the fifth would be held in reserve. Shortly after, two Boeing 707s took off. One of these was designated as a 'hospital' aircraft. It was hoped that the second, back-up aircraft would not be needed. The Boeing pilots had orders to fly to and land at Nairobi, Kenya. Being the Jewish Sabbath it would have normally been unusual for so many military aircraft to be airborne simultaneously and this was bound to attract unwanted attention. Therefore, in order not to arouse unwelcome interest in the operation, the seven aircraft dispersed once they were airborne and took separate routes across central Israel and over the Negev and Sinai deserts to their southernmost staging point. At Ophir, after topping up with fuel and completing the loading of equipment, four of the Hercules resumed the flight, now in formation. Turning over the desert wastes of Saudi Arabia they headed out to sea in a southerly direction, low over the Gulf of Suez, and then on westwards into the African continent, over Ethiopia.

At the Sudanese border, the transport aircraft turned south again, through stormy weather, following the boundary between Uganda and Kenya until, over Lake Victoria, they banked sharply to the west to line up on Entebbe's main runway.

The lead aircraft touched down at 11pm and even before it had come to a standstill the rear ramp was open and the vehicles carried with the raid party were unloaded and moving down the runway. This advance group was tasked with placing emergency beacons by the runway lights in case the control tower shut down all electrical power.

Other commandos now made quickly for the old terminal building where two Ugandan sentries who confronted them were shot down. As they searched for the entrance, another guard was encountered and he too was killed. One of the terrorists momentarily appeared, then, realising what was happening, he retreated inside the building where he commenced to fire at the terrified hostages who were sprawled around on the ground. Pursuing Israeli soldiers shot him dead, along with another of the terrorists, but not before some hostages had been hit.

The girl hijacker, identified by a doorway, was also shot. Regrettably, one of the panic stricken hostages launched himself at the doorway in an attempt to escape. Mistaken for a terrorist, he was cut down in mid-flight by a burst from one of the commando's automatic weapons.

A second assault team entered the old terminal at the point where the terrorists had been quartered. There they came across two men in civilian dress who were not immediately recognised as guerillas. After a moment's hesitation, which provided the opportunity for one of the men to throw a primed hand grenade, they were dealt with by a burst of machine-gun fire. Meanwhile, a third assault party took care of the limited resistance put up by Ugandan soldiers. All opposition ended, the first objective had been achieved within three minutes of landing, before even the three other Hercules had touched down. Unfortunately, Jonathan Netanyahu, who had been supervising the three assault teams was shot and killed by a single bullet fired from the top of the control tower.

Moving freely around the airport on the armoured personnel carriers that were now unloaded from the second and third transport aircraft, the troops backing up the initial assault moved swiftly to secure all access roads to the airport and to take the new terminal and the control tower. A second Israeli casualty was sustained: Sgt Hershko Surin, who had been due to be demobilised from the army that very day.

By now, the fourth, empty Hercules transport had been moved close to the old terminal, ready to embark the hostages. It proved to be unnecessary to commandeer the fuel tanks at the airport, as the crew of the Medical Corps 'hospital' Boeing 707, which by now had landed at Nairobi, was able to advise that all the aircraft could be refuelled there.

Though they were ahead of schedule, the Israeli commandos moved hastily to board the hostages, ready for departure. The bewildered, shaken captives emerged from the building, slowly at first but faster as the soldiers urged them on, making their way to the relief aircraft, again between two lines of soldiers but

Above: **A sobbing elderly woman hugs a relative after the return of the Air France captives to Tel Aviv on 4 July 1976 following the lightning night-time raid by Israeli commandos.** *Associated Press*

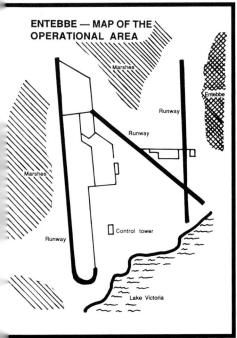

ENTEBBE — MAP OF THE
OPERATIONAL AREA

Marshes

Entebbe

Runway

Runway

Marshes

Control tower

Runway

Lake Victoria

Left: **Map of Entebbe Airport, situated between areas of marshland on the shores of Lake Victoria, showing the key installations, each of which was secured with impressive speed and efficiency in the daring Israeli raid.**

Lufthansa Boeing 737-230 *Landshut* which was hijacked to Mogadishu, Somalia in October 1977. Its maximum fuel capacity of 13,500 litres (3,500 US gall) gave it a range of 2,100km (1,300 statute miles). Frequent refuelling stops were necessary as it followed its erratic route around the Mediterranean and Middle East. *Lufthansa*

this time friendly Israelis. All were taken, the living, the dead and the wounded, as well as Air France AF139's entire crew. By 11.52pm the aircraft was airborne, whisking its cargo of humanity, cold, exhausted and still in shock, away to the safety of Nairobi.

Prior to the departure of the assault force from Entebbe, an infantry team destroyed seven Ugandan MiG fighters on the ground in order to prevent a hostile pursuit. At 12.12am on Sunday, 4 July, the day that had originally threatened to result in such a calamitous finale, the last units of Operation 'Thunderball' finally left Entebbe. At Nairobi, where all the aircraft now assembled, refuelling for the long flight back to Israel was soon in progress with little difficulty and it was not long before the four Hercules and two Boeings were on their way home.

The raid had been a resounding success. All seven hijackers, two West German and five Palestinians had been killed as had 20 members of the Ugandan armed forces. A further 32 Ugandans had been injured. The commando force had sustained only one fatality, Jonathan Netanyahu. Of the hostages, 106 had been retrieved safely, two had been killed outright during the Entebbe fighting, a third died later in a Nairobi hospital. A fourth hostage, Mrs Dora Bloch, who had been taken to a hospital at Entebbe was later murdered there by Amin's troops.

It is not hard to imagine the reception that greeted the returning combat force. The Israelis are, by virtue of their recent heritage, a close-knit nation and they had shared widely and intimately in the concern for the hostages well-being as if they were their own immediate relatives. The relief at their safe home-coming gave way to an outpouring of celebration across the small country on an unprecedented scale and the aircrews and commandos of the raid party were acclaimed as national heroes. There were scenes of great emotion when the hostages and their families were reunited at Ben Gurion International Airport. Significantly, Entebbe was the first major terrorist siege in which hostages were held for political reasons which was successfully broken by direct and forceful military intervention.

Just over a year later, there was a virtual repeat of the Entebbe raid following the hijacking of the Lufthansa Boeing 737-230C, *Landshut* (D-ABOE) during a holiday charter flight from Palma, Majorca to Frankfurt, West Germany.

The main difference between the two episodes was that on the second occasion the hostages had to be rescued from the aircraft out on the runway and not from an airport building, as was the case at Entebbe.

Lufthansa flight LH181 had barely departed from Majorca at 12.55pm (GMT) on 13 October 1977 when four armed terrorists hijacked it in the name of the Organisation of Struggle Against World Imperialism. Aboard the aircraft were 82 passengers and a five person crew. The gang issued a nine-point ultimatum which, among other things, called for:

● the release of 11 members of the Baader-Meinhof urban guerilla group held in West German prisons.

● each of the 11 to be given, on release, 100,000 Deutschmarks, a total of DM1,100,000 (approximately £440,000 at 1993 exchange rates).

● the release of two members of the PFLP, imprisoned in Turkey.

● a payment of $15 million by the Turkish Government.

● arrangements to be made with the Democratic Republic of Vietnam, the Republic of Somalia or the Peoples' Democratic Republic of the Yemen to receive the released prisoners.

● appropriate transport for the conveyance of all the released prisoners and, at the appointed time, the hijackers themselves.

The deadline for accomplishing all this was set at 8am (GMT) on 16 October. If these demands had not been conceded by that time the gang threatened to kill all the passengers and crew as well as Dr Hans-Martin Schleyer, president of the German Industries Federation, who had been kidnapped in Cologne on 5 September that same year.

As the kidnapping unfolded, there followed a bizarre sequence of events as the hijacked aircraft trekked from airport to airport around the Mediterranean and Middle East, principally to refuel but also, it seemed, in search of a country that was prepared to give the terrorists a friendly reception and, in so doing, risk the political, economical and possibly military backlash that would be almost certain to follow.

The first stop was at Rome, followed by calls at Larnaca Airport, Cyprus, Bahrain and then Dubai where it stopped for some 42hr while negotiations took place. Less than an hour before the expiry of the terrorists' declared deadline, the aircraft took off from Dubai heading for the Republic of South Yemen. The government there refused permission to land but, probably because it was already low on fuel, the aircraft was compelled to make a forced landing at Aden, in sandy ground alongside the main runway. This caused damage to the Boeing's undercarriage and broke off the extinguishers attached to the aircraft's two engines.

The Yemeni authorities allowed the aircraft to refuel, after which it took off once again, heading out across the Gulf of Suez towards Africa. It seems that at this point a furious row broke out between the airliner's 37-year old Captain, Jürgen Schumann, and the terrorists. Capt Schumann had at first refused to take-off from Aden because the aircraft's damaged undercarriage could not be relied upon to support the aircraft at its next landing which would have placed all the passengers at an unacceptable risk. Forced at gunpoint to take-off anyway, as soon as they were airborne, Capt Schumann was shot and killed by the hijack gang.

Lufthansa LH181 finally came to a complete stop at its next landing point, Mogadishu, the capital of Somalia. Here, the pilot's body was thrown out of the aircraft down a plastic escape shute and a new ultimatum was set by which time the terrorists' demands had to be satisfied otherwise the aircraft would be blown up with all on board.

The negotiations between the gang and West German officials, which had been in progress at Dubai, were resumed at Mogadishu but it was evident that the group were absolutely fanatical in their commitment to the execution of their purpose and displayed no willingness for compromise in any form. Their ruthless inflexibility extended to a refusal to allow even the sick among the passengers to go, or even the 31 women and seven children. Fearful for the safety of the hostages in these circumstances, some West German Government officials were rapidly reaching the conclusion that a military, commando-type raid was necessary along the lines of that which had been carried out by Israeli commandos at Entebbe in 1976. Unfortunately, the West Germans did not have a comparable amount of time to plan such a raid and with the aircraft's constant movements, it was almost impossible to know which airport's details they needed to study. They did, however, have the benefit of a modicum of co-operation from the Somali authorities; they also received from Israel full details of the Entebbe operation to assist in the planning of a raid.

Timing was of the essence — the situation required rapid intervention and quick decisions. As the detailed plan of action was still being finalised, some 60 members of West Germany's élite anti-guerilla group, formed after the 1972

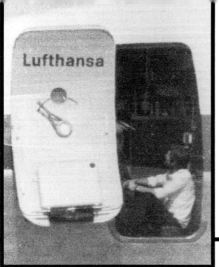

Left: **Capt Jürgen Schuhmann of the hijacked Lufthansa airliner squats at the doorway of the jet as a gunman, behind the door to the left, threatens him with a pistol. The picture was taken during the aircraft's brief stay at Dubai, on 17 October 1977.** *Associated Press*

Below: **Map of the Mediterranean Sea and Africa showing the routes, intended and actual, taken by the hijacked Air France and Lufthansa aircraft.**

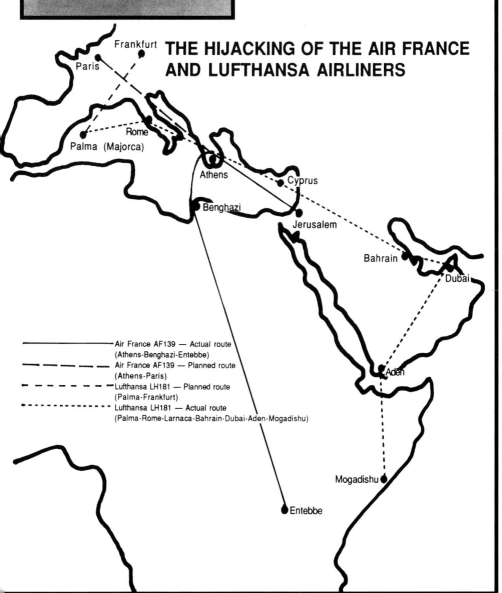

THE HIJACKING OF THE AIR FRANCE AND LUFTHANSA AIRLINERS

Frankfurt
Paris
Rome
Palma (Majorca)
Athens
Cyprus
Benghazi
Jerusalem
Bahrain
Dubai
Aden
Mogadishu
Entebbe

———— Air France AF139 — Actual route
(Athens-Benghazi-Entebbe)
— — — Air France AF139 — Planned route
(Athens-Paris)
- - - - Lufthansa LH181 — Planned route
(Palma-Frankfurt)
· · · · · Lufthansa LH181 — Actual route
(Palma-Rome-Larnaca-Bahrain-Dubai-Aden-Mogadishu)

massacre of athletes at the Munich Olympics, were flown to the Greek island of Crete with their commander, Ulrich Wegener. With them were two members of Britain's crack SAS force. Meanwhile, on the diplomatic front, Chancellor Helmut Schmidt, under intense pressure from the hostage's relatives, and Pope John appealed to the consciences of the hijackers while, simultaneously, volunteering themselves as substitutes for the hostages. The second deadline passed at 3pm (GMT) on 7 October without incident and a third, final deadline was set for 1.30am the following morning.

With barely 90min to go to the expiry of the terrorists' second deadline, the West German anti-terrorist squad, flown down to Mogadishu in complete secrecy, launched a daring last minute assault on the Lufthansa jet, isolated on the airport runway. The attack on the besieged aircraft began at five minutes past midnight, catching the hijackers completely unawares. The hostages too, trying to get whatever fitful sleep they could in their state of total exhaustion, were taken by surprise.

First the Boeing's doors were blown out and then the commandos threw quantities of stun grenades into each of the cabin compartments. These special 'blinding' grenades lack shrapnel but can immobilise a person for six or so critical seconds. Exploding with a blinding flash and a very loud bang, inflicting no more than minor physical injuries, they are excellent at causing disorientation, vital in circumstances such as these where the commandos had to enter the confined space of the aircraft's interior, which was controlled by the terrorists, with no definite knowledge of the disposition of the hostages.

A brief shoot out followed in which all four hijackers, two men and two women, were shot dead. By 12min past midnight it was all over. The hijack of the aircraft and the siege had ended with no loss of life among either the commando squad or the passengers and crew. Ten of the passengers had been slightly wounded, though none of them seriously and none to an extent that prevented their departure, along with all the other hostages, on a special flight to Frankfurt at just after 3.30am that morning.

The mood aboard the returning aircraft was, as it had been the previous year on the Hercules transports taking rescued Israelis back to Tel Aviv, one of stunned silence rather than of noisy and exuberant exultation at the deliverance of the hijack victims. The outpouring of emotions came when the hostages were reunited with their families and friends at Frankfurt.

The Mogadishu raid served West Germany, a country deeply afflicted by violent urban guerilla movements, particularly well, dealing a major blow against these organisations. For the victims there was thankfulness that it had ended without bloodshed and that the siege had not been longer. For the Bonn Government there was a sense of vindication for their policy of 'no surrender'.

The names of Entebbe and Mogadishu, and the operations with which they are associated, enjoy a special place in the annals of the continuing war against terrorism. At their respective times they were a clear, collective declaration that free men need not submit to terrorist blackmail and extortion, no matter how impossible the alternatives may be. Later attempts at employing forceful intervention to resolve sieges, however, were destined to conclude far less auspiciously.

Holding the Netherlands to Ransom

The period between 1975 and 1980 saw terrorist and, by association, siege activity in Europe intensify alarmingly. It seemed that the continent was unremittingly held in a vice-like grip of revolutionary fervour. In the face of this menace, the flow of American tourist dollars into European countries, an income on which so many economies depended, decreased to barely a trickle as visitors stayed away, fearing for their personal safety.

Of all the extremist groups engaged in subversive behaviour at that time, the most obscure was the South Moluccan Nationalists. They appeared to burst upon the scene without warning, a largely unknown organisation with an even less well known grievance. In fact, like so many of the other root causes of terrorist action during that period, the South Moluccan affair had considerable history, fundamentally originating in the closing months of World War 2. Equally, it shared in common with other political disputes the fact that its core issues had not benefited from much of an airing in the ensuing years. Thus, the suppressed energy of years of political frustration was waiting to erupt like a dormant volcano.

For the Dutch, the Moluccan issue had a very immediate significance. The contentious issue of South Molucca was a problem that was both more widely known and understood in the Netherlands for the Moluccas was a former Dutch colony. Not that recognising the problem helped much, for the Dutch found themselves very much the victims when the pent up frustrations of Moluccan nationalism erupted. As the target for these disaffections, it seemed that for a period, between 1975 and 1978, the Netherlands as a whole was held to ransom in a desperate attempt to influence political events on the other side of the world, in Indonesia.

The Moluccan islands, part of the Spice island group, situated between Sulawesi and Irian Jaya, New Guinea in the Ceram Sea, were absorbed into the Republic of Indonesia when it was granted its independence from the Netherlands in 1949.

The confederation of provinces that constituted the new Indonesian state embraced a number of ethnic minority groups including the Moluccans, who had their own separate nationalistic aspirations and who considered that the Netherlands had given undertakings to implement this in recognition of the support that they had given to the Allied cause during World War 2 and because they had been Dutch loyalists during the Indonesian war of Independence.

The formation of the Republic of Indonesia signified, as far as these former colonial minorities were concerned, that the Netherlands had renéged on their promises. In 1953, the Dutch Government pledged that eventually the Moluccan islands would be returned to their own people to form their own sovereign republic. This pledge was not honoured, not that it was necessarily possible once the newly-fledged Indonesian Republic began to flex its muscles and determined to resist the sequestration of any part of its territory.

Resulting from the civil unrest and suppression of the Moluccan independence campaign by the Indonesian authorities, there was an exodus of Moluccan refugees to the Netherlands which the Dutch government felt morally bound to accept; in the circumstances, they were hardly in a position to refuse. The displaced Moluccans set up their government in exile under President Johannes Manusama and set about campaigning for their cherished objectives of freedom and independence. Successive generations of Moluccans, many born and reared in the Netherlands, showed themselves to be less willing to follow the legitimate and, by inference, laborious channels open to them, in pursuit of these aims. They were becoming increasingly vocal, as their faith in achieving progress by any of the official processes or by law-abiding methods waned.

Whereas in 1952 the number of South Moluccans in the Netherlands numbered only 12,000, by the mid-1970s the refugee population had increased to almost 40,000.

The Moluccan dilemma was the classical one experienced by all long-term refugees, a distinction they shared in common with the Palestinians. As displaced persons they do not belong in the country in which they reside and may even be discriminated against there, either because of their race and colour or because they represent continuing instability and a drain on the economy of the country concerned. Yet they are unable to influence world opinion sufficiently to resolve their predicament for, in effect, they have little of interest to offer in the high stakes of world affairs, and, therefore, are left with only two options. Either to return to their homelands, if accepted and with all that entails, probably as inferior citizens, possibly exposed to personal danger, or to take disruptive and extreme political actions to try to influence the situation in their favour.

This was the frustrating predicament that precipitated a sequence of violent activities against civilian targets by a faction of the South Moluccan community in the Netherlands in the mid-1970s.

The first outrage, or pair of outrages, for characteristic to the South Moluccan campaign of terror was the synchronisation of more than one attack on each occasion, occurred on 2 December 1975. Five terrorists hijacked the 9.33am Groningen-Amsterdam train between Beilen and Hoogeveen, taking 62 persons hostage. The train driver and one of the male passengers were shot in the attack, their bodies dumped on the railway track beside the stationary train.

Almost simultaneously, in Amsterdam, another seven masked and heavily armed terrorists raided the Indonesian Consulate in Brachthuyserstraat which doubled as a school, forcing the occupants to the second and third floors where they held them prisoner. The consulate captives numbered 32, of whom 16 were schoolchildren. In the confusion, a number of persons had managed to escape. Later, three Indonesians, who had hidden from the terrorists, made a break for freedom from the building's second floor in the course of which they were injured. One was shot in the stomach by a member of the gang, the other two, covered by police marksmen, were hurt as they jumped to the ground.

There were escapes from the hijacked train as well. On the first day, after dark, five of the younger captives succeeded in getting away. Earlier, an Air Force officer had also managed to slip his custodians. During the next day another 18 hostages managed to escape, including the train's guard, Mr H. J. Brinker.

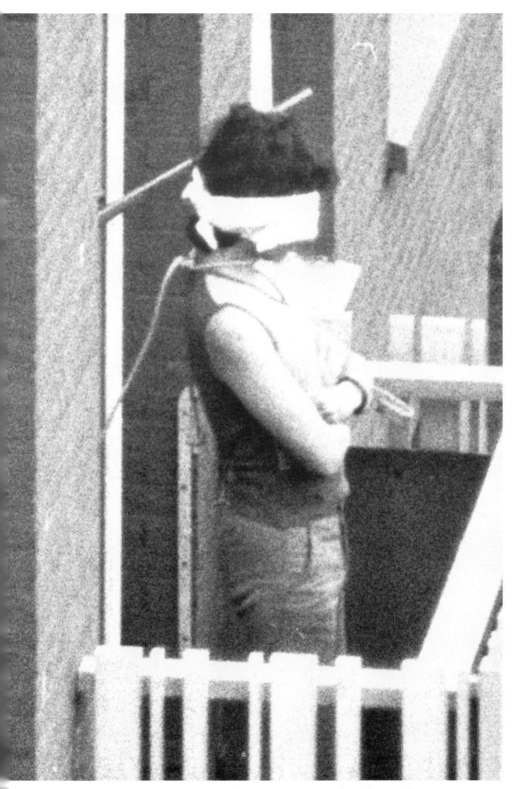

blindfolded hostage from the Indonesian Consulate in Amsterdam is forced to stand at gunpoint on
e of the balconies to reinforce the seriousness of the terrorists' threats. Around his neck is a noose
de from wire flex. *Popperfoto*

Thereafter, the terrorists were rather more attentive to the 38 prisoners who remained on the train.

In both cases, police marksmen and anti-terrorist troops surrounded the train and the Indonesian consulate, besieging the gunmen and their victims.

At Beilen the terrorists voluntarily permitted the release of two women and a child who were used to convey a message setting out their demands. These were fairly predictable and throughout the South Moluccan campaign of urban terror they tended to remain much the same. The demands from Beilen were reinforced by statements communicated by telephone from the group in the Dutch capital.

The terrorists stated that their actions were the result of Dutch and Indonesian refusal to treat seriously their demands for a return to a free South Moluccan republic. They were not, they said, afraid to be killed or to kill to achieve their aims. Later, in a telephone message that was broadcast live over Dutch radio, the gang spokesman pronounced, most ambiguously, 'We are not murderers, the Dutch have made murderers of us'.

The Moluccans listed a number of requirements which they insisted should be met if the hostages were to be freed unhurt. They called for:

● all South Moluccan prisoners in Dutch jails to be released.

● an aircraft to be provided at Schiphol Airport to permit the gang and released prisoners to leave the Netherlands (no destination was specified and it is questionable as to whether there was anywhere they could have gone).

● independence for their Pacific islands homeland which they wanted to have negotiated in talks under the auspices of the United Nations and whichthe Netherlands was requested to initiate.

● the Dutch Government to make a television broadcast, admitting its responsibility in allowing South Molucca to be incorporated within Indonesia when it gave independence to the former colony of the Dutch East Indies.

The Dutch Minister of Justice, Mr Andreas Van Agt, refused to give in to these demands as deaths had occurred which he advised he was regarding as the terrorists' direct responsibility. Shortly after this rejection, Mr Joop den Uyl, the Dutch Prime Minister, spoke about the two sieges saying 'I am very pessimistic about our chances of resolving these situations without the use of violence'. Nevertheless, at both sieges field telephone links were established to permit negotiations by a direct line that could not be cut or tapped into. Both were linked to a crisis control centre in The Hague.

The terrorists in the Indonesian consulate requested the Dutch authorities to supply a mediator, a request which was refused unless the gang agreed to release all the school children held in the building. On the afternoon of 4 December, the five youngest children were allowed to go in exchange for a radio, a television and a megaphone. The Dutch authorities, quite reasonably, felt they could take some satisfaction from this, for it followed the recommended approach to handling terrorist sieges, keeping the gang members on the defensive and exploiting every request, no matter how trivial or no matter how basic its nature, as an opportunity to trade for the much greater prize of the release of hostages.

Any sense of control over the situation was soon shattered, however, as two unrelated incidents served as a measure of the desperation of this particular gang of extremists.

Out on the railway track, the terrorists performed a grisly execution of one of the hostage passengers to convey to the Dutch authorities their unflinching resolve to have their demands met. The passenger concerned, with his hands tied behind his back, was forced to kneel besides the sliding doors of one of the carriages. He was then cold-bloodedly shot in the head and his body toppled out onto the trackside alongside the other two victims, to the horror of all those watching.

Meanwhile, in Amsterdam, a blindfolded Indonesian man was forced to stand for 20min on a balcony of the five-storey consulate building at the point of a sub-machine gun. Around his neck he was secured by a noose of wire flex held by a black-hooded terrorist.

These incidents must have chilled the blood of the captives held at each siege location, who were inevitably suffering immensely from all the typical anxieties and discomforts that these traumatic experiences cause. They were extremely disappointing developments to the Dutch authorities, too, for their uppermost concern all along was to prevent bloodshed.

Their response was to maintain their cool, despite the unpredictability of the Moluccan gang, and to hold steadfastly to the agreed strategy of refusal of the terrorists' demands but remaining willing to negotiate with them wherever this could be linked to concessions. To diffuse the situation at this potentially explosive point, the Dutch authorities conceded to the intervention of mediators, calling on senior and respected members of the South Moluccan community in the Netherlands to help.

At Amsterdam on 5 December, the Rev Semuel Metiari, a Moluccan priest, was allowed to enter the Indonesian Consulate, with an official of the Dutch Justice Ministry, where he talked to the gunmen. Ten minutes after entering, they emerged with three small girls. Half an hour later, two young schoolboys were released; later, two more children were freed into the custody of Metiari.

On the train at Beilen, a doctor among the hostages reported that the terrorists and passengers were extremely hungry. Negotiations for an exchange of food for the prisoners commenced. The terrorists had already allowed the removal of the corpses of the three dead men which were taken away on a Red Cross bus.

On 5 December 1975, before any negotiations through a mediator could commence at the besieged train, there was another incident which heightened the tension. There was an explosion in one of the occupied carriages. This was, as it turned out, only the result of an accidental detonation among the stock of ammunition brought on to the train during the terrorist attack rather than anything more sinister. The South Moluccans appealed for help over the field telephone and this was immediately rendered. An injured terrorist and three of the hostages were removed and taken to hospital in Assen. The released passengers included an elderly couple, Mr and Mrs Van Ter Teer — the man with a broken leg and his wife suffering from shock.

When everything had settled down again, mediators were introduced to the proceedings at Beilen, Mr Johannes Manusama, the self-styled South Moluccan President and the South Moluccan Minister for Education in Exile, Mr Theo Kubuwael. Through these mediators, on 7 December, the authorities were able to agree the release of two more hostages in exchange for a quantity of food, drink, medicine, underclothes, cutlery and cigars. The two passengers who gained their freedom in this deal were an 84-year old retired Protestant clergyman and his elderly wife. A hot meal of meat and potatoes was then delivered.

In their capacity as representatives of the Badan Persatuan, the South Moluccan political council in Holland, Mr Kubuwael and Mr Manusama reminded the terrorists that their actions were placing the lives of their fellow

Above: **Theo Kubuwael, on the right, and another unidentified leader of the South Moluccan community in Holland arrive** **Beilen Town Hall on 6 December 1975, prior to acting as mediators in the nearby siege of a hijacked train.** *Associated Press*

Left: **Map of the Netherlands showing the various locations of South Moluccan-motivated sieges: Amsterdam, Beilen, Bovensmilde, Glimmen and Groningen.**

countrymen in Indonesia at risk, particularly for as long as Indonesian nationals were held at threat of death at the Consulate in Amsterdam. This did not appear to make any great impact on the gunmen and the siege continued, though with less dramatic or volatile overtones.

The West German anti-terrorist specialists who had been engaged in the Munich Olympics affair offered their assistance to the Dutch police in an effort to help bring the siege to a swift and agreeable conclusion. As if to maintain pressure on the terrorist gang on the hijacked train, units of the Dutch Army's 43rd tank division staged a mock attack on an empty four-carriage train that was brought along the track to within a few miles of the hijacked vehicle. It was clearly intended that the terrorists should be aware of the exercise, for even if it could not actually be seen, the fact that it took place was broadcast on the radio and it was known that the terrorists were listening in.

Another breakthrough occurred in the Consulate siege on 8 December when the gunmen there were persuaded to release the last of the kidnapped schoolchildren, a girl of 14 years and three boys aged between 13 and 17. They were allowed to go on the condition that Reverend Metiari saw the Indonesian political counsellor, Mr Soerjadi, on their behalf the following day. The hope was that he could be encouraged to apply pressure on the Indonesian government to free all South Moluccan prisoners in Indonesia as well as to enter into negotiations aimed at concluding a settlement to the independence claim; to this end, that President Suharto should be implored to meet with their leader in exile. But this was to no avail for Indonesia had no intention of agreeing to a deal of any sort or of showing leniency towards its political prisoners. They only reminded the South Moluccan terrorists that their attacks on Indonesian nationals and other innocent civilians in the Netherlands could only result in a crackdown on other South Moluccans in the republic as well as friends and relatives there. In other words they could expect further oppression and little more.

Back in the Netherlands the two sieges dragged on, effectively stalemated, and the boredom of the proceedings was exemplified by the bizarre behaviour that the gunmen on the train began increasingly to display.

Whether it was simply to break the monotony or whether it was play-acting for the world's press camped out alongside the railway line will never be known for sure, but it was certainly very strange. At one point and for no apparent reason, having occupied themselves with tampering with the train's controls, they began to raise and lower a pantograph, the device used to link the locomotive with the overhead power supply. Later, they spent long spells repeatedly and inexplicably blowing the train's horn. More strange still, but hinting at the effects of the long periods of enforced idleness, they amused themselves by taking pot shots at passing birds and wild animals.

Meanwhile, the injured terrorist was charged with murder as he lay in his hospital bed.

At this point, the two sieges could have ended in a number of ways: a sudden, violent flare-up resulting in further fatalities or some degree of concession to the terrorists' demands, allowing a peaceful settlement. Realistically, the South Moluccan gang's demands were not going to be met whatever they resorted to and resignation to this reality must have been growing in both groups. It was no surprise, therefore, when in the end the two confrontations essentially fizzled out, ending at the scene of the hijacked train near Beilen, on 14 December 1975, and at the Consulate in Amsterdam five days later. In each case, having been talked into surrendering by a psychiatrist, the gunmen simply laid down their weapons and walked out into police custody. The relieved hostages who, in the case of the hijacked train had suffered the most appalling insanitary and cold conditions, were attended by paramedic teams and, after a debriefing with the anti-terrorist squads, were reunited with their families. For their part, the terrorists were tried for their crimes and given long prison sentences. But if the Dutch authorities thought that was the end of the matter, they were sadly mistaken.

In the early summer of 1977, the whole South Moluccan issue flared up again, with two more, almost repeat attacks directed against civilian targets. In synchronised raids, on 23 May 1977, terrorists occupied a school at Bovensmilde, three miles to the southwest of Assen, taking 110 children and teachers hostage. At the same time they hijacked the Rotterdam-Groningen express train, in almost identical circumstances to the earlier Beilen attack. The bright yellow locomotive and coaches were stopped on the railway line at Glimmen, six miles south of Groningen, after two of the gang, one a female, who boarded the train at Assen, pulled the communication cord in open countryside at a point where five comrades were waiting. Some 58 passengers were taken hostage on the train. The 13 terrorists engaged in the two raids were distinctive for the broad red head bands each was wearing. These traditionally indicated a Moluccan suicide mission.

At the school, at one point, the terrorists fired over the heads of desperate mothers who tried to approach the building to plead for the release of their children. On the train, at least, all the youngsters and elderly passengers were separated from the rest and allowed to go.

Police and anti-terrorist troops immediately moved in, sealing off the areas concerned and blockading each site to prevent the escape of the Moluccan gunmen. Between each of the sieges, and with the Dutch authorities, a three-way contact was established to permit a dialogue of negotiation but it soon became evident that it was the group on the train who were controlling both situations. In addition to their previously stated terms, the settlement of these new crises depended on the satisfaction of other conditions stipulated by the gunmen. They demanded the release of 21 comrades who had been jailed in 1975, some in connection with the previous siege incidents of that year, the rest for involvement in an unsuccessful plot to kidnap Queen Juliana. Arrangements for them to flee the country with their hostages were again insisted on.

Joop den Uyl, the Dutch Prime Minister, again flatly refused to meet any of the demands and, behind the scenes, the terrorist response team was encouraged to take a firm but measured approach in handling the sieges. Mindful of the fact that a rather larger group of children was being held, none of whom was older than 12 years of age, the first priority was to get them all released unharmed.

The scene at the school was one of great distress, the parents of the captive children visibly anguished. Bovensmilde had a small, close-knit Dutch community and there were few families there which were not affected by the kidnapping. The fact that this group of extremists had previously resorted to cold-blooded murder only served to intensify their anxiety.

The local library was converted into an improvised control and information centre, where most of the parents gathered to await news. When the Dutch Health Minister paid the centre a visit she was devastated by the suffering she encountered there.

Having been successful in extracting concessions from the South Moluccan gangmen in 1975, mediators from their own ethnic community were once more called on to assist with negotiations. Mr Kubuwael flew by helicopter to the school at Bovensmilde and other influential leaders made their way to the hijacked train. The first endeavours were directed at agreeing to the provision of food and drink and, specifically where the children were concerned, more comfortable sleeping facilities.

By comparison with the relatively relaxed and tension-free dealings with the terrorists located at the school, their counterparts aboard the train were more inclined to extreme volatility. This was demonstrated by two occurrences on the 24 May while provisioning arrangements were being established. Following communications between the school's headmaster, the mediators and the gang leader, a supply of camp beds, blankets, food and sweets were accepted by the terrorists and delivered in accordance with mutually agreed arrangements. Suddenly, while this was proceeding, a mentally distraught woman, probably one of the children's mothers, rushed towards the school building. The incident was swiftly diffused though it necessitated two policemen to strip down to their underclothes, to show that they were unarmed, before they were allowed to approach the woman and escort her away.

The climate was significantly more strained at the other siege location. There was a frightening moment when the terrorists had fired off their guns because food was late arriving. When it was finally delivered they would not then risk getting it from where it had been left, outside the train, so everyone on board, hostages and hijackers alike, went hungry.

If it was possible to present the mood or climate of a typical siege as a line graph, plotted in daily increments on the horizontal axis and measured upwards on a vertical scale of antipathy, against datums valued as reasonably conciliatory at the bottom to extremely hostile at the top, it would reveal a peak within the first 24-48hr which, after a day or so, as the siege continued, would begin to gradually fall. This reflects the inability of even the most hardened terrorists to endure the mental and physical strain necessary to sustain the proceedings at a constantly high confrontational level. Flattening out as it comes down, the line would then tend to remain level for long periods, apart from the occasional blip associated with outbursts of frustration on the part of the terrorists, as and when it was felt obligatory to try and impress upon the surrounding forces that it was the terrorists who were calling the shots. It is the endeavour of all teams handling sieges to keep the mood line down once it has fallen to a low level for it is during this period that a rapport can grow between captives and captors which can develop into a regard of an extent that would ultimately inhibit the terrorists from treating their victims aggressively.

There is always the danger, of course, that the mood line could rise again to culminate in another sudden and final peak if attitudes are allowed to harden such that the siege ends in violence. This serves as an indication to siege negotiators that they must, at all times, endeavour to maintain control throughout and not be lulled into a false sense of security.

The second round of South Moluccan sieges was following this typical pattern and, by 25 May, the third day of the siege, the mood was definitely one of malevolence and antagonism. First, the terrorists issued an ultimatum stating that if their wishes were not complied with they would commence to execute the hostages at 2pm. This was duly ignored and at 8.45pm a grotesquely threatening and intimidatory performance was staged for the benefit of the Dutch authorities.

Two blindfolded hostages, a young man and woman, were pushed from the train with their hands tied and nooses drawn tight around their throats. They had been forced to dress in white robes but what significance this had was not clear. Compelled to stand on the top of the embankment in this fashion for some 45min they were then as suddenly and violently dragged back with the ropes, into the train. The sinister symbolism of these mock executions was not lost on the negotiating team.

Earlier, at the school, a group of the children had been lined up at gunpoint in front of one of the windows where they were forced to chant repeatedly 'Van Agt, we want to stay alive!'. This was addressed to Mr Andreas van Agt, the Dutch Minister for Justice, but its impact was mostly felt by the worried parents, whose sense of trepidation grew alarmingly at this frightening development.

Food was again refused, at the school now as well as at the train.

Fearing that it might not be possible to resolve the two incidents, other than by force, contingency plans for paramilitary assaults were drawn up. The UK Government agreed to send a number of SAS troops to the Netherlands to advise Dutch commandos on the planning of such raids. In the final reckoning, it would require permission from the Dutch Government before any sort of forceful intervention could be sanctioned. It was estimated, though rather optimistically, by Lt-Gen Cor de Gragen, the Dutch Army's Commander-in-Chief at the siege scene, that, given the go-ahead, both objectives could be secured in 15sec.

A minor concession was extracted from the gunmen late on 25 May when they agreed to release two of the schoolchildren who had a history of heart illness, a girl of 11 and a boy of seven. The next day a seven-year old girl suffering from severe bronchial asthma was also freed.

It was revealed that there were two pregnant women aboard the hijacked express, one of whom had medical complications and whose life was thought to be in danger. An appeal to the terrorists to permit her to leave was refused. Some medicines were accepted, however, in itself something of an achievement considering the belligerent mood of the gunmen at this time. This was evinced by a repeat of the cruel farce of the previous evening when, during the morning, another hostage was paraded along the railway embankment with a noose around his neck.

A major breakthrough in the twin sieges was achieved during the 27 May when the gunmen agreed to the release of the remaining 102 children held hostage at the school at Bovensmilde. Having refused to accept food for them on the 25 May, the children had become extremely hungry. The following day the terrorists had relented, as much in their own interests as in the children's but within 24hr many of the hostage community were becoming ill through an outbreak of gastric influenza of epidemic proportions. There was a suspicion that the food supplied by the anti-terrorist team had been tampered with but this was vigorously denied. The majority of those affected by the 'bug' were the children and with the sanitary arrangements inside the school incapable of coping with this kind of emergency and with the risk of the illness spreading, if those afflicted were not quarantined, the terrorists elected to take the only precautions open to them and allow the children to go free. Unable to express their relief as they might have done otherwise, due to their being out of sorts, the children shuffled out of the school swaddled in their blankets, accompanied by one of their teachers whose release was also granted.

Demonstrating the greater resilience that seems to be characteristic of young people exposed to trauma or physical danger, the children were quick to reassure that they were none the worse for their experience. Indeed, the biggest problem, apart from having to sleep on uncomfortable camp beds or on the hard floor, was that they had missed their favourite television programmes. As to the treatment they had received from the terrorists, it was soon evident that it had been both

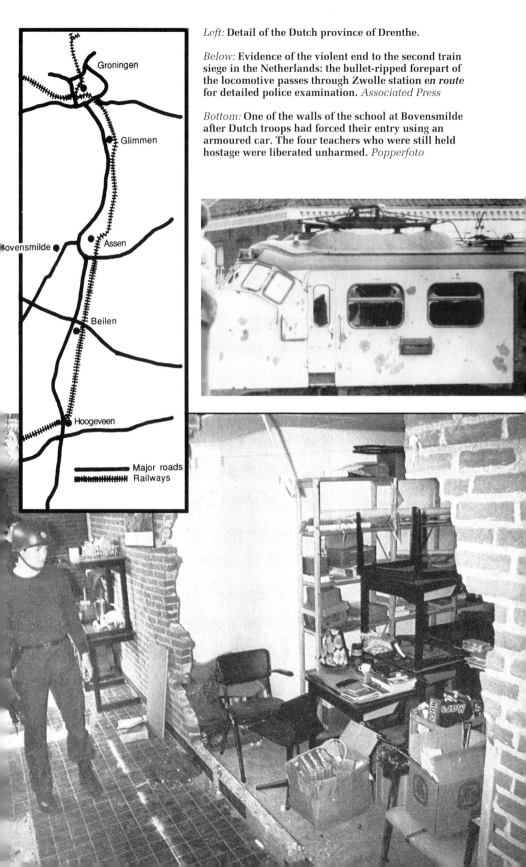

Left: Detail of the Dutch province of Drenthe.

Below: Evidence of the violent end to the second train siege in the Netherlands: the bullet-ripped forepart of the locomotive passes through Zwolle station *en route* for detailed police examination. *Associated Press*

Bottom: One of the walls of the school at Bovensmilde after Dutch troops had forced their entry using an armoured car. The four teachers who were still held hostage were liberated unharmed. *Popperfoto*

Groningen

Glimmen

Bovensmilde ● Assen

Beilen

Hoogeveen

Major roads
Railways

sensitive and sympathetic in contrast to the violent and uncompromising demeanour presented to the outside world. The children explained that the gunmen had been concerned to comfort and reassure them and had taken turns to read them stories. Their waiting parents were relieved beyond anything that words can adequately express. Later, they received reassurances from doctors and psychiatrists that all the children had emerged from the ordeal totally unscathed mentally.

The two sieges settled down around the remaining hostages, the four teachers still held at the school and the considerably larger number that remained incarcerated on the train.

Negotiations between the two sides were deadlocked and there appeared to be little prospect of securing early freedom for the 50 to 60 captives. Continuing requests for the release of the pregnant women were dismissed out of hand and for several days there was a state of almost languid lack of purpose to the proceedings, punctuated only by the occasional flurry of activity when an incident of one sort or another occurred.

The terrorists asked for and received cleaning materials and disinfectants to improve the sanitary conditions at both sieges, to help prevent the spread of disease. By now, the gunmen at the school were also ill with acute stomach upsets. Fearing that more South Moluccan extremists would attempt a break through to relieve four of the men who were most severely affected, the school was enclosed within a high barbed-wire barrier. Rumours began to circulate suggesting that the mystery illness that had broken out among the children was meningitis or lockjaw. The police allowed these groundless suspicions to reach the Moluccan gunmen in the hope that it would have a psychosomatically unsettling effect upon them.

On 31 May the telephone link between the train and the school was severed when faults caused it to stop working. The Dutch Government refused to allow technicians to repair it on the pretext that it would expose them to unacceptable danger. In practice, it suited them to have the two gangs isolated from one another, particularly as the overall direction of the combined operation was apparently vested with one of the terrorists on the besieged train.

Behaviour therapists working with the government team advised that the terrorists were becoming intransigent, stiffening their resolve to resist the siege and that positive action should be taken to avert this. The South Moluccan mediators who had arrived on the scene early on had now withdrawn, being unable to exert any further influence over the gunmen. With a field telephone hotline installed, the gunmen themselves now requested the assistance of new mediators to try to end the sieges. Whereas this request for mediators was broadly accepted, the authorities could not agree to the choice of mediators. Retorting to this, the terrorists advised that the authorities should not waste their time with any more talking unless the discussions concerned a trade-off of prisoners for hostages. In return, the government team advised that what was needed was some inducement from the hijackers, maybe the release of one or two hostages as a token of good faith. And so it continued with move and counter-move but seemingly lacking any impetus that would compel the terrorists to confront the hopelessness of their situation so as to bring the affair to an end.

The continuing, fruitless siege operation, fast threatening to become the longest on record in Dutch criminal history, prompted a number of eminent criminologists and behavioural specialists to voice their concerns. The observations of Dr William Sargant, Honorary Consultant Psychiatrist at

St Thomas' Hospital, London, as quoted in *The Times* newspaper, highlighted these issues most pertinently, amounting to a concise dissertation on the recommended techniques for conducting and controlling sieges:

'The question inevitably arises: are the authorities conducting the siege as they should? Many experts on brainwashing are becoming very worried at the turn events have taken. They have every reason to be concerned. It is one thing to keep the situation off the boil and try to ensure that events run quietly for those who have been kidnapped, but it is quite another to allow the terrorists to fall into a complacent frame of mind.

'In this situation pressure must be continually applied to the kidnappers. All the time the gunmen must be told that their situation is absolutely hopeless. It must be made quite clear to them that if there is any shooting they themselves are almost certain to be shot as soon as it starts. It can be hinted that if they give themselves up they might possibly get a lesser sentence at any trial for their kindness to their sick captives: otherwise their fate is death or a lifetime in jail.

'Human and animal brains, providing the psychological stress is great enough and provided that it continues incessantly, will always become more and more suggestible under such circumstances. Finally, just as the exhausted rabbit turns and runs straight into the mouth of the pursuing stoat, so the kidnappers' brains will go into reverse and they will walk out and give themselves up.

'This technique could and should be applied in the Dutch situation. The present terrible danger in this long Dutch siege is that unless this state of exhaustion is reached soon, some of the captives' minds may become disordered before the kidnappers' and they will act in a way which means that shooting starts, and perhaps spark off a blood bath

'The psychological methods used on the kidnappers must be as intensive and continuous as possible. There must be no restful let-ups and useless conferences.'

Notwithstanding, Dr Sargant's harsh words, the Dutch sieges had not been entirely lacking in progress. On 3 June, the identities of mediators had been finally agreed. They were Mrs Josina Soumokil, the widow of Chris Soumokil, the former Moluccan President, who had been executed by the Indonesians in 1966, and Dr Hassan Tan, a retired chest doctor.

Two days later they secured the freedom of the two expectant mothers-to-be who left the scene of the railway siege escorted by a Moluccan physician, Dr Franz Tutuhatunewa, bound for hospital in Groningen. They were 25-year old Mrs Nelleke Ellenbrock-Prinsen, from Wierden near Almelo, who was five months pregnant and Mrs Annie Brouwers-Korf who was 31 and who came from Nijmegen. She was seven months pregnant.

On 7 June 1977 the joint sieges did indeed finally break the duration record as far as incidents of this kind in the Netherlands were concerned. On the same day the majority of the children who had been held at Bovensmilde resumed their studies at another nearby school. The children from the local Moluccan community were, on their parents' choice, kept away for fear of reprisals. This hinted at a wider issue which threatened to introduce deep and bitter racial tensions to the Netherlands as a whole. Opinion polls and public statements carried in national newspapers revealed that the continuing siege was trying the patience of the Dutch nation and that a race war against the South Moluccan refugee population was on the cards.

The near absence of any dialogue on the 7 June ended when, on the next day and by mutual consent, the deadlocked talks resumed, culminating in the release of another train hostage being secured. But, though Mr Theo van Hattem, whose heart complaint had been aggravated by the prolonged period of anxiety he had endured aboard the besieged train, was able to breathe a sigh of relief as he walked to freedom, this was not in itself a turning point that heralded the end of the sieges. The whole situation remained as tense and uncompromising as ever.

Desperation on the part of the hostages was beginning to reveal itself too. Each of those who had been freed had advised that the others were generally in reasonably good health, bored rather than anything more serious but clearly fear for their survival was always there to some degree, gnawing away in their minds, and could not be suffered for too much longer without the risk of breakdown. As if to support this, on 9 June, one of the hostages in the train flashed a cry for help in morse code using a mirror to reflect the sunlight. Part of his message was an emphatic 'Get us out of here'.

Negotiations remained fruitless, however, and, with the ever mounting concern that the sieges would end in bloodshed if they continued, the military option became inevitable. At dawn on Saturday, 11 June 1977, with all scope for a negotiated solution exhausted, the troops went in, storming the besieged school and the hijacked train simultaneously.

At the school, where Dutch marines punched a hole through the wall of the building with an armoured car, no opposition was encountered. The six gunmen there surrendered with a willingness that suggested that they too were glad it was all over and the four hostage teachers were liberated unharmed. Meanwhile on the railway track at Glimmen things were rather different. The assault was greeted with a barrage of fire which was returned by the advancing troops. By the time it was all over the train was riddled with bullet holes. Six of the terrorists were killed in the battle and there were two casualties among the hostages, a 40-year old man and a girl aged 19. Five other hostages required hospital treatment for their injuries. One of these, a young man named Janneke Wiegers, had been extremely lucky to survive, having been used as a living shield during the assault by one of the South Moluccans who was himself subsequently killed.

The ending of the sieges was warmly welcomed and widely celebrated throughout the country. The hostages resumed their normal lives, though for certain with a totally new outlook; the captured terrorists were tried and sentenced while their dead compatriots were buried in a combined ceremony at the cemetery at Boskamp. It was not quite the end of the South Moluccan reign of terror — a siege at a government building in Assen in March 1978 had to be ended by force after an official there was brutally murdered — but it was almost over.

The danger remains, however, that with the lack of concerted effort to seek and achieve political solutions, that the underlying problem, like a dormant wound continues to fester until it breaks out again at a later date. The extremism of the South Moluccan community in the Netherlands was the ultimate means of expression of a frustrated minority of the younger element of the population. Although they have never seen their ancestral islands in the South Seas, their protest movement is still fuelled by a burning dream of creating an independent republic there, free of Indonesian rule. That dream remains unfulfilled.

The Price of a Presidency

The collapse of the Shah of Persia's rule over Iran, in 1979, precipitated an unstoppable sequence of events, which, in a classic example of the domino effect, had a profound impact on the political fortunes of the leader of another country, ultimately leading to his downfall too. This was Jimmy Carter, the 39th president of the United States of America.

It all began in the late 1970s as opposition to the Shah gathered momentum in the form of public demonstrations and industrial unrest. It was all whipped up, almost deliberately, by religious fundamentalist mullahs who, in turn, derived their inspiration for the riots from the Ayatollah Ruholla Khomeini, the spiritual leader of Iran's majority Shi'ite Muslims who had been exiled in 1963. Following his expulsion from Najaf in Iraq, he was now living at Ponchartrain on the outskirts of Paris, a lion in waiting, sworn to achieving the downfall of the Shah.

The streets of Tehran and other major cities in Iran turned into battlefields as the protests against poverty, repression and the hated national security and intelligence bureau, Savak, reached fever pitch. Waves of strikes brought industrial and oil production to a standstill and the country's economy to the brink of collapse.

The Shah, Mohammed Riza, the latest ruler in the Pahlavi dynasty, the so-called 'Peacock Throne', had attempted throughout his reign to strike a balance in the government of Iran between turning it into a modern 'western' country while at the same time preserving its fundamental Islamic culture and principals. Effort had been concentrated on building up the country's defences with modern armaments and in the modernisation of the cities. In following these policies, though, he had lost touch with the ordinary Iranian people and he was accused of neglecting Iran's predominantly peasant population.

In a bid to appease the widespread discontent, changes were made at the top of the Iranian government as new Prime Ministers came and went but this did nothing to stop the momentum of the slide towards anarchy. A state of martial law was imposed but this only triggered off more violence as fanatical Shia muslims encouraged mobs to go on the rampage, fighting in the streets and destroying property.

As events moved to a climax, it seemed that the Shah's continued reign depended on the loyalty of the army of conscripted troops. While there was no immediate sign of rebellion among the ranks, the soldiers were largely drawn from ordinary Iranian families and it was suspected that they held more than a hint of sympathy for the lot of these citizens who had benefited least from the Shah's programme of modernisation.

A huge demonstration in Tehran on 10 December 1978 confirmed that the end was nigh for the beleagured Shah. Over a million demonstrators in a peaceful column, 30 or more abreast and over five miles long, marched through the city calling for the Shah's abdication and the ending of the month-old military government he had imposed when civilian authority had broken down. The troops did not intervene, even though many in the vast host carried pictures of the exiled Ayatollah Khomeini and chanted for his immediate return.

The inevitable came on 16 January 1979 when the Shah fled from his capital, ostensibly to take a vacation in Egypt with his wife, the Empress Farah, but in reality deposed and fated never to return to Iran. The news of his departure was broadcast to the nation and received with wild celebrations. Revellers in Tehran targetted statues of the Shah and his father which were toppled from their plinths and smashed to pieces. Loyal royalist troops counter-demonstrated the following day but they were in the minority and would soon be silenced.

An interim socialist government was formed under the leadership of Dr Shahpur Bakhtiar but this was immediately threatened by Khomeini's return from exile on 1 February, received in a frenzy of adulation by a crowd of over 3 million supporters. Again, the future of the administration, denounced as illegal by Khomeini, hung in the balance, depending for its survival on the support of the military. But the remaining loyal troops withdrew to their barracks and Bakhtiar's government fell. Declaring that there was no place for democracy in Iran, Ayatollah Khomeini now took control of the government himself, forming a new republican administration comprised of Shi'ite fundamentalists and announcing that Iran would return to strict observance of extremist Muslim codes of behaviour. The Iranian Islamic revolution was complete.

It soon became evident that under the new régime all aspects of former Iranian life would be purged; officials and representatives of the previous governments and their various official authorities would be rounded-up and tried by revolutionary courts; reprisals would be taken against organisations with links with the west and their funds confiscated in the name of the people. Top-ranking generals in the armed forces and former premiers among others, were executed.

As part of a campaign of restoration of the impoverished Iranian economy, the revolutionary government announced that all industries that remained in private hands or foreign ownership were to be nationalised. The extradition of the former Shah was also sought, primarily for him to stand trial for crimes against the Iranian people but also to obtain the surrender of his huge personal fortune. To the relief of the Egyptians, who feared a fundamentalist backlash within their own population, the Shah flew to the United States where he underwent medical treatment — an operation to remove his gall bladder and biopsies on tissue samples which confirmed that he had advanced cancer of the lymph glands. Egypt was already suffering criticism from hard-line Arab states for engaging in peace talks with Israel which challenged the fundamental hostility towards the continued existence of the Jewish state that was central to Muslim extremism.

Even as he lay in his hospital bed, the demands for his return to Iran, urged on by Iran's so-called 'hanging-judge', the Ayatollah Khalkhali, led to demonstrations outside the New York nursing home, with blood-curdling calls for him to be dragged from the building, sick as he was, to be dismembered in the street.

Arising from the fact that the Shah was now in America, the United States became the target of Iranian venom, castigated as the 'Great Satan' and blamed for the spiritually demoralising materialistic values of the Shah's Imperial Iran, which were now spurned by the Shi'ite fundamentalists.

Towards the end of 1979 Iranian demands for the extradition of the Shah were intensified. Unable to do more, from a distance, than pour ineffectual abuse on the United States, attention was turned to the one American target within Iran that could be physically violated — the United States Embassy in Tehran.

The first attempt to occupy the Embassy by Revolutionary Guards ended swiftly when the Ayatollah Khomeini ordered the so-called 'students' to leave but their action had demonstrated the vulnerability of the residence of the American Ambassador, which at one-time had been the seat of United States' power and influence in the Middle East.

On 4 November 1979 the Revolutionary Guards, backed up by a baying mob screaming anti-American rhetoric, stormed the Embassy a second time. Swarming over the Embassy's walls they brushed aside the guard of US Marines, who were understandably unsure how best to repel safely the incursion without further inflaming the situation, and occupied the sprawling buildings within the vast Embassy grounds taking nearly 100 members of the diplomatic staff hostage.

The hostages, men and women alike, were rounded up and placed together under close guard, some of them held in basement rooms, handcuffed and blindfolded. The Embassy gates were locked tight and all access to the compound placed under the control of more of the heavily armed fundamentalist revolutionaries. Meanwhile, the mob outside presented a macabre foretaste of what awaited the Shah, if and when he returned to Iran, for the benefit of the foreign newspaper correspondents and TV cameramen who had been following the extraordinary scenes. A mock gallows was constructed and erected, complete with noose. Attached to the dangling rope was a placard with the legend 'For the Shah'.

At the same time, to the hysterical cheers and thunderous applause of the crowd, a number of American flags were burned. More placards were produced, too, with deliberately provocative messages on them, such as 'USA, we want the Shah soon' and another which boasted, more sinisterly, 'When Khomeini fights, Carter trembles'.

The American Government was outraged by the illegal incursion into what was effectively their property, its sovereign recognition and protection governed by the Geneva Convention. The Iranian threat to kill the Embassy staff unless the Shah was returned to face the justice of the Islamic Revolution only served to amplify this wrathful indignation. The Iranian Ambassador was summoned to the White House where he was advised by President Carter, in no uncertain terms, that the USA expected swift intervention by the Iranian authorities to end the incident which otherwise threatened a dangerous confrontation between the two powers.

Shrewdly, Khomeini's government ministers implied that the fundamentalists occupying the Embassy were operating outside their control or authority, that police action to end the occupation might, therefore, prove to be inflammatory and could put the hostages' lives at risk and that the best solution to bringing the unfortunate incident to a rapid and peaceful conclusion was the quick return of the Shah to stand trial.

In reality, of course, the extremists enjoyed the tacit approval for their actions of the Ayatollah Khomeini and his government. Indeed, it was almost certain that the 'spontaneous' move against the Embassy had been deliberately orchestrated by government officials acting on Ayatollah Khomeini's instructions. Certainly no effort was made to intervene and reverse what had happened. Later, it became transparently clear that the siege was, as suspected, politically motivated, sanctioned with the full authority of the Iranian leader.

The only positive sign for America at this time was the resignation, in protest at the siege, of the Iranian Prime Minister, Dr Meldi Bazargan, who had been appointed by Khomeini as Bakhtiar's replacement and who had been in office for less than nine months.

It was the run-up period to the US presidential elections. For President Carter, seeking his second term in office, the hostage crisis had come at the worst possible time. This tricky incident would have tested the skills of the most astute politician but it caught Carter unprepared and he struggled to do other than react to events. When he most needed to come across as an effective and assertive statesman, able to command the respect of the international community and to deal decisively with this diplomatic affair, it threatened instead to humiliate both him and the US. The American Goliath had been given a very public bloody-nose by the Iranian David and all the signs were that he would get away with it.

Economic sanctions were imposed which were designed to strike at Iran, with its impoverished economy, where it hurt most. First, Carter ordered the cessation of all US imports of Iranian oil. Next, in further retaliation for the Embassy occupation, all Iranian assets in the US were frozen. Tehran was quick to respond. The Iranian Economics and Foreign Minister, Abol Hassan Bani-Sadr, declared that, at a stroke, all of Iran's foreign debts had been rendered void. Khomeini, too, retorted menacingly by threatening to put the hostages on trial as spies. Simultaneously, the US pursued other moves to terminate the siege under the auspices and influence of the United Nations. On 9 November 1979 the Security Council duly called for the immediate release of the American hostages but all this made little impression on Iran.

For some of the hostages, at least, captivity within the besieged Embassy, turned out to be gratefully shortlived, ended by Khomeini's decree on 17 November that all women and blacks should be immediately released. In the event, two of the women remained with the hostages for the duration of the siege.

Four days later, fearing US military intervention, the Iranians warned that if anything of that sort was tried all the hostages still detained in the Embassy would be killed instantly.

For the 53 remaining hostages it was the beginning of an ordeal of extreme dimensions. At 444 days duration, by the time that it ended, it was one of the longest sieges of its kind on record. It would be futile to try here to describe the feelings or the daily experiences of the hostages as this protracted incarceration under extreme duress unfolded. Relying on the mutual support of the group to see each other through, the over-riding concern for the hostages was one of coping with the sheer monotony and boredom of the experience as day after day passed with a restricted routine and inadequate means to stimulate the brain or keep physically active.

Of course, it was not just a matter of relieving the enforced idleness — after all, a régime of routine duties was, as far as possible maintained. The fact was that underlying this imposed normality were tensions fed by real concerns and anxieties. Arising from their near total isolation there was a continuous niggling fear of the unknown insofar as what might be their ultimate fate. Who could tell with certainty what awaited them in the hands of these unstable fanatics who clearly showed no respect for international conventions or protocols? More than anything, though, it was the isolation from the outside world that affected the hostages — little news from the family back home to find out how they were handling the situation or to know that everyone was well and no means of communicating back to let them know that, in spite of the constant threats and the degrading treatment as individuals, the siege was being endured and that their resolve to survive was unquenchable. There was always the danger that, even collected together as a mutually-supportive group, as time progressed with no sign of release and in the total absence of news, the will to endure would be undermined by a growing sense of impotence and abandonment.

Further evidence was soon forthcoming that Iran's Islamic fundamentalist régime would pursue its intentions anywhere in the world, regardless of the constraints of international codes of conduct and with no regard for the law of any of the countries in which they operated. In Paris, on 7 December 1979, Capt Shariar Chefik, the deposed Shah's nephew was shot dead. Later, similar attempts would be made to assassinate former political leaders who had also sought sanctuary abroad.

Meanwhile, the Shah, having been discharged from hospital, was granted temporary asylum in Panama. An application to remain in the US had not been received sympathetically.

Efforts to obtain the release of the hostages continued. On 17 January 1980, at the request of the US Government, Kurt Waldheim, the UN Secretary General paid Iran a visit for talks on the crisis. Though the freedom of the hostages was the top item on his agenda, the Secretary General was unable to make substantive progress towards achieving this. However, he agreed to the formation of a UN Commission to investigate the former Shah's activities, on the conclusion of which, the position of the hostages would be reviewed. To the chagrin of President Carter, the Iranian renegades were still calling the shots.

While the Commission was being set up and as it commenced its work, little more happened to advance the resolution of the crisis. Having embarked upon this approach to achieving a settlement of the affair, it had to be given a meaningful chance to produce results before alternative options were resorted to, even if the American public objected strongly to this apparent, if temporary, continuation of the illegal imprisonment of its diplomats. The appointment of Bani-Sadr as the Iranian Republic's first president seemed to provide grounds for optimism especially as he was granted increased powers by Ayatollah Khomeini specifically for dealing with the American captives.

Any hope for a settlement were soon dashed, however, when the Iranians demanded from Carter, in a new bid to humiliate him, that he should publicly apologise for US 'actions in Iran in the past' in return for securing the hostages release. Carter bluntly refused, whereupon co-operation with the UN Commission of Enquiry was largely withdrawn by the Iranians.

A request for the Commission team to visit the hostages, to determine if they were being treated correctly and to provide a minimal courier service for messages, was refused by Khomeini's Government unless the Commission's members first expressed condemnation of the 'crimes' committed by the Shah and by the US. Instead, Kurt Waldheim ordered the Commission to leave Iran with its work still incomplete. This sinister new development left the stranded diplomatic staff as far as ever from regaining their liberty. It confirmed, too, as had been suspected all along, that the hostages were being held against their will not by the revolutionary 'students' occupying the US Embassy but by the Iranian Government on whose behalf the 'students' were acting as agents of anti-American subversion.

The frustration and disillusionment within the Carter administration at this turn of events was immense. It was summed up by Jodi Powell, the President's Press Secretary, when he said 'The Iranian Government's ability to function as a (legitimate) government and to fulfil the commitments it has made is now seriously in doubt'. To cap it all, as the UN team was departing from Iran, it was subjected to a further indignity when it was advised that only when its findings had been published and only if these were favourable to Iran would the team be allowed to meet the hostages. As to whether this would also elicit the hostages' release was not even mentioned.

President Carter was confronting a growing dilemma. As the months had passed he had been subjected to increasingly bitter criticism from the US media for his vacillation over the hostage crisis, yet he had little means at his disposal, other than military intervention with all the risks that entailed, to bring meaningful influence to bear on the situation or to pressurise the Iranians into agreeing to his demands and to those, almost without exception, of the international community.

Almost as if the immediate hostage crisis was a minor and inconsequential distraction, the Iranians continued to concentrate their efforts on getting the Shah's return. He, in turn, was endeavouring to stay one step ahead of his adversaries, even as his health was rapidly failing. Just a day before Iran was due to serve a request for the Shah's extradition, he left Panama, returning to Egypt.

As the siege entered its sixth month, rumours abounded that the US was about to resort to military action to free the hostages. Realistically, confronted by Iran's obstructive and recalcitrant attitude, short of abandoning the captives to their fate, President Carter had no other option left to him. In a final effort to use political and commercial pressure to bring the siege to a peaceful conclusion before resorting to more extreme measures, diplomatic relations with Iran were severed on 7 April and a further package of punitive trade sanctions was announced.

Pressure on President Carter to take more aggressive action was mounting. US pride had been severely dented and irritated by Iran's impudence and in earnest to see the Islamic revolutionaries put firmly in their place, American public opinion clamoured for the military to embark upon a campaign of retribution and reprisal. In the growing atmosphere of jingoism, it seems that little thought was given to the possible implications of military action to the victims of Iran's illegal actions, the very hostages whose freedom was desired. Equally, the hostage crisis had aroused a powerful surge of partisan solidarity for the cause of this group of American citizens illegally incarcerated on foreign soil. It was as if the potent symbolism of the Liberty Bell, which had been fundamental to the shaping of the US constitution, had been rediscovered, renewing an impoverished sense of national, spiritual comradeship. Ordinary Americans everywhere registered their allegiance to the hostage vigil by attaching thousands of yellow ribbons, the American symbol of home coming, to trees, flagpoles and lamp-posts throughout the Union.

Little opportunity was, therefore, afforded in this atmosphere of gauging whether Carter's package of economic measures would have the desired effect. On 24 April, with the full endorsement of the President and under a cloud of secrecy, the long anticipated military intervention by US forces was launched. Codenamed Operation 'Eagle Claw', a raiding party of 90 commanders from a crack anti-terrorist unit known as the 'Delta Force' or the 'Blue Light Squad', was assembled under the leadership of Col 'Charging' Charlie Beckwith. Their objective was to storm the Embassy compound, recover all the hostages and fly them out to safety. Enough fire power and equipment was carried to permit the containment of whatever resistance could be expected from the Iranian revolutionaries holding the Embassy. The intention was to get in and out before any more concerted opposition could be mustered from regular troops.

On this basis, the force, comprising eight Sikorsky and Boeing helicopters and six Lockheed C-130 Hercules transport aircraft, was first to make for a temporary airbase to be established in the desert at a suitable point on the outskirts of Tehran within a short ferrying distance of the Embassy. The aircraft headed into Iran under cover of darkness, the helicopters from the aircraft carrier USS Nimitz, operating in the Persian Gulf, and the transports, so it was reported but not confirmed, via Bahrain from a base in Egypt.

Given the diplomatic manoeuvring that had preceded the military directive and the fact that all pre-planning was a closely guarded secret, it is impossible to know just how long the US force was given to prepare for the operation. It was claimed that it had begun as early as the previous November. If so, then the pre-inspection of equipment to clear it for the exercise left a lot to be desired.

What is certain is that either through inadequate pre-planning or poor pre-flight checks, given the vital nature of the operation, things started to go badly wrong even as the flight to Tehran was underway. Three of the helicopters developed mechanical faults and the entire force was compelled to re-appraise its capability to complete the operation after landing at a refuelling point in a remote area of desert some 200 miles southeast of the Iranian capital.

The first helicopter to experience problems was abandoned in the desert where it had made an emergency landing. Its crew was picked up by another of the squad which then proceeded towards the planned assembly point. A second machine that developed faults was obliged to return straight away to the carrier Nimitz. When the remaining helicopters reached the pre-arranged refuelling point it was discovered that a third helicopter had suffered component failures which, because they could not be fixed, reduced the serviceable strength of helicopters to five machines which was inadequate to complete the mission. It was decided, therefore, to abandon the operation totally in the hope that, if the raid remained undiscovered, the exercise could be repeated at another, early opportunity.

However, it transpired that even the ability to launch a second surprise attack had been fatally impaired when it was realised, on the flight in, that a group of Iranians in a bus had spotted one of the Hercules transports. The aircraft landed and the 50 Iranians were taken prisoner, the intention being to hold them until the mission was complete. They were later released, unharmed.

Having decided to abort the mission, orders were given to refuel the aircraft ready for take-off and return to their bases of departure. In the process of getting airborne, the force suffered a further, catastrophic mishap which turned the operation from a failure into a fiasco — an embarrassing and humiliating disaster that was bound to be emblazoned across the front pages of all the world's newspapers. The die was cast when, as one of the remaining helicopters took off, it collided with a transport aircraft causing it to crash to the ground where it exploded and burst into flames. Eight commandos were killed outright. With no means of remedying the situation, or concealing the evidence of the débâcle, the remaining units of the force had no option but to abandon the scene as quickly as possible, leaving the desert littered with the flaming wreckage of the destroyed aircraft and the bodies of the dead.

It was a matter of considerable regret that the remnants of the force had insufficient capacity even to recover the bodies of the victims. Subsequent developments, when the Iranians gave their public reaction to the aborted and calamitously bungled raid, only compounded the debasement of the American

Debris and bodies litter the Iranian desert as a testament to the catastrophic outcome of Operation 'Eagle Claw', the mission to rescue the US Embassy hostages. Beyond the body of a dead commando is the remains of a Lockheed C-130 transport's starboard wing. In the background stand various helicopters, a Sikorsky Sea Stallion, on the left and a Boeing Chinook further back, on the right. *Popperfoto*

nation in the wake of the wretched episode, as Iran revelled in its disrespectful and irreverent treatment of the dead commandos. News of the failed rescue attempt, after it had been broadcast to the Iranian people, was greeted with unbridled jubilation. The remains of the killed Americans were flown to Tehran where they were contemptuously put on public display. Later, during a press conference presided over by Ayatollah Khalkhali, they were ghoulishly mutilated.

The militants holding the remaining hostages let it be known, in no uncertain terms, that, if another rescue attempt was made, they would all be executed. Pointedly castigating and mocking the hapless American President, Khomeini added to Carter's misery by declaring the raid 'an act of stupidity which could have sent the hostages to hell'. The Soviet Union, too, through the organ of its news agency, Tass, had its own tough commentary on the failed US rescue mission. It accused President Carter of having taken the world to the edge of war for the sake of a purely selfish interest in the forthcoming Presidential elections.

The disastrous outcome of the attempted rescue was a bitter personal and political blow for President Carter. It was universally regarded as an act of desperate political imperative by a beleaguered and unpopular President searching for the means to boost his flagging political fortunes. Now confronting yet greater scorn and derision, for his failure to organise and implement successfully the daring rescue mission, than he had suffered hitherto for his indecision and oscillation in the handling of the crisis over the preceding months, he forlornly presented himself to the shocked American nation on breakfast-time television on 25 April.

Announcing the terrible outcome of the unsuccessful raid he declared publicly his personal atonement for the disaster, taking full responsibility for its consequences. In sombre tone, he confessed 'It was my decision to attempt the rescue operation; it was my decision to cancel it when a problem developed in the placement of our rescue team. The responsibility is purely my own'. As to the justification for launching the raid in the first place he explained that he had viewed it as 'a necessity and a duty'. He continued 'I ordered the rescue mission prepared in order to safeguard American lives, to protect America's national interest and to reduce the tensions in the world that have been caused among many nations as this crisis has continued.' 'It was a consequence too,' he said, 'of the steady unravelling of authority in Iran and the mounting dangers that were posed to the hostages themselves'. In conclusion, President Carter advised that his administration would revert to recognised political mechanisms in its continuing pursuit of a settlement to the hostage crisis; the prospect of further military intervention was clearly ruled out. 'We will seek to continue to find along with other nations and with the officials of Iran, a prompt resolution of the crisis without any loss of life and through peaceful and diplomatic means'.

It was a brave endeavour and an honest declaration of accountability at the highest level that should, perhaps, have been viewed in a spirit of national reconciliation. But it was in reality, the symbolic hammering in of the final nail in Carter's coffin for it was, in effect, an admission that he had not, in all truth, acted according to his own judgements but rather that he had allowed himself to be manipulated by public opinion, a weakness that could not be tolerated in the character of the person who occupied this, the most senior political office in the world. Thus, from that moment, Carter's future political career was condemned.

Behind the scenes, concerted efforts continued to be made to gain the hostages release but, it seemed that Carter himself remained the stumbling block as the Iranian leaders sought to ensure that he was not re-elected. The successful ending of the siege at the Iranian Embassy in London, on 5 May 1980, brought the lingering business back once more into the spotlight. Trying to feed off the positive and determined tackling of the London incident, a stern tone was once again briefly adopted by the Carter administration. The Iranian Government was emphatically reminded that it alone was held responsible for the safety and well-being of the US captives. It was pointed out, too, that the culmination of the siege at the Iranian Embassy in London acted as a sharp reminder of the abhorrence felt by the international community for terrorist acts against the diplomats of any nation.

It was of little consequence, though. In the end, it took an act of aggression by Iran's neighbour Iraq, coupled with the death of the former Shah to deflect the attention of Khomeini's government on to more pressing matters. By providing the Islamic extremists in the streets with a new target for their rhetoric it proved possible for the crisis to be resolved peacefully.

The Shah died of cancer in Cairo on 27 July 1980. He was buried in a Cairo mausoleum after a state funeral with full honours and 'all due respects' but it was a valedictory ceremony that was conspicuous for the absence of world leaders both from Arab and western countries who would normally have been represented on such an occasion. The fact was that they had not been invited by Egypt, thereby saving them the embarrassment of having to decline for fear of making themselves the focus of Iranian antagonism. Tehran Radio's only contribution to the proceedings was to describe the former Shah as 'the bloodsucker of the century'.

On 17 September 1980, President Saddam Hussain of Iraq precipitated a territorial dispute with Iran by abrogating the 1975 border agreement between the two countries. A war of bloody attrition was triggered which was to embroil the two countries for the next five years. In the short term it largely demoted Iran's campaign of anti-Americanism to a matter of secondary importance, to the considerable relief of the west.

Negotiations for the release of the remaining 52 hostages — a single, sick hostage, Richard Owen, had been released back in early July in a token gesture of humanitarian benevolence — were well advanced by the time of the American Presidential elections on 4 November. As expected, Carter was soundly defeated by his Republican opponent, Ronald Reagan, but the size of Reagan's landslide victory was staggering. Compared with four years earlier, when Carter had wrested the Presidency from Gerald Ford by 297 electoral votes to 241, Reagan had secured 489 votes to Carter's meagre 49, a decline of popularity without precedence.

Acting on behalf of the US Government, the Algerian Government commenced to apply intense pressure on Iran, in concert with the UN, the Palestinian Liberation Organisation and Pope John Paul, in a bid to conclude the hostage business once and for all. A deal was finally secured when the US agreed to freeze all the assets of the late Shah, to unfreeze Iranian assets and to end all trade sanctions. A ransom of £10,000 million was refused.

To complete the political assassination of Jimmy Carter, Ayatollah Khomeini still delayed the agreed-upon release until 20 January 1981, the date of Ronald Reagan's inauguration, the beginning of the term of office of the new President.

Taken aboard an Algerian-registered jet, the hostages, smiling broadly and evidently delighted to be free at last, were flown to Algiers. They arrived there early in the morning of 21 January, stepping from the aircraft to freedom, displaying a mixture of exhaustion and euphoria. The first to disembark was the most senior US captive, the Chargé d'Affairs, Bruce Laingen. He was followed by the two women who had remained within the Embassy for the duration of the siege, Elizabeth Ann Swift and Kathryn Koob. They wore yellow ribbons in their hair in recognition of the many similar symbols of their long awaited homecoming that had been put up on their behalf all over the US. On leaving Algiers, the hostages were flown to Wiesbaden in West Germany where they were greeted by the former President, Jimmy Carter, who had tried for so long but in vain to secure their release.

Back in the USA, the hostages' release was greeted everywhere with pealing bells and hooting sirens. A sign that had been erected in New York, on which the days of the siege had been counted, was replaced with a new sign which read: 'Free at last — thank God; Free at last — Never again!'.

As it turned out, President Carter was not the last casualty of the domino-like chain reaction of political events which had been triggered in 1978 with the drive to unseat the Shah of Persia from his throne by Islamic extremists. In June 1981, Mr Bani-Sadr proved to be yet another shortlived Iranian premier when he was first ousted and then impeached. Four months later, on 6 October 1981, the most tragic victim of the extreme Islamic fundamentalism unleashed by Ayatollah Khomeini was gunned down in Cairo. This was Anwar Sadat, the Egyptian President, assassinated for his part in concluding a peace accord with Israel and for his complicity with the former Shah by aiding him in avoiding the justice of the Islamic Revolution.

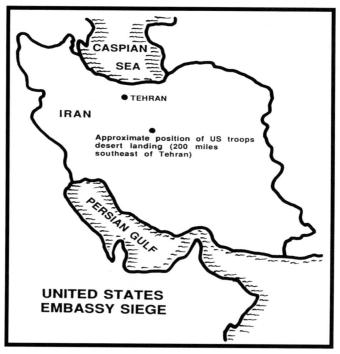

Map of Iran showing the capital, Tehran, and the point in the desert where Operation 'Eagle Claw' came to calamitous grief.

Who Dares Wins

Viewers of BBC Television's popular situation comedy *Only Fools and Horses*, which features as its central character aspiring socialite and street trader Derek Trotter, may perhaps be curious about or even have forgotten the origin of one of his popular catch phrases: 'Who dares wins'. This is, in fact, the motto of the Special Air Service (SAS), an élite Royal Air Force regiment created in World War 2 for clandestine insurgency operations behind enemy lines in North Africa and now employed as a crack counter-revolutionary warfare team.

The SAS motto is now far better known than the service it belongs to, brought to prominence through a dramatic siege-cracking assault in London in May 1980 while the regiment itself, by necessity, remained shrouded in deep secrecy.

Inevitably, the explosion of Islamic fundamentalism and Arab extremism in the Middle East provoked disturbances in many western countries as reactions and counter-reactions erupted among small pockets of displaced and expatriate persons, exiles, students and others who were domiciled abroad. These groups, representing both liberal and radical points of view, vented their support or opposition to the dictatorial régimes in their own countries in public disturbances on the streets of the country in which they were living, often to the bewilderment and irritation of the domestic population. Though this usually took the form of demonstrations, occasionally more extreme forms of behaviour were resorted to, leading to physical violence and requiring the active intervention of the police authorities. This was twice the case in London during the 1980s when clashes between rival ideological factions resulted in the siege incidents described here.

On 28 April 1980, at 11.30am, five armed men entered the Iranian Embassy in Princes Gate, Knightsbridge, swiftly taking control of the five storey building and holding 26 persons hostage. Given the continuing siege at the US Embassy in Tehran by Islamic revolutionaries, it was a classic case of the biter being bitten.

With two major embassy violations within six months of each other it seemed that an epidemic of diplomatic hostage taking was set to continue unabated into the new decade. Quite apart from the London siege, the first few months of 1980 had seen similar incidents at Bogota and Ajaccio while the crisis of the US Embassy hostages at Tehran persisted with no end in sight.

Since the taking of diplomatic hostages had commenced in earnest in 1969, with the kidnapping of the US Ambassador to Brazil, the practice had increased relentlessly over the succeeding years. There had been examples all over the world but by far the biggest concentration was in Central and South America. The year 1979 saw no fewer than 26 embassies, consulates or legations, forcefully occupied. In the first two months of 1980, a further 10 occupations had occurred, threatening to make 1980 the worst year on record for this type of crime and signifying a near total breakdown of respect for the status of diplomatic missions as afforded them by the Geneva Convention.

There were attacks on embassy buildings in Peru, El Salvador, Mexico, Guatemala, Colombia, Panama, Belgium and Corsica. Although, since then, there has in fact been an overall reduction of diplomatic kidnappings and assaults, the practice still continues. As late as early 1993, three gunmen took and held a group of 19 hostages in a violent raid on the Nicaraguan Embassy in San José, the Costa Rican capital. They threatened to destroy the building in a fireball by igniting gallons of gasoline that they had taken into the embassy with them. The suicidal vow 'victorious or dead' was heard to be shouted to police surrounding the building, echoing the menacing challenges that have taunted the authorities on so many other, earlier sieges.

The take-over of the Iranian Embassy in London was apparently carried out by a group who were said to represent the interests of Iranians living in the oil-rich, partly Arab-speaking southern province of Khuzestan, a region seeking political autonomy. They declared themselves to be members of an organisation variously described as the Group of the Martyr or the Mujahedeen al Nasser which was vehemently opposed to the Shi'ite Islamic fundamentalism advocated by Ayatollah Khomeini. They were demanding the release of 91 political prisoners held in Khuzestan, which they referred to by the alternative name, Arabestan. To demonstrate their basically pro-Western, pro-American affiliations they also offered to free the hostages they had taken if the Iranian Government reciprocated with the release of the US diplomats held in the Embassy at Tehran. To reinforce their demands, the gunmen threatened to blow up the Embassy and kill the hostages if there was no sign of a positive response after 24hr, a familiar enough ultimatum. This first deadline and another, set two hours later, passed uneventfully enough.

The 26 hostages included four British persons, among them an armed 41-year old police constable, Trevor Lock, from Scotland Yard's diplomatic patrol group. He had been overpowered and bundled inside by the gunmen while he guarded the front entrance, the speed of the assault giving him no opportunity to reach for his weapon which, for this type of duty, was routinely kept concealed beneath his tunic. Two of the other Britons were members of a BBC news and documentary film unit who had been at the Embassy to apply for visas to visit Iran where they were to carry out a special current affairs assignment. Christopher Cramer, 32, was a news organiser and Simeon Harris, 33, was a sound recordist. It transpired that Christopher Cramer had been injured when shots were fired by the gunmen when they first occupied the Embassy. The final British hostage, 47-year old Ronald Morris, was employed at the Embassy as a clerk and messenger.

The identities of the other hostages, Embassy staff and visitors, only emerged as the siege proceeded. The Iranian hostages, the majority of those held, included Dr Gholam Ali Afruz, the most senior of the diplomats confined in the Embassy building. A Syrian journalist, Mustapha Karkouti, was quickly identified as being among the non-Iranians being held.

Police cars arrived at Princes Gate soon after the gunmen had entered the Embassy. Two girls, who had run out soon after the occupation began, appeared to have raised the alarm. Within a short period of time, police marksmen and observers wearing bullet-proof vests were in position on adjoining roofs and in the gardens at the rear. Other officers found suitable observation points in the shelter of entrance porches at the front of the Embassy building and other adjacent diplomatic missions. All the surrounding buildings were evacuated as a strict cordon was thrown around the area. Road blocks were erected in Kensington Road, alongside Hyde Park, sealing all the approaches to Princes Gate. The police were dug in ready for a long siege in a manner to which they were becoming increasingly accustomed.

The first exchanges between the hijackers and the outside world were taking place just as police negotiators were also endeavouring to establish an understanding with them in a bid to resolve the incident peacefully. At 2.45pm the Syrian journalist Mustapha Karkouti telephoned the BBC's external services headquarters, advising of the terrorists' demands. This was followed by the transmission of two telexed messages, both approved by the gang leader, to the BBC newsroom, the first detailing how the group had burst into and taken control of the Embassy, the second apologising to the British people for the siege but also complaining that the police had refused a request for a doctor to examine Christopher Cramer's injuries.

In fact, a doctor had been called to the scene where he was referred to the police forward control unit. Food was also delivered to the hijackers and hostages. Later that afternoon an unidentified young woman was released though what elicited the granting of her freedom was not established. She was rushed to hospital, thought to be suffering from severe shock.

The truth was that there was more than a hint of sympathy for the gunmen's aims, as confirmed by the statement made by Sir David McNee, the Metropolitan Police Commissioner, the day after the start of the siege: 'The gunmen inside the Iranian Embassy must know that it is not within our powers to meet all of their demands whatever our views on the rights and wrongs of their cause may be. I appeal to them to remain calm. Hasty action may cause even more suffering to their own people in Iran.' This last comment alluded to the reprisals threatened in the official Iranian Government response to the gunmen's demands.

Sadeq Qotbzadeh, the Iranian Foreign Minister, who, meanwhile, had been telephoned at the Iranian Embassy in Abu Dhabi, where he was on an official visit, warned the gunmen in London that 'if the attackers shed one drop of blood of any members of the embassy staff, the same number of prisoners whose release they are seeking would be tried and executed'. He added, with a certain irony given the wider situation prevailing at that time, 'My country will not submit to blackmail whether from the super powers, any country or any small group of terrorist gunmen'. Asked what would be the reaction if any of the Iranian diplomats were shot, he advised that it was believed that anyone who died for Islam went straight to heaven. He felt confident that loyal Iranian people would rather die than see a true Islamic government concede to threats. On this basis Iran was quite prepared to accept the killing of the hostages. Submission was clearly regarded as weakness; a martyred death as an act of great valour — no doubt the US authorities closely following this new drama took careful note of these inflexible viewpoints and wondered whether their own hostages predicament could ever be peacefully resolved.

The Metropolitan Police set about tackling this siege on exactly the same basis as that employed so successfully on the two previous occasions, basically keeping tempers cool while applying unrelenting psychological pressure. This involved following the advice repeatedly given by doctors to develop nervous fatigue and exhaustion in the terrorists through a combination of pressure, tension and lack of food. As weariness grows, from the pursuit of this process, so too does suggestibility and the kidnappers may then be persuaded to surrender without violence, regardless of their potential punishment. As Sir David McNee put it 'All my officers engaged in this incident are concerned to do what we always try to do, resolve the situation without loss of life. We must show patience and perseverance; that is what we propose to do'.

This may have been the intention, most rigorously applied where the handling of the siege itself was concerned, but, confronted with a totally new and unexpected dimension of civil disorder on the streets outside, a dimension which compelled the firmest treatment, they were the last qualities the police displayed in dealing with this ancillary problem.

As news of the siege at the Iranian Embassy had circulated, so gangs of rival demonstrators had congregated at the scene confronting each other and the police, creating a distraction that the authorities could have well done without. Contemporary newspaper accounts described the scenes as 'near-carnival' and 'farcical', which was partly true at times, but there were also moments, too many as far as the police were concerned, when the mood between the rival groups of chanting demonstrators became ugly and hostile. The pent-up nationalistic fervour, for the most part vented vocally, threatened to spill over into physical violence.

On the one hand, there were pro and anti-Khomeini Iranian nationals challenging each other, the former group over 400 strong. On the other hand there were some 100 British and American demonstrators, led by a number of students from Imperial College, who were taking advantage of the opportunity to protest against Islamic fundamentalist repression in general and to focus condemnation in particular on the continuing plight of the US hostages trapped in Tehran. As the Iranians repeatedly shouted their slogans in ritual fashion, led by a mullah whose convenient appearance encouraged the co-ordination of their ranting chorus, so they were answered by renditions of 'Rule Britannia' and the British and US national anthems. The students had brought a piano along to provide accompaniment but this had to compete with the dharma-drum beating of a band of saffron-robed Buddhists. The Buddhists were there to pray for peace. In contrast, the Iranian extremists, openly declaring their blind allegiance to the Ayatollah, had slogans printed in red on their white smocks or held aloft on placards with messages like: 'We give our last drop of blood for Khomeini' and 'We are your soldiers, Khomeini, ready for your orders'. One Englishman in the crowds, joining in the proceedings just for the fun of it, had, as far as he was concerned, a much more earnest cause. His banner simply said 'Arsenal for the Cup!'.

The police were frequently called upon to intervene as scuffles broke out, suffering injuries among their own ranks in the process. While, on the face of it, the gang who had taken over the Embassy represented the claims for autonomy of a minority ethnic group in Iran, it was widely thought that their act of terrorism had been influenced by other sources. One rumour suggested that the raid had been encouraged by Iraq whose border dispute with Iran was then intensifying. There was certainly no love lost between the neighbouring Muslim states.

For their part, the Iranians were convinced that the incident was west-inspired, a tit-for-tat exercise to give the Iranians a dose of their own medicine. Relations between Iran and Great Britain were already strained and, mindful of the danger of counter-seizure of British diplomatic staff in the Embassy in Tehran, the British Government endeavoured to reduce tension by pledging to the Iranians that they would take firm action to deal with the London Embassy terrorists. It provided a salutary opportunity, too, in so doing, to reaffirm British views concerning respect for the sacrosanct status of diplomatic institutions which required both an appropriate level of protection and unequivocable condemnation of any act that violated that status. The Prime Minister's message, fully endorsed by Government and Opposition alike and delivered through Sir John Graham, the Ambassador in Tehran, stated, among other things: 'This intrusion constitutes an act of terrorism and an infringement of the immunity of diplomatic staff which the British Government finds totally repugnant and is acting firmly to counter'.

Of course, having stressed this line of unmitigated endorsement and strict observance of the statutory rights of diplomatic missions, as expressed within the Geneva Convention, there was now the danger of this becoming an instance of shooting oneself in the foot. This could seriously hamper the operation by precluding the police authorities from taking certain steps to resolve the affair and, in particular, the option of direct intervention in the event that the circumstances deemed this course of action to be necessary. The Geneva Convention prohibits the use of force to enter an embassy unless permission is first granted by the head of the diplomatic mission concerned. In the case of the Iranian Embassy this was Dr Gholam Ali Afruz who himself was one of the hostages.

It was premature, though, at this point, for such extreme action to be even in the minds of the senior officers conducting the siege operation under the leadership of John Dellow, Deputy Assistant Commissioner, and through chief negotiator, Superintendent Frederick Luff. Negotiation remained both the policy and the main tool employed by the police. There were, however, certain complications arising from differences between this siege and those that had been experienced previously which required the police to adapt their plan of action, as appropriate, although its fundamental aims remained unchanged. Though contact had been rapidly made with the terrorist gang and no strong ideological hostility had been encountered, these men had not been trapped in the Embassy while being pursued, as had the IRA gunmen at Balcombe Street or the criminal burglars at the Spaghetti House. Having launched their assault deliberately, they had not been compelled, therefore, to adjust to a situation of siege in which they unexpectedly found themselves. Equally, they were not contained within a single room which could be more readily monitored. Instead, they had the unrestricted freedom of movement throughout the entire five storey building, although this was not entirely to their favour either for it meant that they were also required to remain more vigilant, having to keep watch on many fronts.

Although there was an absence of intensive ideological motivation to complicate matters, the gunmen were nevertheless committed to definite political objectives in association with which they had presented demands which could only be satisfied by parties who were beyond British control or influence.

All this made it imperative for the police to establish a mutually trustful dialogue with the gunmen, to glean information on the identities of the gang members and determine how they would be likely to react to given circumstances. Knowledge of the interior layout of the Embassy was also required, along with some indication of the diplomatic routines to which the senior officials among the kidnapped may attempt to adhere in a bid to maintain a semblance of normality.

Paramount to the intelligence gathering effort, routinely undertaken in these situations, was the building up of a detailed picture of the hostages — their total number, their sexes, their nationalities, their disposition and location within the building and any other facets of information, peculiar to certain individuals, that could be exploited during negotiations or for which special contingencies would be required if the police elected to storm the Embassy. There were a number of obvious questions that needed answering. Were any of the women prisoners pregnant? Did anyone have a heart illness or other debilitating medical condition? Were there any individuals whose status, nationality or publicly declared beliefs could make them a more vulnerable target for abuse or violence from the terrorists?

Critical to this was the careful interrogation of any escapees or released hostages, along with the attachment on any available surfaces of fly-on-the-wall snooping devices. In the case of the Iranian Embassy, being situated in a terraced block, ultra-sensitive microphones and miniature TV cameras were set into the dividing walls on either side.

On this occasion, the police had several possible sources of intelligence, for no less than four persons had left the Iranian Embassy and their combined testimonials ought to provide all the information they needed — the two girls who had escaped when the siege began, the unidentified woman who had been released during the afternoon of the first day and Christopher Cramer who, because his injuries needed urgent medical attention, was also freed within the first day of the siege. Unfortunately, all four had left the Embassy before things had settled down inside so they were only able to provide limited help with the police enquiries. There was uncertainty as to the precise numbers of both gunmen and hostages or the nature of the weapons held by the former. They could confirm that there were Iranian and non-Iranian hostages, including a small number of women but, most critically, they could shed no light on where they were being held inside the building.

Details made available after the siege was over showed that there were, in fact, only five gunmen and that the hostages that remained in captivity numbered 23, of whom six were women. They were all kept at the back of the building, on the second floor, the men in one room and the women in another. At all times they were kept under close guard. The women reacted emotionally to their forceful imprisonment, evidently fearful for their lives, and occupied long spells wailing and shouting. This proved to be very distressing for the men who were powerless to provide them with either comfort or reassurance. In contrast, the men had, as one, confronted their attackers with an impassive demeanour, determined to conceal the anxiety that lay beneath the surface.

In spite of the significant warmth of the early spring weather, PC Lock wore all his clothes throughout the siege, including his overcoat, as this was the only way he could keep his gun concealed. When extended the opportunity to take a bath, as were the other hostages, he declined the offer to the considerable surprise of the terrorists though, luckily, this did not arouse suspicion.

Food and bedding proved to be problematic. In the first stages of the siege, the hostages were given oranges and apples to eat. Later, hamburgers, rolls and shepherd's pie were sent in from outside. It was mainly only the British captives who benefited from this sustenance until this source of supply was interrupted by the terrorists when, from the night of Saturday, 3 May, they refused all further offers of food. A stock of biscuits found within the Embassy was consumed but thereafter there was nothing to eat.

The hostages slept on the floor on improvised beds made from chair cushions. There were no covers to keep warm with in the middle of the night. The women, who were wearing light summer clothes, suffered particularly as a consequence, denied the sleep and rest they most urgently needed. Had the authorities been fully aware of the emotional state of the women hostages this would undoubtedly have been a matter that would have triggered the alarm bells. Coping with the stress of a hijacking or kidnapping, including the post-trauma after effects, are issues of deep concern. Certainly, the state of mind of siege hostages is a sensitive barometer which must be very closely monitored by the medical personnel attached to anti-terrorist teams.

Coincidentally, the findings of an important study on the after-care treatment of hostage victims were published at the very time of the Iranian Embassy hostage crisis. The study, undertaken for the Dutch Government by the Department of Psychiatry at Leyden University, had investigated seven incidents of hijacking and terrorist occupation. Both victims and their relatives had been interviewed and short-term and long-term after effects analysed. It revealed close similarities to the experiences disclosed in earlier studies of wartime imprisonment.

The short-term effects of being held hostage, those that are likely to surface within the first four weeks or so after release, include insomnia, tenseness and the development of phobias. These symptoms are more strongly present in women than men. Longer term effects tended to be suffered by fewer victims, the likelihood being almost directly relative to the length of the period of captivity. Among these effects are irritability, vague and groundless physical complaints and a vivid preoccupation with the fact of having been personally taken hostage which was inclined in some cases to develop into a persecution complex. Former hostages also complained of feelings of being misunderstood and of lost confidence. Again, women experienced these symptoms more than men but there was also evidence to suggest that these negative after-effects tended to be less pronounced in older and educated persons.

The report stressed the need to encourage people who survived hostage incidents 'to see the relativity of things', by helping them to keep the experience in perspective. It was evident that, in the majority of cases where problems arose, the predominant effect of being held hostage was to revive or expose suppressed fears and anxieties. Central to the study's recommendations was the formulation of proper post-experience care policies, rather than hit-or-miss short duration treatment practices that may not provide enough help or even the right kind of help. It was important to give the victims the opportunity to talk without restriction about their experiences immediately following the end of their ordeal. Assistance to reorganise their lives was also critical to the repair process, helping to commence a resumption of normality as quickly as possible. Above all it was vital to accentuate the positive, by encouraging constructive diversions and morale-building outgoing activities. Continuing contact with fellow hostages was, it was discovered, a particularly beneficial form of recovery therapy.

The weekend of 3-4 May 1980 witnessed an intensification of diplomatic activity in support of the police effort to end the siege. The gunmen themselves had requested the involvement of a number of Arab diplomats who could act as mediators between the gang and the British Government and police authorities. The Ambassadors of Algeria, Jordan and Iraq were called upon to assist, along with representatives of the International Red Cross. In the event that any of the aforementioned diplomats were unavailable, the Ambassadors of Libya, Kuwait and Syria were proposed as alternatives. Following discussions at the Foreign Office and negotiations with the gunmen under the stewardship of the senior officers handling the crisis, three further releases of hostages were secured.

First, the gunmen freed a three-month pregnant woman who worked at the Embassy as a secretary, Mrs Haj Deah Kanji. She was followed by a Pakistani man, Ghanzansan Gull. Later, the 37-year old Syrian journalist, Mustapha Karkouti, was allowed to go. He was clearly weak and suffering from the protracted tension, finding it difficult to walk from the building as he emerged from the front entrance, momentarily clutching at railings to steady himself. With his arms raised above his head, he stumbled unsteadily towards armed policemen who appeared in doorways further down the terrace. He was swiftly shepherded into the safety of one of the evacuated buildings nearby.

These breakthroughs were viewed as hopeful signs that the siege was moving ever more swiftly towards an altogether peaceful conclusion. Regrettably, however, the fanatical rhetoric of the Iranian Islamic fundamentalists constantly threatened to undermine progress, its stridently uncompromising and antagonistic tone inclined to induce a reciprocally stubborn resistance to surrender by the gunmen. Typical of this was the message sent to the Iranian hostages from Mr Sayf Ehdaie, the Iranian Consul General. Passed to 'The Times' for publication and broadcast over radio and television networks, it stated in part:

'Since it is a fact that the whole of the Iranian nation is prepared for martyrdom for continuity of our glorious revolution and will in no circumstances yield to any kind of force and pressure exerted by imperialism and international Zionism, we feel certain that you are also ready for martyrdom alongside your nation and do not accept that the Iranian nation pay ransom to the agents of world imperialism.

'You must be rest assured that we shall save no effort for your release and should you so wish, and if need be, tens of thousands of Iranians are just ready to enter into the premises of the Embassy, not with weapons but with cries of 'Allaho — Akbar' ('God is Great').'

The impassioned message certainly roused those devout disciples of the Ayatollah Khomeini in the streets around the location of the siege, compelling the police to quell yet another round of unnecessary civil disturbance. Although no restraints had been imposed upon the press and news media in their coverage of the drama, the publication of this message raised the question of responsible reporting at a time when the whole business of what was described as deliberately sensationalist and provocative news broadcasting had become the subject of political criticism. Hinting at curbs on the freedom of the press, the question was being asked increasingly 'Is the news being reported or is it being made?'.

One thing was for certain, concerning the news coverage of the Embassy hostage crisis. With the formidable array of television and press cameras covering the scene, along with the army of reporters, the Iranian Embassy was as much under siege from the media as from the police. The BBC and ITN had each hired giant hydraulic cranes, known as 'cherry-pickers', which, when fully extended, towered 60ft above the scene to give their respective cameras unobstructed, though probably identical, views of whatever events unfolded.

As feared, the releases of hostages did not continue and the prospects for ending the siege peacefully began to recede. By now the terrorists had relaxed their demands and were now only asking for safe passage out of Britain. Superintendent Luff still hoped to talk the gunmen out without resort to violent means of ending the incident. Indeed, such a conclusion would represent a measure of failure on the basis of the policy the police were endeavouring to pursue. Nevertheless, sensing a changing atmosphere, the first hints were made that a Special Air Service regiment team might have to be called upon to intervene as a last desperate measure should the mood of the continuing stand off turn really sour.

On Monday, 5 May, negotiations between the police and the gunmen had resumed with an apparent air of optimism. Later, around 2pm, things changed dramatically for the worse when, even as discussions were continuing on the field telephone link, a series of gun shots were heard fired within the Embassy. It later transpired that this had been the sound of the summary execution of one of the hostages, later identified as Abbas Lavasani, a 25-year old press counsellor.

It was not clear what had provoked this sudden and serious deterioration in the dealings aimed at concluding the siege. Later, some of the hostages revealed that, at this point, the gunmen had begun to display profound unease. It is possible, given their interception of mixed signals, on the one hand from press sources, reporting the official British and Iranian Government lines, and on the other, the more persuasive and placatory tones of the police negotiators, that the gunmen became confused in their growing state of fatigue. This in turn could have provoked an attitude of irritation and instability rather than one of suggestibility and acquiescence, as desired.

There was another factor that may have induced this unheralded and alarming collapse to the negotiations. Although the police prognosis for a successful outcome to the siege had been expressed as favourable that morning it is, perhaps, more likely that, based on previous experience, they actually had serious misgivings about the way the situation might develop. Thus, they had already initiated, in part at least, contingency arrangements for a physical intervention. Certainly, the timing of the subsequent course of events would support this. But, if this was so, it perhaps only served in turn to fuel the growing distrust among the gunmen. Simeon Harris later described how the gunmen became increasingly troubled by noises they could hear in buildings on either side of the Embassy.

Whatever the cause of the breakdown, the police team was anxious to limit the damage. To placate the gunmen, Sir David McNee, who had spent most of the day at the scene, wrote a personal message to the terrorist gang which was delivered through the Embassy letterbox. It explained his policy and his objectives as far as resolving the dispute were concerned. He advised that, unlike in other countries, his force operated independently of politicians and Government; that they sought only to achieve a peaceful solution to the incident and that it was not police policy to carry out a witch-hunt against those responsible or to vindictively seek retribution for what had occurred. He appealed to the hostage-takers not to feel threatened or frightened, asserting that they had nothing to fear provided they did not harm those held in their custody.

The gunmen's response, callous and ruthless in the extreme, was not long in coming, serving without the need for any spoken words to confirm the gravely downward spiral of the turn of events. At 6.55pm the front door of the Embassy was briefly opened and the dead body of the executed man was pushed out. From that point it was evident that there was only one way for the siege to end.

As the minutes ticked by the tension became electric, for those watching and waiting outside as well as for the hostages who had rapidly become aware of the day's sinister developments. At 7pm the hostages learnt from a news bulletin, heard on the terrorists' transistor radio, of the execution of the young Iranian diplomat who had earlier been led away and of the brutal ejection of his body. They were chillingly informed that the next killing would follow in 45min and that, thereafter, if the police did not co-operate, additional hostages would be executed.

Simeon Harris scrambling to safety across a balcony wall as the flames from the burning Iranian Embassy rapidly spread behind him. *Press Association*

At about 7.10pm, the terrorists were contacted by the police on the field telephone to engage them in what were, on the face of it, earnest discussions on the method of implementing their demands. The suggestion was that these had been conceded in full but, in reality, it was a deliberate diversionary tactic. The gunmen, ever suspicious, correctly anticipated an attack at any moment but, seeking to stall it, called on PC Lock and Simeon Harris to communicate with the authorities in an attempt to delay the inevitable. Imploring the gunmen to remain calm, on the pretext that a raid would never be launched in daylight, the two Englishmen duly spoke on the telephone with no warning as to what was to happen next. Hardly had they returned the telephone handset than the raiding party burst in upon them from all directions. Within an hour the legendary reputation of the SAS was to be firmly established.

Only minutes after receiving the authorisation to strike from the Metropolitan Police Commissioner, duly approved by the Home Secretary, black-uniformed figures wearing balaclavas suddenly appeared from nowhere on the balcony at the front of the Embassy. After blowing in a window with a frame of explosives, further explosions heralded the detonation of stun grenades and gas grenades as the SAS squad commenced to storm the interior. Simultaneously, at the rear of the once-smart, cream-painted Georgian villa, more SAS officers, who had gathered on the roof, abseiled down the walls, swinging in through the windows and detonating more explosive devices to cover their entry. Almost immediately, flames and smoke began to billow from the windows as fires rapidly spread from the curtains which had been ignited by the bursting grenades.

To the casual observer, certainly many television viewers among them who found normal programmes interrupted to allow live transmission of the dramatic operation at Princes Gate, it gave all the impressions of being a scene of complete mayhem and confusion. In fact, from the SAS point of view, everything was going like clockwork, absolutely according to a carefully prepared plan.

Even as the SAS units were going in, the first of the hostages began to emerge, struggling along the balcony at the front, away from the licking flames and intense heat behind them. BBC man Simeon Harris, recognised as one of the first captives to escape, was seen scrambling his way to safety.

Meanwhile, inside, bursts of automatic fire could be heard, first as the terrorists turned their guns on the hostages, killing a second Iranian diplomat and seriously injuring three others. Then the SAS force opened fire in return on the Iranian extremists, the rattling bursts of their weapons reverberating all around. By the time it was all over four of the five terrorists were also dead, the fifth only surviving because one of the women hostages, taking pity on him, pleaded with the SAS to spare his life.

The leader of the terrorists, a man apparently identified by the word or name 'Own', would certainly have killed the first SAS soldier to enter the Embassy had PC Trevor Lock not tackled him first. After struggling with him on the floor, the SAS officer instructed PC Lock to step aside with which 'Own' was promptly despatched by a series of perfectly aimed shots.

Dozens of policemen now moved forward behind the military units, their faces obscured by the grotesque shapes of their gas masks, worn to combat the effects of the dense cloud of tear-gas. Behind them came ambulancemen and firemen. In the garden behind the Embassy, as the hostages were crudely bundled out, they were subjected, by necessity, to some quite rough treatment until their identities were established beyond doubt. Tied up with locking straps, searched and told to remain quiet, they were left lying face down on the ground as the mopping-up operation continued inside the building.

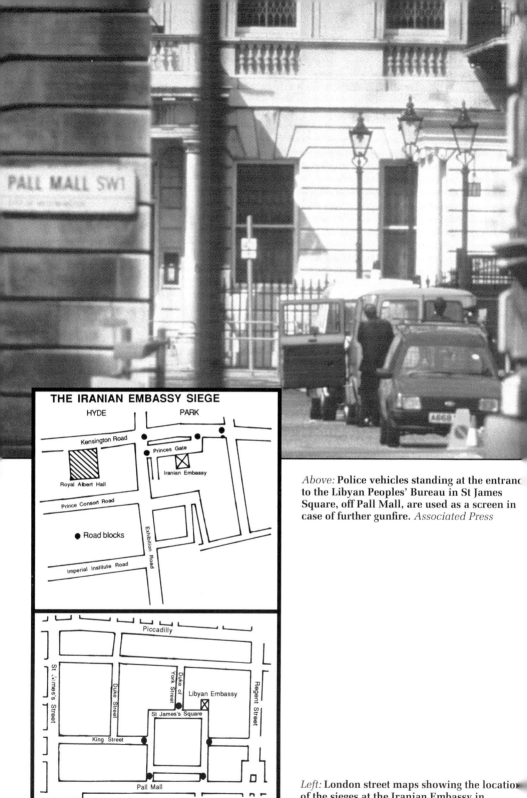

PALL MALL SW1

THE IRANIAN EMBASSY SIEGE

HYDE PARK

Kensington Road

Princes Gate

Iranian Embassy

Royal Albert Hall

Prince Consort Road

Exhibition Road

● Road blocks

Imperial Institute Road

Piccadilly

St James's Street

Duke Street

Duke of York Street

Libyan Embassy

St James's Square

Regent Street

King Street

Pall Mall

LOCATION OF LIBYAN EMBASSY

● Road blocks

Above: **Police vehicles standing at the entrance to the Libyan Peoples' Bureau in St James Square, off Pall Mall, are used as a screen in case of further gunfire.** *Associated Press*

Left: **London street maps showing the location of the sieges at the Iranian Embassy in Knightsbridge and the Libyan Peoples' Bureau in Mayfair, with the positions of police road blocks.**

After some 15min it was all over. As the sound of explosions and gun-fire began to subside, a white flag appeared, first at one window and then at another. With the last signs of resistance dealt with, the hostages were now ushered from the Embassy and the back gardens, many of them needing to be supported by police officers.

Even as the hostages were being transferred to hospital, the SAS squad, its work completed with professional efficiency, faded away and disappeared as secretively as it had arrived. The precise strength of the raiding party was never made known publicly.

The SAS raid had successfully freed 19 hostages, 14 men and five women, at a crucial point when mass token killings seemed to be on the cards. While the siege at the Iranian Embassy had been ended in a fashion which the police negotiators would not, by preference, have desired they could still take considerable comfort from knowing that, when all else failed, they had such a potent contingency force available to call upon.

Just four years later, in April 1984, the Metropolitan Police were called on to deal with a second embassy siege in the capital. Whereas this incident also originated through a demonstration against the repressive system of government in another Arab country it was considerably different from the Iranian Embassy affair for other reasons associated with the diplomatic privileges enjoyed by the missions of foreign governments. In this case it was not so much a question of these rights being violated by outsiders invading the embassy as of the diplomats themselves abusing the immunity from British law and authority to which their diplomatic status entitled them.

The embassy or legation in question was the so-called Libyan Peoples' Bureau, situated in St James's Square, near Mayfair. The bureau had increasingly become the target of the disaffections of moderate Libyans exiled in the UK who were opposed to the extremist régime of Col Moammar Khadafy (Gaddafi).

Khadafy had seized power in Libya, with a group of revolutionary army officers, in September 1969 when he ousted the 70-year old King Idris, who was abroad in Turkey, in a bloodless coup. Khadafy created a revolutionary socialist republic which was violently opposed to colonialism and, as the years passed, Libya became a hot-bed and focal point of all forms of terrorism and subversion, not just in association with the continuing conflict in Palestine.

On 17 April 1984, during a peaceful student demonstration on the street outside the Libyan Embassy, one of the diplomatic officials inside opened fire on the crowd with a sub-machine gun fired from a window in the building. Spraying the helpless students and their police escort with a hail of bullets, eleven demonstrators were injured and WPC Yvonne Fletcher, a young policewoman, was fatally hit, collapsing and dying on the pavement.

The police immediately surrounded the Embassy, blocking all access roads into St James's Square and covering the building from the surrounding rooftops. The occupants of all the nearby office premises and private residences were hastily evacuated. Though the murdered policewoman's body was removed soon afterwards, her uniform hat remained on the ground where she had been cut down, a constant and sad reminder of the criminal attack to the millions of viewers who followed the progress of the ensuing siege on their television screens. Later, a memorial to WPC Fletcher was unveiled in St James's Square to mark her selfless sacrifice in the line of duty.

Though the primary aim of besieging the Embassy was, apart from containment, to try to force the Libyan officials into ejecting the individual guilty of the shooting, they were in fact powerless to compel such an outcome. In spite of police fury and public anger over the murder as well as the evident abuse of diplomatic privilege by the use of the mission for terrorist activities, they could do no more than demand that the occupants vacate the Embassy and close it down in conjunction with the severing of all diplomatic relations with Libya.

Thus, the Government gave the extremists and professional diplomats holed-up in the Peoples' Bureau seven days to quit. The Home Secretary admitted that, realistically, neither the police nor any other department under his authority had the means of establishing the identity of Yvonne Fletcher's murderer without the co-operation of the Libyans. This was patently not going to be forthcoming.

The Libyans duly complied with the demands to leave, offering no resistance as 30 of their number were deported to Tripoli on the 27 April and taking vital evidence with them, contained in their diplomatic bags. In the final reckoning the British authorities were unable to take other than token measures to respond to the Libyan diplomats' crime, particularly as a lack of endorsement from NATO allies inhibited the taking of any form of military reprisal. Instead, economic sanctions were imposed while a policy of international cooperation was agreed with the US, France, West Germany, Italy, Japan and Canada to assist in the fight against state-sponsored terrorism. While this permitted a crackdown on terrorists masquerading as diplomats, it did little to end the campaign of terror being waged by the extremists operating out of the safe haven of Khadafy's Libya. The odious bombing of innocent passengers aboard the Pan Am Boeing 747, flight 103, over Lockerbie, Scotland on 22 December 1988, with the deaths of all 259 passengers and crew and at least 11 villagers, was a sickeningly graphic reminder of this failure.

A memorial tablet to WPC Yvonne Fletcher was unveiled at the spot where she was killed on 17 April 1984. More than the overall criminal behaviour of the Libyan diplomats, it was her death that sparked off the siege of the Bureau. *Hulton Picture Co*

128

Piracy on the High Seas

Some two to three centuries after the era in which brigandry on the high seas was at its peak, an act of piracy occurred which quite shocked the world, the more so in that it involved a commercial passenger ship carrying a full complement of civilian passengers. Unlike earlier acts of piracy, though, this act of terror did not have loot and pillage as its objectives. Rather, it was aimed at focusing world opinion on the plight of Portuguese citizens living under the dictatorial regime of Dr Antonio de Salazar, both in the home country and in the African colonies of Angola and Mozambique.

The modern, steam driven 20,900 gross ton passenger vessel *Santa Maria*, owned by the Compania Nacional de Navagacao and registered under the flag of Portugal, was at the centre of the drama. Built in 1953 by the Cockerill Ougrée shipyard at Hoboken in the Netherlands, she was routinely engaged on a scheduled route that took her from Lisbon to ports on the northern coast of South America and in the West Indies. Occasionally, she made cruises to the Antilles beauty spots. Apart from her service as a passenger ferry, her cargo holds in the forepart of the ship were regularly used to carry Portuguese manufactured products outward and the produce of the countries on her route back home. In early 1961, nine days after the start of the new year, the *Santa Maria* departed her home port bound for Vigo, Madeira, Tenerife, La Guaira and Curacao, continuing to Port Everglades on a winter sunshine cruise. Normally, she would then have sailed back to Lisbon direct. The ship was carrying 612 passengers, all of them, on the face of it, normal, innocent travellers but, unknown at the time, the passenger list contained the names of 24 political revolutionaries operating as a group under the leadership of one Henrique Carlos Malta Galvao.

Galvao was a colourful character, a former army Captain and a prominent opponent of the Portuguese régime, given to an exuberant and, to some extent, scandalous lifestyle. An occasional novelist and big game hunter, he was also a perennial champion of democratic values. He had escaped from prison two years earlier while serving a 16-year sentence for incitement to revolt.

Galvao was in league with another exiled former Portuguese Army officer, Gen Humberto Delgado who had taken refuge in Brazil where he was now residing in the city of Rio de Janeiro. Delgado, the President elect of the Portuguese Republic had, it was claimed, been fraudulently deprived of his rights by the Salazar government. He had been the defeated candidate in the 1958 presidential elections.

At La Guaira and again at Curacao, the *Santa Maria* took on several hundred additional passengers while a similar number disembarked. In the course of this exchange, more anti-Salazar revolutionaries undoubtedly boarded the ship,

Left: **Map showing the route taken by the *Santa Maria* from Lisbon to the West Indies and, after the hijacking, on to Brazil.**

Below: **The Portuguese passenger liner *Santa Maria*, captured by anti-Salazar rebels in 1961.**
World Ship Photo Library

THE ROUTE OF THE *SANTA MARIA*
Lisbon-Vigo-Madeira-Tenerife-
La Guaira-Curacao

UNITED STATES
OF AMERICA

Vigo
Lisbon

Madeira

Tenerife

St Lucia

Miami

Cuba

Jamaica

Curacao

La Guaira

Recife

SOUTH AMERICA

including Henrique Galvao himself, swelling the group's numbers to about 70 in total. The ship sailed from Curacao on 21 January 1961 bound for Port Everglades via the Lesser Antilles. Apart from her passenger complement which was once more in excess of 600, her crew numbered 370.

Galvao's men made their move at 1am on Sunday, 22 January while the *Santa Maria* was in the vicinity of the French island of Martinique. The rebels made their way up to the bridge armed with machine guns, pistols and grenades where they aimed to forcibly seize the liner. A fight ensued, in which the Third Mate, Nascimento Costa, was fatally shot as he tried to raise the alarm. Another bridge officer and the Second Purser were also wounded in the exchange. Capt Mario Simoes Maia, who had been asleep at the time when the gang struck, was summoned to the bridge where Galvao advised him that his ship had been taken over and that he was directed to sail the *Santa Maria* to wherever they commanded. His refusal to agree to these instructions resulted in him being imprisoned. An alert radio officer had managed to transmit a brief message advising of the ship's plight. This was swiftly followed up by a detailed announcement broadcast by Galvao himself in which he confirmed the reported act of piracy and set out his objectives as well as the measures he would resort to if attempts were made to interfere.

Galvao stated that all was normal aboard the seized vessel and that all passengers were well and safe. He added 'I will land them safely at a neutral port, but which port depends on whether efforts are made to intercept the ship. I seized the ship myself as a first step in freeing all of Portugal'. In fact, the *Santa Maria* had been commandeered in the name of the 'international junta of Liberals', an organisation which was apparently presided over by the exiled Delgado. Without giving a clear explanation of his intentions, he warned those listening that if warships approached the *Santa Maria* he would scuttle her and the responsibility for loss of life among the passengers, who included women and children, would rest with those who precipitated such an action. 'If we are followed by Portuguese or foreign warships,' he said, 'we will not surrender, nor will we stop. United States' passengers and others understand perfectly the legitimacy of our struggle for freedom and liberty. We are no tyrants but adversaries of all forms of totalitarian government'.

Whether or not the passengers truly supported these commendable sentiments was not known but one thing was for certain — the method of securing those objectives, by terrorising innocent civilians, many of them foreign nationals, was totally intolerable and was repudiated by all the democratic governments whose citizens were caught up in the affair.

Early on 23 January, the *Santa Maria*, which had been dubbed 'Santa Liberdade' by the rebels, made a call at Castries, the main port of the British island of St Lucia, where one of her lifeboats was launched. This landed eight members of her crew, two of whom were the men who had been injured in the gunfight. The launch also conveyed ashore the body of the dead officer. The *Santa Maria* immediately put to sea again before the authorities could investigate.

Meanwhile, the wounded crew men were carried aboard the British frigate HMS *Rothesay*, which was visiting St Lucia at the time, where they were interviewed by the Administrator of St Lucia and the Senior British Naval Officer, West Indies. Following this conference, all naval ships in the region were ordered to intercept the *Santa Maria*.

The *Rothesay* sailed in pursuit shortly after midday the same day. She was joined in the chase by the United States Navy ships USS *Damato* and *Robert L. Wilson* from their base in Puerto Rico. Progressively other vessels joined the hunt, the Dutch frigate *Van Amstel*, the American nuclear submarine *Seawolf*, two more United States destroyers, the *Gearing* and *Vogelsang*, which had been visiting the Ivory Coast, and a second British ship, the destroyer HMS *Ulster*. In addition, the long-range reconnaissance aircraft of several nations, scoured the ocean expanses out into the Atlantic to the north and east of the South American continent in search of the hijacked liner.

It was a siege of two dimensions. In the first place the passengers on the *Santa Maria* were in effect besieged aboard the ship by their captors. Equally, the ship itself, with its band of insurgents, was to be trapped gradually within the closing circle of pursuing vessels, resulting in a bizarre situation in which the dramatic process of negotiations for the release of hostages, typical of various sieges on land, was to be played out on the high seas.

This was still some days off, though. Taking advantage of bad weather, under a blanket of low cloud, and with the full benefit of her superior speed, Galvao had ensured the escape of the *Santa Maria* for the time being at least. Unsure of his intentions and unable, therefore, to focus their search immediately, quite apart from being hampered by meteorological conditions, the pursuers were experiencing difficulty in tracking the liner. For more than a day, it was a question of where had the *Santa Maria* gone?

All ships were requested to keep a look-out for the abducted liner and report observations. Simultaneously, radio tracking stations, intercepting the occasional transmissions from the ship, were working to get a fix on her position. In the event, the breakthrough came when she was sighted at sea. At 3.15pm on 25 January a report was received from the Danish merchant vessel *Vibeke Gulwa* advising that a ship fitting the description of the *Santa Maria* had been seen. Her position was approximately 930 miles east of Trinidad and she was heading towards Africa at a speed of about 20kt.

All of the tracking aircraft and ships were diverted to this sea area and, once she was positively located, the *Santa Maria* was kept under constant surveillance ready for the time and opportunity when she could be intercepted. It had been calculated that she was carrying sufficient fuel for 12 days steaming at her present speed. Based on this and given her course and bearing, it was presumed that Galvao was planning on taking the *Santa Maria* to Angola.

With the intention being to accost the seized ship at the earliest and most favourable moment, it is interesting to compare the respective orders issued to the pursuing Royal Navy and United States Navy warships, bearing in mind that Portugal had, by now, officially requested assistance from both the British and US governments to detain the *Santa Maria* and arrest her hijackers.

The rules of engagement applying to British naval vessels involved in the hunt, called for them to try to arrest the liner if this could be done peacefully 'without loss of life or the risk of scuttling'. By contrast the orders issued to American naval vessels went further. They were instructed to 'visit and search' the *Santa Maria* and, if they found evidence of piracy, to escort the ship to the nearest US port. In both cases, the orders only applied if the liner was intercepted in international waters.

A US Navy spokesman explained his country's position. He stated that they were acting under the well-defined terms of international law governing piracy and insurrection aboard ship. This meant, he explained, that the actions they were taking were completely legitimate provided, at the time of the arrest of the mutineers, the vessel was not in territorial waters. In that situation no action would be taken whatever. Later, to assuage concern as to what the US action might be if and when it occurred, a further statement was issued which moderated the apparently strong line that had been expressed earlier: 'Our instructions are to continue shadowing her and to report her position. We have no intention of taking any action that might endanger the passengers on board'.

Meanwhile, concerns about the rather more restrained British policy were being voiced nevertheless in the House of Commons. It was argued that Britain had no obligation to interfere in a case of political rebellion against a sovereign country. Also, it was suggested that if the affair was to be treated as a matter of piracy, Britain should not hand over any arrested persons to any authority against whom they might be in rebellion and any request for political asylum would need to be considered carefully before any hand over or extradition was agreed upon. The Admiralty promised that the legal implications would be studied closely before any further action was taken. As it turned out, this proved to be unnecessary, as the British ships signalled their intention of breaking off the pursuit as they needed to return to port to refuel.

Although it was not known at the time, the circumstances aboard the *Santa Maria* for the hijacked passengers were not immediately threatening, indeed they were actually quite relaxed. The details of the bloody take-over of the ship had gradually filtered out to the passengers who had already become aware of the ship's change of direction as well as the strained atmosphere among members of the crew. At times, the passengers witnessed disturbing fights between the hijackers and the crew who were clearly resisting the occupation of the ship insofar as they were able. Occasionally, the rebels were seen waving their weapons at crew members coercing them into performing some task or other that the latter were reluctant to carry out. The terrorists remained armed at all times throughout the crisis.

Food and water were rationed, although the amounts provided were in fact quite sufficient, and generally the passengers were allowed to do what they liked. Nevertheless, there remained the nagging doubts as to the eventual outcome of the strange episode which in itself caused considerable strain on the passengers. Sooner or later the hijacking would be brought to an end but whether it was to be resolved peacefully or in a violent climax, either through the ship being shelled or assaulted by an armed party, remained an open question.

Galvao issued a communiqué to the passengers during the voyage which informed them that his main preoccupation was to land them safely. He invited them to appoint, as representatives, two persons from each class who could meet with him regularly to present passengers' complaints or needs. This committee of passengers' delegates remained in existence until the end of the siege and was instrumental in diffusing a number of tense and potentially explosive situations. As one passenger put it later 'It was like walking on dynamite all the time'.

As the hours and days passed, the *Santa Maria*'s relentless progress out into the Atlantic Ocean towards Africa was plotted. On 26 January her position was given as 1,000 miles east of Trinidad; by 27 January she was placed 600 miles north of the northeastern tip of Brazil; the next day she crossed the Equator at a point 800 miles to the east of Belem.

By this time, US officials, notably Rear-Adm Allen Smith, the Commander of the US Caribbean Sea Frontier, had established a fairly healthy dialogue with Captain Galvao by radio telephone. Smith concentrated on the matter of getting the passengers off the ship and pressed Galvao as to his intentions in this respect. Galvao's response signified that, in principal, being anxious to rid himself of this liability, he was willing to disembark the passengers on land, at an agreed point, or to transfer them at sea. With the latter possibility in mind, the dock-landing ship USS *Hermitage* was diverted towards the *Santa Maria* in order to make possible an ocean rendezvous.

Progress in the negotiations had also reached the point where Galvao had indicated his willingness to accept a US Navy escort, provided he was given an assurance that no hostile action against the *Santa Maria* would be taken and on the condition that, if necessary, the escort would provide protection against Portuguese warships that were also pursuing the liner. It was known that the frigate *Pero Escobar* had been instructed to join the search for the *Santa Maria*, although her precise whereabouts could only be guessed at. The Portuguese Navy Ministry, which had also been working at getting a fix on the *Santa Maria*'s course and position, from intercepted radio traffic, later announced that two more destroyers and another frigate had left Lisbon bound for the coast of Africa. They had undisclosed orders.

There was an unwelcome turn of events at one point which caused considerable concern, given the delicate nature of the interlocution between the *Santa Maria* and Rear-Adm Smith. The unexpected announcement by the Portuguese Government on 29 January that its ships had been given orders to sink the *Santa Maria*, if necessary, after the passengers had been disembarked, threatened to undermine the tenuous understanding that had been fostered with Galvao. Such a move could also have placed the Americans in an invidious position, perhaps compelling them to take direct steps to neutralise a lawful military counter measure directed against the *Santa Maria* by warships of her own flag nation, the very same sovereign power whose interests they were supposed to be representing.

With these complications in mind, the efforts to resolve the *Santa Maria* incident assumed a new urgency. The Brazilian Government was known to be sympathetic to the rebels' cause even it it too had publicly announced that its naval vessels were under orders to halt the *Santa Maria*, if she was encountered. Nevertheless, Rear-Adm Smith invited Galvao to take the *Santa Maria* to any port in northern South America — in effect to Brazil. Galvao responded affirmatively stating, however, that while he could not advise the actual port of destination, the Americans should still believe that his desire to disembark the passengers was sincere. He was evidently uneasy as to what might await him if he over declared his hand. 'We go to the port where we can see our desire accomplished,' he said, adding 'I will be very glad to cable you for a conference when we are near that port'. Seeking to reassure him, the US Defense Department advised that it would take no action against the ship if she voluntarily entered port to disembark the hostages. Nor would it be attacked after the passengers had been released.

From this point things began to happen quickly. The *Santa Maria* changed course, first southward and then westwards towards the coast of Brazil. Portugal was persuaded not to aggravate the situation and a conference aboard the *Santa Maria* was arranged for dawn on 30 January 1961 when the ship was expected to reach a point 35 miles to the east of Recife. President Janis Quadros, the newly inaugurated leader of Brazil and a personal friend of Capt Galvao, had already advised that Brazil would not intern the *Santa Maria* if she entered Recife. He was represented at the meeting which took place on board the ship by Rear-Adm Fernandez Diaz, in the role of mediator to assist Rear-Adm Smith and Capt Galvao as they conferred.

Of course, the entire episode of the *Santa Maria* had been followed attentively by the world's press with committed reporters and photographers determined to get as close to the action as they could. Having followed the hunter as it stalked its prey, there was keen competition to be the one to scoop the moment of climax as the 'kill' was made, and there were, it seemed, no limits to the lengths that they were prepared to go to achieve this end. One resourceful French photographer, Gil de la Marre, working for a press agency, hired an aircraft and parachuted into the sea alongside the liner. His hopes were fulfilled when he was helped from the water on to the liner where he was able to record for posterity the final acts of the drama. Another pressman who tried the same stunt was less successful. He was rescued by a navy launch only to be taken to one of the nearby destroyers.

The talks aboard the *Santa Maria* were fraught with difficulties and threatened to become deadlocked. Galvao listed his terms for the release of the passengers:

- That the *Santa Maria* should remain in his hands and that none of his rebel group should be detained.
- That only the passengers and those crew not considered necessary for the running of the ship should be allowed to disembark.
- That he should be granted authorisation to take on food, water and fuel (Delgado had already flown to Recife from Rio de Janeiro to organise this for him).
- That he should be granted authorisation to carry out repairs to one of the vessel's turbines.

Neither the Brazilian authorities nor the US Navy would accede to the last two requests and they were equally insistent that all the passengers and all the crew should be released. Fearing for their safety, a number of Portuguese crewmen had already jumped off the ship and swam to nearby warships.

Galvao was reminded that, even while they deliberated, his path to the open sea was being blocked and that, despite the promises given, the US Navy was not in a position to guarantee the safety of the *Santa Maria*. President Quadros had advised Galvao and his men that they would be granted political asylum in Brazil provided that the ship was returned and he implored him to abandon his crusade there and then.

Gradually worn down by the pressure upon him, Galvao agreed to take the *Santa Maria* into Recife's inner harbour. With low reserves of fuel and unable to replenish them, in danger of now turning the sympathetic publicity he had received against himself, he was also at risk of losing the support of Brazil on which he was currently able to depend. His demands were moderated, too, but he remained reluctant to abandon the ship. As he explained, in words of desperate defiance but tinged with a note of resignation to his imminent defeat, it was a question of principle and honour: 'Our patriotic intentions are to free our enslaved country.... The ship is considered to be the first part of our liberated territory. We demand the recognition of states for our revolutionary act'.

The *Santa Maria* dropped anchor inside the breakwater at Recife harbour at 2.27pm (GMT) on 2 February. Even now, Galvao resisted tying up at the dockside. Here, the protracted deliberations to end the siege threatened to continue had it not been for two separate events.

First, the frustrated passengers, by now consumed with anxiety and impatient for the affair to be ended, decided to take matters into their own hands. A spontaneous demonstration erupted as passengers gathered outside Galvao's cabin. Furniture and other objects readily at hand were hurled over the ship's side and the disturbance required the intervention of Capt Helio Leite and fellow Brazilian officers on board the liner to prevent the incident developing into a violent clash between the hijackers and hostages. Thereupon, and accompanied by immense relief, evacuation of the passengers commenced.

Later that night, before disembarkation of the passengers had been completed, a detachment of 87 armed Brazilian marines boarded the *Santa Maria* and took up positions all over the ship. They encountered no resistance from the rebels. Simultaneously, the crew initiated a sit down strike. Between them, they had made it impossible for Galvao to take the *Santa Maria* back to sea. At 9.15pm (GMT) on 3 February, Capt Galvao and his band of rebels surrendered to the Brazilian Navy and were taken ashore into the custody of the naval authorities. The hijacking of the *Santa Maria*, an act of piracy unequalled in modern times, was over.

The *Santa Maria* was returned to her owners and, following minor repairs, she returned to Lisbon under the command of Capt Maia. Her passengers had gone on ahead aboard the *Vera Cruz*, the *Santa Maria*'s sister ship. Galvao and his men were, as promised, granted political asylum in Brazil and Portugal abandoned all interest in them. A Portuguese Government spokesman said 'The men who attacked the *Santa Maria* are not politicians or ideologists. They are just outlaws'. Having said that, they indicated that no application for extradition would be made. The responsibility for investigating the crime, it was stated, including the murder of an officer, lay with the country offering political asylum.

On reflection, it is difficult to see what material progress towards the overthrowing of the Salazar régime was achieved by the seizure of the *Santa Maria*, especially as it was not planned in conjunction with, or as a preliminary to, a popular revolution against the Portuguese dictatorship. As so often seems the case where sieges of this kind are concerned it amounted to little more than a futile and potentially counter-productive gesture.

A quarter of a century later a similar case of terrorist piracy occurred when the Italian cruise ship *Achille Lauro* was seized by Palestinian extremists outside Alexandria harbour during a Mediterranean cruise.

Shortly after the liner had departed from Alexandria, on 8 October 1985, bound for Port Said, a band of Arab terrorists under the leadership of the Palestinian guerilla Mohammed 'Abul' Abbas seized the vessel in a violent raid.

The *Achille Lauro*, a 26-year old, 23,600 gross ton motorship, originally built for a Dutch shipping company, had arrived at Alexandria from Genoa, her home port, at 7.30am (local time) on 8 October. She had then proceeded to disembark 664 of the passengers who were making an overland excursion to Cairo. Two hours later the ship sailed for Port Said where the sightseers were intended to rejoin her. Another 180 passengers remained aboard with the 331 crew while the ship was repositioned.

When the *Achille Lauro* had reached a point about 30 miles north of Alexandria, in international waters, the Palestinian gunmen, numbering only four, commandeered the ship in a lightning strike, spraying a hail of automatic gunfire to terrorise and intimidate passengers and crew alike. Capt Gerardo de Rosa was advised that his ship had been hijacked by the Palestinian Liberation Front (PLF) and that he should co-operate fully otherwise he would be personally responsible for any harm inflicted upon the passengers. At 9.45pm, Capt de Rosa instructed his radio operators to notify the Egyptian authorities that his vessel had been seized by an armed group. He advised that the terrorists were demanding freedom for 50 political prisoners held by Israel and were threatening to blow up the *Achille Lauro* if these demands were not met or if the ship was approached by any rescue craft, despatched to intercept her.

Contact between the Egyptian authorities and the Palestinians was soon lost as the *Achille Lauro* sailed northwards away from the coast and out of radio range. The Egyptians were left to absorb the gravity of the situation and determine how they should best respond given the intransigence over such matters that was fundamental to Israel's anti-terrorist policy. The Italian and Israeli governments were informed of the situation and, once the nationalities of the passengers aboard the cruise liner were identified, so too were their respective governments. There were in fact 28 Italians, 52 Swiss, three British, 16 Americans, 22 Germans and Austrians and 11 Belgians amongst the hostages; quite a mixed bunch. The crew comprised mainly Italians plus some Portuguese and British.

Aboard the *Achille Lauro*, the guerillas had made no attempt to spare the passengers undue suffering, indeed it appeared that alarm and panic were deliberately and maliciously fostered among them. This suggested either that, with a cruel lack of regard for the well-being of the hostages, the hijackers actually took pleasure from tormenting them with death threats or that, equally cold-bloodedly, they were planning to use the hostages as an expendable commodity to be traded crudely to achieve the terrorists' objectives. By performing token executions they could perhaps apply pressure on the international community to force through concessions.

This callous intimidation was directed primarily at the British and American passengers who were separated from the rest and surrounded by cans of petrol. They were left under no illusion that these would be ignited if there was trouble or if other circumstances warranted it. Bravely, some of the male hostages attempted to confront their tyrannical oppressors, challenging the guns and grenades with which they were threatened with their own weapons of courage and dignity. Particularly vocal was an elderly New York Jewish man, Mr Leon Klinghoffer, a cripple who was confined to a wheelchair. To silence this challenge and reinforce the menace of their threats, the terrorists dragged Klinghoffer out onto the open deck where he was cold bloodedly shot twice in the back and his body dumped over the side of the ship. The remaining passengers, horrified at this nightmarish act of brutality, were condemned to silence at the risk of inciting more of the same.

By this time, the *Achille Lauro* had arrived off the Syrian coast, near the port of Tartus, where her anchor was dropped. The gunmen now proceeded to issue further demands to Syrian Government officials. These were revealed in detail by the Christian Voice of Lebanon radio station which had intercepted the ship-to-shore communications: 'In a conversation with the Syrian authorities in the port of Tartus, the gunmen demanded a Red Cross ship to carry the ambassadors of the United States, West Germany, Italy and Britain, as well as other Western diplomats, to approach and negotiate with them. The gunmen also demanded to talk with a delegation from the Arab Liberation Front.'

This met with a completely negative response for the Syrians had no desire to become associated in any way with this criminal act of terrorism and piracy. In the face of this cool reception from fellow Arabs who themselves were known to have had connections with extremist organisations in the past, the Palestinians had little choice but to move on. Consequently, the *Achille Lauro* was taken back to Port Said where she arrived some 20 miles off the port entrance on 9 October.

Egyptian officials at Port Said refused clearance for the *Achille Lauro* to enter the port. The Palestinian guerillas for their part repeated their threat to blow up the ship if their demands were not met and according to Guilio Andreotti, the Italian Foreign Minister, they were now insisting on the release of prisoners held in various other countries including Italy. They persisted too with their call for negotiations with the Italian, US and West German ambassadors.

The spotlight of international concern over the *Achille Lauro* affair was now focused well and truly on Egypt. Egypt was not, it has to be said, an extremist

THE HIJACKING OF THE *ACHILLE LAURO*

——— Route of liner *Achille Lauro*: Genoa-Alexandria-Tartous (Syria)-Port Said

——— Route of Egyptian Boeing 737: Cairo-intercepted south of Crete- Catania (Sicily)-Rome

Below: The passenger liner *Achille Lauro.* The ship and her occupants were effectively held under arrest, at Port Foad, off Port Said, Egypt, pending the completion of police investigations. *World Ship Photo Library*

Right: Map of the Mediterranean Sea showing the route of the *Achille Lauro* during her cruise to Alexandria and after the subsequent hijacking. The map also shows the route of the Egyptian airliner which attempted to take the surrendered terrorists to Tunis.

Arab nation and enjoyed good relationships with both the West and with her fellow Arab states. This pivotal position, which gave Egypt an enviable status as a mediator in Middle East affairs, stood to be challenged in these circumstances for Egypt could not afford to be other than equivocal in its handling of the situation without risking alienation from one side or the other. Anxious to extricate itself from the dilemma, the Egyptians elected to concede to at least one of the terrorists' demands by arranging a meeting aboard the ship between interested parties.

An Egyptian naval vessel, conspicuously identified for the purpose, ferried a party of International Red Cross representatives, Egyptian and Italian officials, along with a PLO delegation, out to the bright blue liner, anchored out on the horizon. During the discussions that followed a deal was struck that permitted the Egyptians to announce, on their return, that the siege aboard the *Achille Lauro* would end at 5pm that day with the surrender of the gunmen. Having elected to take what it saw as the line of least resistance, the agreement that had been concluded provided for the release of the ship and all passengers and crew in exchange for safe conduct out of the country for the terrorists. Regrettably, for all its merits, it did not take into account the backlash of American public opinion which followed the disclosure of the murder of Leon Klinghoffer.

The *Achille Lauro* docked during the morning of 10 October, bringing the brief ship-board siege to an end. But the incident as a whole was far from over. The freed hostages were quick to inform the Italian and US ambassadors in Cairo of what had happened during the hijacking. Yet, even as they were making known these revelations, the four terrorists had been surreptitiously transferred to Cairo Airport where they boarded an Egyptian Boeing 737 airliner bound for Tunis, the agreed destination. President Husni Mubarak later excused these actions by stating, with little plausibility, that the Palestinian terrorists had already left the country before Egypt knew of the murder of the American hostage. It was hinted too, though not from official sources, that the death may have resulted anyway from other than violent causes.

When, on 13 October, the body of Leon Klinghoffer was recovered from the coastline near Tartus where it had been washed ashore, the two bullet wounds confirmed the act of murder reported and witnessed by the released hostages. It was handed over to US Embassy officials in Damascus.

The Americans determined to capture the men responsible, not only to account for this particular murder but also because they had been identified as senior terrorists wanted in connection with a series of other atrocities. Special forces that had been deployed in the eastern Mediterranean, ready to storm the liner *Achille Lauro* had it proved to be necessary, were now activated in a bid to capture the wanted gunmen. Suspecting what was about to happen and therefore monitoring the air traffic control communications at Cairo airport, four F-14 fighter aircraft were launched from the aircraft carrier USS *Saratoga* to intercept the Egyptian airliner. They caught up with it after take-off as it banked to the east in international airspace over the Mediterranean Sea.

The commercial jet was headed off, south of the island of Crete and despite the pilot's repeated insistence that he should be permitted to land at Tunis or alternatively Athens, which Greek officials refused anyway, he was compelled to accede to being escorted into the NATO military air base at Sigonella, near Catania, Sicily where it landed at 00.30am on 11 October.

Unfortunately, having accomplished successfully such a daring intervention, the whole operation backfired as a result of a lack of accord between the Italians and Americans. Once it was on the ground the intercepted airliner was surrounded by two rings of troops, Italian Caribinieri on the inside and US Marines and special force personnel on the outside. Instead of jointly accosting the terrorists, the two lines of soldiers stood confronting one another face to face, each side refusing to let the other move. Italy had charged the four Palestinians with premeditated murder, hijacking, kidnapping and illegal possession of arms and explosives, insisting that, as these crimes had taken place on an Italian flag vessel in international waters, they should be tried under Italian law. The Italians were incensed at the Americans' cavalier behaviour, particularly their failure to respect appropriate protocols by taking such provocative actions on the territory of a sovereign state and without the consultation of an ally. They also asserted their right to arrest the hijackers on Italian territory.

The Americans, having hooked the fish and anxious not to let it slip through the net, had almost certainly exceeded their rights, both legally and diplomatically. The US Justice Department had obtained an arrest warrant for Mohammed Abbas, leader of the PLF, alleging that he had masterminded the hijacking of the *Achille Lauro* and charging him with a range of federal violations including hostage-taking, piracy, conspiracy and murder.

Not surprisingly, the Egyptian Government added its voice to the widespread condemnation of the American action. Their statement said it deplored both the hijacking of the *Achille Lauro* and the interception of their airliner. It expressed surprise and regret at the United States' action.

All that could be said about all this was that the terrorists caught up in the middle of this diplomatic fracas could only have taken comfort from the evident lack of cooperation at national level in the fight against terrorist crime.

The Italian argument concerning jurisdiction over the gunmen ultimately prevailed and the terrorists were taken into their custody. The Americans protested but resigned themselves to ensuring the detention of the Palestinians pending a request for the extradition of Abbas to stand trial in the USA in order to secure a justice that was regarded as the only one acceptable to their citizens. Meanwhile, the Egyptian Boeing 737 shuttled between Rome and Sicily with its complement of Egyptian diplomats and secret service officers and the two PLO representatives that had accompanied the terrorists from Cairo. This pair also happened to be of interest to the USA. In the course of this, the Palestinians, one of whom was positively identified as Abbas, were allowed to leave for Belgrade in Yugoslavia much to the indignation of the USA. Inexplicably, the prize fish had been allowed to wriggle off the hook.

Sources within the Italian government justified the releases by saying that the Palestinians had been held 'without motive and longer than necessary'. This did not prevent the government of Bettino Craxi being toppled by the tidal wave of condemnation that followed. More importantly, though, nothing happened to remedy the international community's failure to develop a spirit of meaningful co-operation in the war against terrorism. The *Achille Lauro* hijacking served as a timely reminder of the consequences of failing to agree mutually the necessary international policies and protocols that would allow terrorism to be combatted wherever it occurred.

As a postscript to the *Achille Lauro* incident, in making a concerted bid to restore its reputation with the west, Egypt elected to take a hard line in dealing with the hijacking of one of its aircraft by Palestinian gunmen which occurred a month later. Egyptian commandos stormed the airliner as it stood on the tarmac at Malta's Luqa airport but despite the good intentions behind this uncompromising intervention, the raid backfired and 59 persons were killed.

Apocalypse Now

While the majority of sieges so far described in this book have had a nationalist or political dispute as their root cause, issues of religious conflict involving fanatical or extremist cults have also precipitated confrontations and it is to these subjects that the attention of this final chapter is turned. The fact that martyrdom is regarded as the most estimable self-sacrifice by many of the world's religions, particularly by the fundamentalist orders of certain religions and some obscure fanatical sects, the breaking of the stalemate of sieges which have such a religious origin has invariably proved impossible to achieve without violence and extensive loss of life.

The birth of the states of Pakistan and India in August 1947 was accompanied by the outbreak of widespread communal, secular violence, particularly between Muslims and Hindus, but also between numerous minor religious groups as each expressed its aspirations for religious or ethnic independence. Fired by deeply felt hatred and bigotry, there was indiscriminate slaughter among the many groups of mobile refugees' and horror stories abounded as innocent victims were hacked and beaten to death.

This all left a legacy of disputed areas along the borders between the two countries, notably Jammu and Kashmir, over which there have been regular outbreaks of armed conflict since. India itself is a country of numerous religions each with its own holy shrines and centres of worship. Over 80% of India's 850 million population are practising Hindus. A further 90 million or so are Muslims. There are, approximately 20 million Christians and around 15 million Sikhs, followed by smaller numbers of Buddhists, Jains and many other faiths.

The Sikhs, a proudly monotheistic, insular warrior people are concentrated in the state of Punjab on India's northwest frontier. Notorious for their defiant opposition to the power of authority of the British Raj they are equally opposed to the rule of the Federal Republic from New Delhi, demanding independence for the Sikh homeland of Khalistan. The cultural and spiritual centre of the Sikh religion is in the city of Amritsar ('tranquil pool of nectar', as it is translated) where the holiest of shrines, the Golden Temple of Harmandir Sahib and the holy sanctuary of Akal Takht, the seat of immortal power of the Sikhs, are located.

Amritsar has had a long history of violent bloodshed inherited from the years of resistance to and demonstration against British rule. The most infamous incident under the Raj occurred in April 1919 when troops under Brig-Gen Dyer massacred more than a thousand protesters, including many women and children, machine-gunning them to death in the Jallianwala Bagh district of the city as they demonstrated against repressive new security laws.

Some 60 or so years later, freed from the British but still engaged in a continuing dispute with the federal Indian authorities, Sikh militancy re-emerged with new energy in 1982 with the launching of a campaign of agitation in support of their demands by the Akali Dal, the so-called immortal party. It flourished with a fresh vitality under the leadership of Sant Harchand Longowal, the party president, and Sant Jarnail Singh Bhindranwale, the high-priest of the Sikh extremists.

Ironically, Bhindranwale's rise to pre-eminence in the Sikh religious hierarchy had been contrived by the Congress Party when he received their sponsorship as a young politician in a bid to undercut the Sikh leadership by dividing the Akali vote between the moderates and fundamentalists. Unexpectedly, just as the monster turned on Dr Frankenstein, in Mary Shelley's story, so the young Bhindranwale turned on his sponsors, becoming an inspiration to the very terrorists whom the Indian government had hoped he would weaken or demoralise.

The Sikh's agitation for self-determination, in fact, had as much to do with political power as religion. Following India's independence, the Sikhs had been left as a minority within their own state of the Punjab. Thus they campaigned for a smaller state in which they would predominate. This was achieved in 1966 when the mainly Hindu areas of Haryana and Himachal Pradesh were carved out of the greater Punjab, leaving the Sikhs as the dominant population of the remaining area. The Sikhs remained dissatisfied, however. This was because their perceived under-representation had continued as a straightforward consequence of Punjabis exercising their free democratic rights. Enough of the state's citizens voted either for the Congress Party, the Communists or for right-wing Hindu candidates to deny power to the Sikhs other than that shared through coalitions. The solution was to press for full autonomy under which a suitably weighted constitution could be drafted that would guarantee the prevalence of Sikh values in all aspects of Punjabi life.

From early in 1984, violent confrontations against the Indian Army increased alarmingly as the campaign for regional autonomy was intensified. Wide ranging powers of search and arrest were introduced by the Government. At the end of May, under the orders of the Indian Prime Minister, Mrs Indira Gandhi, a determined offensive was launched against the Sikhs in a concerted effort to suppress the militants and end their murderous activities once and for all. All that this achieved, though, was to drive the heavily-armed Sikh extremists, with their leader Bhindranwale, and other senior priests, into the inviolable sanctuary of the Golden Temple where they were besieged for four days from 2 June.

It should be stressed that the conflict was only with a minority of fanatical Sikhs. The majority of Sikh citizens, many of whom held positions of respect and importance within the Indian Civil Service and the Indian armed forces, disapproved of the conduct of the militants while maintaining their desire for a separate existence from the Indian federation.

According to a government minister, the besieged Sikhs immediately resorted to provocative action against the Indian troops, who were in fortified positions surrounding the temple complex. The militants opened fire on the security forces with medium machine guns and mortars, killing a soldier and a civilian. Endeavouring to show restraint, given the dangers associated with any form of military intervention and anxious not to offend Sikh sensitivities by firing on the Golden Temple, the Indian army's retaliation was limited. Instead they concentrated on making loudspeaker appeals to the militants to surrender while

The domed structure at the entrance to Amritsar's Golden Temple, the Sikhs' holiest shrine, showing the damage caused by machine-gun fire and shelling during the battle of 6-7 June 1984 between religious zealots and Indian troops along with units of the Central Reserve Police Force. *Associated Press*

the army also reinforced its positions around the Temple, constructing more sandbagged emplacements and brick pillboxes.

A total curfew was imposed to back up the security force's moves to restore law and order within the Punjab as a whole. This was enforced with particular vigour in the key centres of opposition but this too only served to generate antipathy in the wider community. Considerable hardship was caused as people were trapped in their homes unable to access markets to obtain provisions. As the simmering heat climbed to more than 110°F, so pent-up passions rose remorselessly to boiling point.

The security clampdown also extended to the expulsion of all foreign news correspondents from the state along with any Indian nationals who were engaged working for foreign media organisations. Journalists were rounded up at their hotels and driven in military vehicles to the state boundaries where they were put down and advised in the strongest terms not to return. Other correspondents, already outside the exclusion zone, were stopped from entering the area by road-blocks on every highway at which they were informed that they were in danger of being shot if they attempted to proceed further. The Indian authorities explained that this had been done simply to protect foreigners from the risk of physical harm but it was suspected that the real motivation behind the clamp down was to ensure that, if the army was left with no choice but to storm the Golden Temple, it should not happen with the eyes of the press looking on.

Government statements had repeatedly emphasised that, while there was a desire to ending the siege quickly, the authorities wished to achieve this without recourse to armed force and without directly entering the Golden Temple. This policy was reinforced in an interview with Mr K. K. Wali, the Home Minister in the central Government, who was quick to put down rumours and suspicions. 'The overall objective,' he said, 'is to avoid taking any action of a military nature unless it is absolutely unavoidable'. The fact was, though, that the Government had already given the authorisation for the army to enter the Temple provided that the besieged occupants had been given adequate opportunity to surrender and provided that the local authorities (that is the State Government administrators in Amritsar) also believed there was no realistic alternative.

Whatever its concerns of presenting a moderate, restrained and religiously tolerant impression of their handling of the siege to the world at large, in the final analysis the Indian Government was confronted with an irreconcilable conflict of interests. Whichever move the Government took, it would be condemned.

On the one hand, if the sanctuary of the holy shrine was respected and the Sikh militants were not tackled this would be seen as weakness on the part of the Government and the problem of religious terrorism would increase, not only with the Sikhs but with other, unsettled minority factions throughout India. On the other hand if military intervention was sanctioned, to end the siege by force, flush out the extremists and subject them to the due process of law, there was always the danger of a backlash among the moderate elements of the Sikh community. In carrying out such an assault the troops would clearly have to avoid causing damage to the Golden Temple, they would have to endeavour to limit any bloodshed and avoid anything else that hinted, even remotely, of wanton violation or disrespect for the sacred shrine. It seems to be human nature for peoples of common ancestry or cultural stock, who may hold quite polarised attitudes over their domestic affairs, to close ranks in the face of what is perceived to be a common adversary. Quite patently, it was impossible for the Indian troops to be sure whether they could sufficiently prevent any of these

Left: Map of India showing the location of Amritsar and the Punjab.

Below: Mrs Indira Gandhi lies in state at the Teen Murti House in the Indian capital, New Delhi, after her assassination by Sikh soldiers from her personal bodyguard. Her body was conveyed to the funeral on top of a howitzer carriage. *Associated Press*

consequences when they were facing tenaciously and suicidally committed defenders who were armed with a veritable arsenal of powerful, modern weapons.

The Saudi Arabian Government had been confronted with a similar dilemma in late November 1979 when renegade Shi'ite fundamentalist fanatics occupied the Great Mosque at Mecca, the holiest place in all Islam, holding thousands of pilgrims as hostages.

After consulting with religious leaders, Royal forces were ordered to storm the Mosque to end a seven day siege. In bloody hand-to-hand fighting, as Muslim confronted Muslim, the holy shrine was finally secured but only after heavy loss of life. This incident had arisen from conflict within the same religion, the Shi'ites, followers of the same sect as Ayatollah Khomeini's Islamic Iranian revolutionaries being opposed to the orthodox Sunni sect of Islam as practised by Saudi Arabians. The siege in the Punjab, by contrast, pitted Hindus against Sikhs — a yet more explosive mixture.

On balance, considering all the implications, the Indian Government determined that, if the respect for its authority was not to be constantly challenged, there was no choice but to send the troops in to clean out the assassins sheltering within the Golden Temple's holy precincts. Early in the morning of 6 June 1984 the security forces were given the green light to launch their offensive, code named Operation 'Blue Star'. As anticipated, they met extremely stiff resistance, finding it necessary to fight bitterly for every inch they secured.

The strength of Sikh resistance — a measure of both their fanatical zeal and the failure of the Indian Army intelligence services to assess properly their strength — came as a total surprise. Driven by their conviction in their cause and with faith in their own immortality, and aided by their intimate knowledge of the tunnels and passageways of the Temple complex, the Sikh militants proved to be difficult to dislodge. Casualties on both sides were very heavy, the Indian soldiers suffering particularly during the push on the Harmandir Sahib because they were reluctant to fire on the gold covered shrine in which, normally, priests read continuously from the Guru Granth Sahib, the holy book of the Sikhs, from an altar in the centre of the temple's lake. This area was held by 23 terrorists who finally surrendered to the invaders after inflicting heavy losses on them. Another group of militants, occupying the basement of the Akal Takht, refused to give themselves up and were only finally driven out after several salvoes of tear-gas canisters had been fired in amongst them.

Left with no alternative, if Operation 'Blue Star' was to accomplish all its set objectives, the army sent in tanks and commandos to hasten the end of the siege and the fighting. Extensive damage was caused and hundreds killed.

When it was all over and the situation was fully assessed, it was soon evident that the storming had resulted in a bloodbath. Externally, the Golden Temple displayed all the tell-tale signs of the ferocious battle, its walls pock-marked with cannon and shell hits. Over 700 of the Sikh extremists were dead, including Sant Bhindranwale, his military leaders — Narinder Singh Bhuller and Shahbeg Singh — and all the leaders of the All-Indian Sikh Students Federation who had been among the prime movers of the terrorist campaign along with the high priests. Another 450 Sikh fundamentalists were captured and imprisoned.

The Indian army fatalities were high too. Lt-Gen Ranjit Singh Dayal, the military adviser to the Governor of the Punjab, gave the army's losses as one officer and 47 other ranks killed, 10 officers and 100 other ranks seriously wounded. A further 12 soldiers were said to be missing presumed dead.

The army operation had not been confined just to the Golden Temple in Amritsar. Elsewhere in Punjab State, as part of a wide-sweeping campaign of crackdown, troops had attacked 38 other Sikh shrines, including the temple of Tarm Tarn, a few miles from Amritsar, five Hindu temples and a Muslim mosque. The Government was pointedly serving notice to all concerned that it would not tolerate civil disobedience and terrorism any longer.

The barbarous outcome of the offensive on the Golden Temple met with widespread condemnation. The assault was widely regarded as as an act of desecration of a sanctified place of worship and it enraged even those moderate Sikhs who were sickened by the extremist's campaign of terror. Like a scorpion, the fateful assault on the Golden Temple proved to have a powerful and fatal sting in its tail.

Mutinies among Sikh troops were reported almost immediately. Despite warnings that she should no longer trust the Sikh contingent of her personal bodyguard, Indira Gandhi did not act on the advice, preferring to ride out the storm, concerned not to alienate Sikh opinion further. On 31 October 1984 the 66-year old Prime Minister paid the price for her misguided faith in their loyalty and in a clear act of revenge for Operation 'Blue Star' she was assassinated, shot 10 times as she walked in the garden of her New Delhi home. One of her killers was himself shot dead, the other was wounded.

Mrs Gandhi's successor, her 40-year old son Rajiv was immediately sworn in while bloody riots swept across India as Hindus exacted revenge on the Sikhs for the murder. The Sikhs in turn retaliated and at least 1,000 people died in the wake of the assassination as victims from both religious factions, invariably innocents caught up in the mayhem, were horrifically slaughtered within the teaming city slums. Rajiv Gandhi appealed for calm but was compelled to order soldiers into the inner-city residential areas to quell the violence. Fired by such deeply held religious passions it took some time before the almost ritual bloodletting was exhausted and any semblance of order was reinstated.

Rajiv Gandhi was himself the victim of a political murder in 1991, which arose from continuing religious tension and rivalry between India's Hindu, Muslim and Tamil communities.

Another, quite different, religiously-influenced siege occurred in the United States of America in early 1993. Centred on the potent mixture of America's free-and-easy gun laws, the hell-fire and brimstone doctrines preached by the many obscure churches in America's new wave of religious evangelism and the gung-ho heavy-handedness of law enforcement agencies, as exhibited in the tactics frequently employed to deal with social disturbances, it presented a major challenge to the newly inaugurated President Bill Clinton.

The most famous siege in American history had occurred in February 1836 at the Battle of the Alamo, when the legendary heroes of the American West, Will Travis, Davy Crocket and Jim Bowie, along with a small garrison of Texas Rangers, were besieged by 3,000 Mexican soldiers under Gen Antonio Lopez Sant Anna. When the small Franciscan mission called the Alamo was finally overrun, after repeated assaults, all 184 within it were killed but only after hundreds of Sant Anna's troops had also been slaughtered. The mission fortress of the Alamo, now a museum and national heritage centre, is located at San Antonio, Texas.

Almost two centuries later, the second most famous siege in American and Texan history took place at Waco, some 160 miles from the site of the Alamo. In the later siege, those captive and surrounded within their fortified compound were, rather than freedom fighters whose exploits would provide inspiration for future generations, naïve religious zealots led, like lambs to the slaughter, by a fanatical self-styled reincarnation of Jesus Christ and former pop-recording star — David Koresh. Realistically, because of the dominant influence of his personality on the proceedings, the Siege of Waco was in essence the Siege of Koresh.

Koresh was a bizarre, mentally unbalanced and complex character. He was a product of America's Bible-belt with its many born-again, fundamentalist Christian denominations and hell-fire evangelical churches, each claiming to own the monopoly of knowledge on the true path to salvation in the hereafter. As one newspaper put it, referring to the messianic fervour with which he was imbued, 'In layman's terms, David Koresh is a nut!'.

Born in Houston, Texas in 1959 as Vernon Wayne Howell, he changed his name as an adult adopting the stage name David Koresh in pursuit of his originally intended career as a rock musician.

His childhood seems to have been characterised by obsessive, if not disturbing, behaviour. Born illegitimately when his mother was still only 15, he was brought up by his grandmother as a member of the mainstream Seventh Day Adventist Church. As a child he displayed an intensive and disquieting propensity for religious matters, typified by his ability, by the time he was 12, to memorise long passages of text from the New Testament. His mother later described how 'he would come home from school and go out to the barn where he would pray for hours'. She added, 'I've often seen him kneeling by his bed, crying and praying'.

At school he was described as an 'average ability student' with a friendly disposition but remembered more as a loner than anything else. A disastrous love affair in his teens, with the minister's daughter from the family church, led him to severing his ties with the orthodox Seventh Day Adventists. In 1976, following this, he joined the Branch Davidians. Created in the 1930s by a Bulgarian emigré, who believed the return of Christ was imminent, this was a heretic, splinter Adventist sect which had been expelled from the mainstream faith because of its extreme interpretation of the Bible's message. By 1984 Koresh had taken partial control of the cult following a split into two rival factions. The Koresh group moved to a town called Palestine. Three years later he was involved in a violent leadership struggle between the two factions, a struggle which ended in a shoot out and a court appearance where he was charged with the attempted murder of George Roden, the leader of the other group. Koresh was tried and acquitted of the charge.

Koresh had moved around quite a lot as a young man, particularly during the period when he was trying to establish himself as a rock guitarist. As a result he had lived in several cities in east Texas and in many foreign countries. After assuming the leadership of the Branch Davidian sect, he occupied its base, Mount Carmel, a 77-acre ranch at Waco, 90 miles south of Dallas, where the cult was established as an isolated commune within a compound which he proceeded to fortify intensively. Koresh's authority over the small community was absolute, the product of his magnetic personality and his indisputable and extraordinary knowledge of the scriptures. Free love was believed and practised by the Branch Davidians and Koresh apparently demanded and obtained sexual gratification from all of the women who joined the sect, bedding girls as young as thirteen. Many of the women were taken as his concubines and it was claimed that he had fathered the majority of the children living in the compound.

The population of the compound began to swell for other reasons too. Koresh frequently travelled abroad preaching his gospel and winning converts to his

148

faith. New members came to Waco from Britain, Hawaii, New Zealand and Australia. By early 1993, there were more than a hundred persons in total, men, women and children, living in the compound, almost a third of them of British nationality.

The fortification of Mount Carmel continued apace, with the stockpiling of food, water and huge quantities of weapons. In terms of fire-power the compound was a veritable arsenal, a matter which, as it became known, was of great concern to the Texan law enforcement authorities. Over the years since the group arrived at Waco there had been more than a few minor scrapes between Koresh and the police, relating to weapons offences, but this sinister process of arming the group to the teeth aroused particular concern. It led ultimately to the intervention by a group of agents from the Bureau of Alcohol, Tobacco and Firearms (ATF) in a secret raid on 28 February 1993. The intention had been to take the compound by surprise in order to avoid any hostile resistance, allowing officers to serve warrants for firearms offences, to search for illegal weapons, of which there were probably many, and to investigate alleged sexual crimes committed against children in the congregation.

The raid, involving as many as 200 ATF agents, was disastrously bungled. Koresh appears to have been tipped off and was waiting, fully prepared when the police officers approached. A ferocious battle broke out in which Koresh's men employed automatic weapons and a 50mm howitzer to defend the compound. Four ATF officers were killed and another 16 were wounded. From two to six persons from within the compound, reports varied on this, also died. Koresh claimed in a telephone call to his mother that one of the dead was his son. One of the cult members definitely shot in the raid was a 28 year old British male, Winston Blake, who came from Nottingham.

The ATF operation aroused considerable criticism and debate. It was asked, not unreasonably, why they had chosen to storm the Branch Davidian compound in military style, when Koresh, the prime target of their enquiries, who was known to regularly jog around the area unaccompanied, could have been readily intercepted and arrested at any time.

The US Bureau of Alcohol, Tobacco and Firearms, a unit of the Treasury Department and essentially a Revenue organisation, had been around since 1919 when the Volstead Act, the 18th amendment to the US Constitution, introduced a total ban on the manufacture and consumption of alcohol. Its most famous member was Eliot Ness, leader of the 'Untouchables', a squad which relentlessly pursued the bootlegging mobs of Al Capone and other gangsters during the 1920s, earning their nickname from the unbreakable moral integrity which was a fundamental requirement of the character of the force's officers.

Since the end of Prohibition, in 1933, the ATF had declined in importance to become something of a second-line crime fighting organisation by comparison with the larger agencies such as the Federal Bureau of Investigation (FBI), the Drug Enforcement Administration (DEA) and the Internal Revenue Service (IRS). As the years had passed its members had not received the breadth or sophistication of training necessary for this type of work. The bureau's tactical capability and competence was open to critical questioning, a matter of vital significance given that the ATF was permitted to operate freely under its own command structure and without strict day-to-day supervision by its parent department. The Waco débâcle appeared to confirm all the fears expressed by other law enforcement officers.

However, this was not the right and proper time to carry out a post-mortem on the failed raid. Having caused the deaths of a number of ATF agents, Koresh's

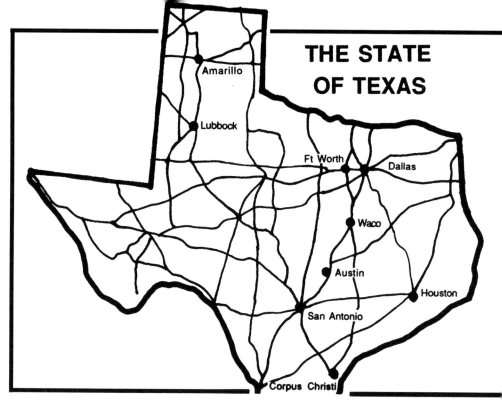

Above: **Map of Texas showing Waco and San Antonio, the scene of the legendary siege of the Alamo.**

Right: **During the court appearance in 1988, when he was charged with the attempted murder of George Roden, religious fanatic David Koresh handles a rifle, presaging the bloody gun battle and siege that were to happen in the spring of 1993.** *Sygma*

Below: **Plan of the Branch Davidian compound at Waco showing the main features, the points where fires broke out and where the Abrams tanks, with their battering rams, knocked holes in the walls of the buildings.**

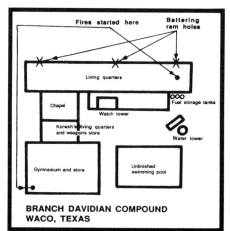

Fires started here   Battering ram holes

Living quarters

Chapel   Watch tower   Fuel storage tanks

Koresh's living quarters and weapons store   Water tower

Gymnasium and store   Unfinished swimming pool

**BRANCH DAVIDIAN COMPOUND
WACO, TEXAS**

Branch Davidians were now wanted for other, more serious reasons. Facing the prospect of further, heavy casualties if another frontal assault was attempted, the ATF instead besieged the ranch, bringing in hundreds of reinforcements to completely encircle it, in the hope that they could persuade the compound's occupants to surrender peacefully. More than 500 police and federal agents took up position with support from helicopters and armoured vehicles.

The total number trapped within Mount Carmel was 132 of whom at least 31 were known to be British. Back in Britain, the families of those concerned seeing the drama unfold on their TV screens, became extremely anxious about the safety of their relatives. Knowing from first-hand experience of the powerful influence that Koresh could exert over his impressionable followers, many of whom had been drawn like unsuspecting flies into his spider's web, and of the psychotic conviction he had in his belief that he was the reincarnated Christ, the Lamb of God, they feared that the siege could only have a violent outcome.

It is perhaps surprising that the members of the Branch Davidian sect, all of them fundamentally law-abiding citizens, did not revolt against Koresh's leadership now that they had become accessories, with him, to the crime of murder, the breaking of the sixth commandment. The fact that they did not serves to demonstrate how absolute his control was over them. It was not so much a question of their being browbeaten or intimidated by Koresh, so much as that he had convinced them that he was indeed the Son of God — like Jesus Christ, his side had been pierced by his enemies; he too was ready to die and rise again; he alone could unravel the mysteries of the Seven Seals in the Book of Revelations; this was the long-awaited Apocalypse that instruction in the Bible's message had taught them to expect.

If ever there was a siege that required delicate but firm handling, according to all the well-established rules of engagement for these types of incident, this was it. The authorities had to impose their superiority on the situation; they had to dictate the course of events in order to control and manoeuvre them to achieve a clearly defined end objective. They had to control the psychology of the situation and they had to be able to override Koresh's personality and emphatically win the war of persuasion.

While recognising the extreme difficulty that any organisation would have had in negotiating with an unstable individual like Koresh, the reality at Waco was in fact far removed from this ideal. The ATF policy for handling the siege was ambiguous; it lacked decisiveness and had a muddled operational strategy. Above all, it seemed to be unduly influenced by the fear of a repetition of the Jonestown massacre of November 1978. At that time, another religious fanatic, the Rev James Jones, persuaded 913 of his disciples to commit mass suicide after a group of American congressmen and investigators, who had managed to locate the People's Temple — the cult's remote headquarters deep in the jungle of Guyana — had been murdered.

In these circumstances, the Waco siege dragged on for 51 days with the ATF authorities uncertain of which way to handle the problem and constantly being outwitted and humiliated by the devious Koresh. On 2 March, in a 58min radio broadcast that he had been permitted to make, Koresh promised to surrender with all his followers but this amounted to no more than an empty gesture. Three days later he advised that he was awaiting instructions from God before considering his surrender intentions.

Some progress was made early on in persuading the Branch Davidians to allow the younger members of their community to go free. By 15 March they had released 21 children, three of whom were British, along with two elderly women.

Another 25 juveniles remained in the besieged ranch and arrangements were made to deliver a consignment of six gallons of fresh milk for these youngsters. Other than this, the stock piling of provisions over the preceding months meant that there was no shortage of food available to the trapped cult and it was considered that, if they wanted to, they could hold out for months. A deep well inside the compound ensured that they had a plentiful and continuous supply of water.

More than anything else, it was uncertainty as to the actual extent of Koresh's available fire power that kept the ATF team on the defensive. Some indication of the range and power of the weapons in his armoury had been gleaned from shipping documents that investigating officers had uncovered, These revealed that he had no less than:

- 100 AR-15 assault rifles equipped with armour-piercing ammunition;
- 200 other rifles;
- 50lb of gunpowder;
- 200 rifle grenades;
- 20,000 rounds of ammunition;
- dozens of bomb-making kits;
- parts for hundreds of automatic and semi-automatic weapons.

In response to Koresh's claim that he also had rocket launches, four M1-A1 Abrams tanks were called to the scene to reinforce the lighter-armoured M60 military vehicles already on site. It was also believed that the windows and doors of the ranch had been booby-trapped to forestall another attempt at an armed incursion.

The hours and days passed. The siege operation, now placed under the direction of the FBI, through its director, William Sessions, constantly vacillated between a high level of indulgence on the one extreme, presumably aimed at trying to win Koresh over, to a much tougher stance, as patience seemed to be exhausted, on the other. On reflection, an excessive media presence had been permitted by the authorities which was totally counter-productive in that it was encouraging Koresh to perform to an audience.

On a more positive note, further evacuations had been achieved and by 23 March the total number released had increased to 37. Another Briton, Victoria Hollingworth, was among the most recent group voluntarily to leave the compound while Livingstone Fagan, who was also British and who was identified as one of the cult's ringleaders, also surrendered to the waiting lawmen.

After having permitted David Koresh to broadcast on radio and to make unlimited telephone interviews, in which he invariably degenerated into shouted histrionics, the police authorities decided to deny him further access to the media. Having recognised that he craved publicity and that the more he got the longer the siege was likely to continue, they determined to gag him.

But this was first challenged by lawyers, who claimed that it also denied Koresh his right of access to legal advice, and by a sympathetic and, at best, well-intentioned but irresponsible radio talk show host who wanted to give him air time. Later, the authorities themselves undermined their own resolve by allowing Koresh to conduct negotiations for a book contract with lawyers in New York. Apart from using the opportunity to play games with the FBI, Koresh was apparently trying to establish just how lucrative an income he could derive from auctioning the rights to a best-seller, further evidence of his egotistical, self-centred personality.

Frustrated with all this, the authorities decided to step up the heat. A Hostage Rescue Team was deployed at Waco to reinforce the FBI capability. A ring of steel was thrown around the besieged compound as huge coils of barbed-wire fencing were put in place. In clandestine night time moves, special units attached to the federal forces wired the compound with high-tech listening devices in order to eavesdrop on the conversations going on inside. They also secured control over the compound's electricity supply so that this could be deliberately interrupted at any time to create inconvenience and to undermine Koresh's declared immunity to any outside interference.

Horns began to sound over Waco, too, but not the trumpets of angels as presaged in Koresh's dream of an apocalyptic end to the world. As part of a raucous, mind-shattering wall of noise intended to disturb any attempt at sleep, the compound was bombarded with everything from grating jazz trumpet improvisations and heavy-metal guitar solos to inane pop music, sound effects and Buddhist chants. The sound effect noises were perhaps the worst, with successive doses of wailing police sirens, ticking clocks, barking dogs, chiming bells, crowing cockerels, hooting cars and ringing telephones — a selection from every persons list of most detested sounds — and all played at ear-splitting volume. Accompanying the din were searing strobe lights from lamps on the ground and sweeping shafts of floodlight played over the buildings from helicopters hovering overhead.

Yet, incredibly, all this was completely unproductive. Koresh and his tribe of zealots somehow managed to resist all this psychological warfare and remained firmly dug in. On one occasion Koresh appeared briefly at an entrance, brandishing a weapon, hurling abuse and a fire-brand in the direction of the federal agents perhaps hoping to provoke a trigger happy reaction. This certainly seemed to be his aim, only prevented by the alert calls for restraint of a perceptive officer, anxious to prevent any act of martyrdom.

Koresh had long prophesied that he would meet a glorious death when he reached 33, the same age as Jesus was when he was crucified. Former associates advised the authorities that he had expressed a belief that his holy mission would only be fulfilled if he got himself killed during a shoot out with government agents. The concern was, would he try to take all his fellow cult members with him in such a battle or would he even now resort to a Jonestown-type pact of ritual suicide. Letters received from Koresh added to the growing anxiety. In one he talked about the commands of a vengeful God 'who authorises his chosen people to punish unbelievers'.

Two days later, in a further twist to the bizarre affair, Koresh unexpectedly promised that he would surrender after he had finished a book about the Apocalypse. The authorities doubted this, not because they now believed this to be his latest stalling tactic, but rather because intelligence gathered from the snooping devices appeared to suggest that a hideously terrifying, Domesday-style climax was looking increasingly in prospect.

On the basis of these judgements, the FBI elected to go on the offensive, committing their men to making peremptory moves in order to avoid a symbolic and sacrificial bloodbath. Having said that, even at this critical point, the FBI actions in fact remained hesitant and indecisive. Operations of the kind they were planning, a physical assault on the building, depend absolutely for their success on the elements of speed and surprise. Both these ingredients were missing.

Just before dawn on 19 April, at around 5.30am (local time) the Branch Davidian compound was contacted by telephone and demands were made for the total surrender of the occupants. An ultimatum was issued advising that, unless there was full compliance with this order, the FBI was about to take direct action to end the confrontation. This was the first mistake for it gave the religious extremists warning of what to expect and they were able to prepare their resistance.

Not surprisingly, the response from the compound was belligerent and defiant. The telephone was ripped out and thrown through the window.

At 6.04am an Abrams tank fitted with a 36ft extension and a battering ram smashed down the front door of the main building. Under fire from inside, it propelled 15 canisters of non-toxic, non-inflammable CS gas into the building. Nine minutes later, having enlarged the aperture, a further 15 canisters were lobbed inside. Later still, at around 6.48am, the process was repeated with another tank at the side of the building where, after battering down the wall, more salvoes of gas shells were fired inside. It is believed that Koresh's people were able to cope with the tear-gas without undue discomfort, however. Enough opportunity had been given to issue gas mask, and the tunnel complex under the buildings offered numerous pockets of clean air in which the group could shelter.

Incredibly, the FBI took no follow up action, their second mistake. It can only be assumed that, on the basis of this limited offensive, they expected everyone inside simply to walk out with their hands up. If so, it was a massive under-estimation of the nature of the beast with which they were dealing.

For four hours the FBI did nothing to directly expedite the ending of the siege. They *did* find time to have at least two press conferences to inform the media of what they were doing — yet another error — for it was quite probable that news could still be received inside the compound on battery-powered devices.

At around 10.50am, still dithering, another gas attack was carried out followed by another long pause until, just before noon, smoke was seen rising from the second floor windows in the compound's living quarters, first at one end and then the other. The sect's headquarters had been constructed of tinder dry wood which, once fire had broken out, burnt readily. Within minutes the entire building was engulfed in flames.

Two men, who were seen outside the walls and who were captured alive, were believed to have deliberately torched the building. Soon burning fiercely, fanned by the high winds and accompanied by explosions as the pyrotechnic stock pile inside fuelled the fiery holocaust, the entire compound was totally consumed by fire as the attacking force and the world's press could only look on helplessly.

It was calculated that the temperature inside this terrible inferno would have risen to around 1,000°F, incinerating everything and everybody inside. Despite some wishful claims that there would have been protection in the bunkers deep below the ground or that it had been possible for escape to be made from the rear, it was soon evident that, apart from a small number of persons who had been captured, there were no survivors. The fire claimed 87 victims including 25 children. Steven Sneider, the cult's second in command, was dead as was David Koresh, the mad prophet himself, perhaps as he had intended all along 'in a blaze of glory, in the flames of Hell!'.

Among the dead were 27 Britons whose families at home, who had been following the drama on television, watched their screens aghast as the horror unfolded before their very eyes, relayed live from Texas, knowing that their loved ones were perishing as they looked on. The anguish was indescribable. The slaughter of their brothers, sisters, wives and children had been unwittingly conveyed to them in a ghoulish picture show. Samuel Henry of Old Trafford, Manchester, whose wife and five grown up children had been trapped in the compound tried in vain to describe this terrible experience: 'Realising my family, my flesh and blood, are inside, I cannot find words to describe my feelings. I am still hoping and praying that they will come out alive and that I will see and talk to my family again'. Mr. Henry's prayers were not answered. Instead, like many others, he was forced to reconcile himself to the awful reality of what had happened.

So what of the aftermath? The tragic end of the Waco siege, culminating in the massacre of 25 innocent young children, triggered enormous repercussions. In the wake of the disaster there was claim and counter claim as those involved sought to deflect the spotlight of criticism off themselves and onto someone else. The FBI held to its theory that the fire had been a deliberate act of mass suicide motivated by a madman that they could have done nothing to prevent. The few survivors, among them the British men Derek Lovelock (37) and Renos Avraam (29), both charged as material witnesses, refuted this. They claimed that the fire had been started accidentally when kerosene lamps, used for light since the electricity supply had been cut off, were knocked over by the tanks as they punched holes in the perimeter walls.

It was also suggested that the child victims had been injected with a lethal substance to spare them the agony of a fiery death. Other reports claimed that they had been shot first by their fanatically indoctrinated mothers, as had any other faint-hearted cult members who attempted to escape. The evidence, what little there was of it, lay in the ashes of the destroyed compound. It would be difficult enough to identify the dead, let alone to ascertain their precise cause of death.

Having said that, the police investigators did recover some bodies which showed clear evidence that executions had taken place, much to the relief of the beleaguered federal authority for it remained the focus of much of the criticism. With such a devastating conclusion to the siege coming hard on the heels of the pronouncement by Bob Ricks, the FBI's chief negotiator, that the authorities were committed to avoiding injury or harm to the compound's occupants, it still took some explaining why the local fire brigade had not even been alerted as part of a contingency to deal with any eventuality. The first fire appliances did not reach the scene until around 1.40pm (local time) by which time the compound was little more than a heap of charred and smouldering remains.

Sensing that the blame for the abortive assault was being directed at him personally, William Sessions, already under investigation for alleged corruption, fought back. 'Let's face facts,' he said, 'those children are dead because David Koresh had them killed'.

The political flack struck wider and higher still, with criticism levelled at the newly elected Democrat administration, including President Clinton himself. He had been reported as being horrified at the ATF's bumbling at the original raid on the Waco compound and had ordered the FBI chief to avoid any more unnecessary bloodshed. Before the flames of the inferno had died down and the smoke had cleared, he was already preparing to speak to the shocked American nation. Clearly shaken, he told his audience, 'We did everything we could to avoid loss of life'. Only later did it transpire that he knew of and had approved the planned siege-busting operation. His Attorney General, Janet Reno, in a concerted effort at damage limitation, announced that it was she and not the President who had authorised the assault but, as Americans are keen to point out, the buck stops at the top. Bill Clinton, already suffering an inauspicious start to his term in office, experienced a further drop in the opinion poll ratings as his competence was brought into question.

The fact is though that all this smacked of hypocrisy. The point should perhaps be made that, in pursuing a witch hunt after the event, Americans wanted it both ways. The Waco affair was not so much an example of political or institutional mismanagement as a symptom of a society which in some respects is rather sick. When given the choice, Americans reject the tightening-up of liberal gun laws, yet at the same time they insist on preserving the right of all manner of freaks and weirdos, who may well turn their readily obtained weapons on innocent bystanders, to have the freedom and opportunity to indulge, with impunity, their perversions and anti-social practices. It is the dangerous incompatibility of this constitutional cocktail, a misguided indulgence to the legacy of the frontier values of the Old West that are no longer safe or appropriate to the modern world, that is the root cause of tragedies like Waco.

To the foreign observer, the Bible-thumping religious hot-head, who is as likely to serve up guns as gospel in equal measures, is a quintessentially surreal American manifestation. He represents a particular dimension of American society in which life seems to be lived as if it were part of a stage or film drama; in a sense, where life is mirroring art rather than art mirroring life. Another spin-off of the Waco disaster gives credence to this hypothesis.

Before the siege had even neared its tragic end, a leading film company had started to produce a 'docu-drama' of the incident for American prime-time TV consumption. Using a mixture of real-life newsreel footage, including scenes of the devastating fire, interwoven with a trite, soap-opera plot played out by a cast of 'Dallas'-type wooden actors, it has contributed to this blurring of the edges between fact and fiction, distorting the American perception of this particular human tragedy.

As for David Koresh, he had written a verse in one of his failed rock songs which served as a suitable epitaph both for himself and the many other extremists who had been at the centre of siege stand-offs:

'There's a madman living in Waco
Praying to the Prince of Hell
Won't you help us now, Oh Lord?'

For Waco, read Entebbe, Assen, Munich, Mogadishu, Amritsar or any of the many other scenes of frightening sieges which have been related in this book.

Bibliography

Books

The Siege of Berlin; ARNOLD-FORSTER, Mark (1979)
Berlin Airlift - An Account of the British Contribution; BARKER, Dudley (HMSO, 1949)
Fifty Famous Liners; BRAYNARD, Frank, O. and MILLER, William H. (1982)
Passage Perilous; DAY, Beth (1962)
Bridge in the Sky; DONOVAN, Frank (1970)
Berlin Airlift; JACKSON, Robert (1986)
The Jew in the Modern World; MENDES-FLOHR, Paul and REINHARZ, Jehuda
The Floating Revolution; ROGERS, Warren, Jr. (1962)
The Iranian Rescue Mission; RYAN (USNI Press)
Malta Convoy; SHANKLAND, Peter and HUNTER, Anthony (Fontana Books, 1976)
The Shah's Last Ride; SHAWCROSS, William (1988)
Pedestal — The Malta Convoy of August 1942; SMITH, Peter C. (1987)
Winged Dagger; STIRLING, David
Voyage of the Damned; THOMAS, Gordon and MORGAN-WITTS, Max
The Berlin Blockade; TUSA, Anne & John (1988)
Entebbe Diary; (*IDF Journal*, Vol II No 3) WILLIAMS, Maj Louis
To the Ends of the Earth; YALLOP, David (1993)

also:

Lloyd's Lists; *Lloyd's Weekly Casualty Reports*; *RAF Yearbooks*; *The Times*; other newspapers — various editions and dates

Films/Videos:

In the Line of Duty — Ambush in Waco; *Raid on Entebbe*; *The Yangtse Incident*; *Voyage of the Damned*

Acknowledgements

My thanks are extended to the following for their help in the preparation of this book:

Joan Fisher, Dena Bowers and the staff at Associated Press; Colin Cruddas of Flight Refueling Group; the staff at the Guildhall Library, London; Ronald Wilson of Historical Aviation Services; the staff at the Imperial War Museum; Israeli Defence Forces; Landesbildstelle, Berlin; Norman Hooke at Lloyd's Intelligence Services; Lufthansa A. G.; Times Newspapers; Ronald Wheatman; and the World Ship Photo Library

Index